THE JOB ANALYSIS APPROACH
TO AFFIRMATIVE ACTION

THE JOB ANALYSIS APPROACH
TO AFFIRMATIVE ACTION

CLEMENT J. BERWITZ
Doctor of Public Administration
Formerly Chief,
Occupational Analysis and Industrial Services
Manpower Services Division
New York State Department of Labor

A WILEY-INTERSCIENCE PUBLICATION

JOHN WILEY & SONS

New York / London / Sydney / Toronto

Copyright © 1975 by John Wiley & Sons, Inc.

Library of Congress Cataloging in Publication Data:

Berwitz, Clement J   1905–
  The job analysis approach to affirmative action.

  "A Wiley-Interscience publication."
  Originally presented as the author's thesis, State
University of New York, Albany, 1973.
  Bibliography: p.
  Includes index.
  1. Personnel management—United States. 2. Discrim-
ination in employment—United States. 3. Job analysis.
I. Title.

HF5549.2.U5B46 1975   658.31′4   75-11660
ISBN 0-471-07157-9

Printed in the United States of America

10 9 8 7 6 5 4 3 2 1

To Sylvia

PREFACE

The development of the Wagner College Affirmative Action Plan is an example of technical assistance given by a government agency to an employer engaged in fulfilling statutory requirements. Although this is primarily a case study of Affirmative Action, it also encompasses public administration: the study was begun at the request of a government contractor who needed assistance because the government guidelines were insufficient for practical implementation. The problem was so compelling that the United States Manpower Administration, a unit of the Department of Labor (which has other units responsible for Affirmative Action implementation) recommended that state employment security agencies provide necessary technical assistance to employers on request. This recommendation is included in two releases cited in Chapter 6.

If Affirmative Action leading to equal employment opportunity is to achieve the optimum utilization and allocation of the nation's human resources, it must become the cornerstone of manpower policy. The Wagner experience allowed the author to generalize the findings of the study in these directions. In developing the study, the author brought to bear his long experience as Principal Administrative Analyst in charge of Planning, Methods, and Procedures for the Field Operations Bureau of the New York State Department of Labor's Division of Employment (now the Manpower Services Division), and more recently, his experience as Chief of the Occupational Analysis–Industrial Services Section of the same Manpower Services Division.

CLEMENT J. BERWITZ

New York, New York
April, 1975

ACKNOWLEDGMENTS

With deep thanks I acknowledge the valuable assistance provided in preparing this material, when it was initially developed as a dissertation, by many individuals concerned with or interested in the study. These include M. Charlyne Cox, Director of Personnel at Wagner College, for her dedication to Affirmative Action and her vision and capacity for creative, practical innovation; Lorraine Mrozinski and Anne Mochnik, Wagner College personnel technicians, for their indefatigable patience and willingness to dedicate themselves over and above regular job assignments, to learn and to apply imaginatively a complex technology; Nelson F. Hopper, Director of the New York State Department of Labor's Manpower Services Division (which includes the New York State Employment Service), for his understanding, support, and encouragement; Leon Lewis, Chief of the Occupational Analysis Branch of the U.S. Manpower Administration, and Adeline Padgett of the same organization (which developed the USES Job Analysis Formulation and the *Dictionary of Occupational Titles*), for their cooperation over a period of years and their readiness to share their knowledge; the following members of my staff in the New York State Department of Labor's Manpower Services Division, who prepared most of the position descriptions: Jack Berkman, Gustave Greis, Normal Kalenson, David Knapp, Harry Levitt, Erwin Mark, and Peter Thomas; special thanks to Gustave Greis for the additional assistance he provided so graciously; and to Lawrence Ruscher for his ready help whenever requested; Gen Callanan, my former secretary, and Reba Johnson, my present secretary, for their patience and cheerful cooperation in typing the drafts; Janice Hines for her typing and clerical support from time to time; and the members of my dissertation committee for their invaluable assistance in improving the thrust and contents of the work: Professor Walter L. Balk, Chairman, and Professors Melvin Bers, Lester Hawkins, Orville Poland, and Ronald Stout.

After completing the Wagner study, I was invited to present several lectures and workshops on the USES Job Analysis Formulation and the DOT, at the School of Industrial and Labor Relation's of Cornell University, in a course developed and conducted by Professor Frank Miller and I gratefully acknowledge his valuable suggestions.

Finally, I gratefully acknowledge the cooperation, understanding, and goodwill of the officials of Wagner College and those members of the staff who were exposed to Affirmative Action in all its dynamic dimensions.

C. J. B.

CONTENTS

THE JOB ANALYSIS APPROACH
TO AFFIRMATIVE ACTION

INTRODUCTION

Even the most casual observer must sense that change is the great dynamic of the contemporary scene—that the country, the employer community, and the individual are in transition.

Politics, clothing, social and moral values, jobs, civil rights, virtually everything within sight and sound reflect and represent a reaching out toward new equilibria whose dimensions are but dimly perceived. People want more, expect more, demand more, and are prepared to fight to get more of the elements of the good life. Most feel that their expectations are equitable, feasible, and just.

The roots for a better balance of nature's goods probably began with the dawn of life and vitality, perhaps on a tropistic basis. Whatever the predisposing factors, a new reality and sense of imminence pervade the air. Government began to perceive this reality and to prepare for it with the enactment of the Employment Act of 1946. That act affirmed the intention of the government to create and maintain conditions

> . . . under which there will be afforded useful employment opportunities, including self-employment, for those able, willing, and seeking work, and to promote maximum employment, production and purchasing power.

The later Manpower Acts of the 1960's provided occupational training and work experience for many who had previously been unable to obtain a foothold in the economy or to continue their progress in it. The Civil Rights Act of 1964, with its amendments and successive orders, was designed to stimulate and to ensure equal employment opportunity at least as a civil right.

Because experience indicated that many employers practiced "tokenism," that is providing jobs to minorities and women in relatively lower skill levels, government reaffirmed its intentions by requiring employers with government contracts to provide equal employment opportunity across the entire occupational spectrum. Goals were to be established in quantities to approximate the proportion each group bore to the population and within the area surrounding each particular government contractor.

More importantly, workers were to be given at least equal consideration in every personnel transaction, such as hiring, counseling, and promotion. But government did more than that by recognizing that just any job was not good enough. It declared in most of the manpower enactments that jobs should be meaningful and should utilize individual talents so as to lead to the workers' occupational self-fulfillment.

From these developments one might subsume that government now recognizes that workers are entitled to meaningful employment, which will provide them with opportunities for growth and development consistent with both aspiration levels and employer production needs.

Many employers have undoubtedly subscribed to this principle and implemented it for many years. The identification of these precepts and practices over time and the resulting experiences and findings would make a valuable contribution to human resources theory. So too would an exploration of the reasons for employer failure or resistance in these directions. However such endeavor are beyond the purview of this book. Instead, my objective is to describe a case study in the development and implementation of an Affirmative Action Plan in all of its aspects at Wagner College, Staten Island, New York. My main thrust is to indicate that a basic unifying technology is essential to achieve these ends—a technology that is applicable to many of the facets of personnel management and human resources planning. In fact my thesis is that Affirmative Action means good personnel management and nothing more; that once Affirmative Action—or good personnel management—is achieved through job analysis and objective employer attitudes, government prodding through legislation will no longer be necessary.

This book shows how government assisted one employer to establish a plan which might serve as a prototype for others. In developing the plan, I utilized my long-term experience and training in government in the field of occupational analysis and administrative management. While many of the techniques and devices described have been used in the same or different formats in government in the past, I freely made adaptations of these devices and broadened interpretations of some elements of the statutes and regulations. For these reasons the views expressed in this book, and my adaptations, do not in any way represent the endorsement of any government agency whatever. It is my hope and expectation that further experience will document the worth of these approaches and that replication of this plan will indicate the new directions needed to fulfill and implement the search for a more equitable fulfillment of achievable job-related objectives.

CHAPTER 1

ASSUMPTIONS

One purpose of the Civil Rights Act of 1964 was to ensure that equal employment opportunity became a reality throughout the United States. Many employers did not hasten to comply, and a customary ploy was to limit hiring of minority workers and women to the lower reaches of the occupational spectrum, forcing the government to issue a succession of Executive Orders to overcome this response. The most recent, Revised Order No. 4,[1] provides that establishments receiving government contracts of $50,000 or more and having 50 or more employees are required to take "affirmative action" when statistics indicate that "minorities"[2] and women with requisite skills are not employed in relation to their availability in the area near the establishment. That is, they must prepare a plan outlining the steps they will take to secure a more balanced work force, which is taken to show that equal employment opportunity has been achieved and will continue to be achieved.

At first sight, the provisions of Revised Order No. 4 seem to comprise a collection of *arbitrary directives* to government contractors. For example, the order requires contractors to compile and to interpret a variety of statistics relating to employment, unemployment, and the ethnic characteristics of the male/female population residing near the establishment, for comparison with the composition of the contractor's work force. The objective is to provide a basis for setting goals for hiring minorities and women. Additionally, the order requires contractors to develop and to utilize certain personnel management techniques that many employers never had been compelled to use before. These include preparing position descriptions, pre-

4

paring sufficiently detailed worker and job-seeker records to enable the personnel department to consider every worker for each promotional opportunity as it occurs, providing counseling to workers, and adopting some of the other more modern personnel measures ordinarily found in large establishments staffed with innovative personnel technicians.

A careful review of the provisions of Revised Order No. 4 might lead to a somewhat different conclusion concerning the degree of arbitrariness involved. The order was created to remedy the "tokenism" practiced by many establishments following the enactment of the Civil Rights Act of 1964. Apparently the order was designed to overcome the gaps in the preceding orders and to assure the achievement of equal employment opportunity, as required by Title VII of the act; however, the order does not indicate how its provisions are to be implemented.

The order necessarily utilizes language designed to supply compliance officers with ammunition for requiring "deficient" establishments to take more specific actions to realize equal employment. A detailed review of the provisions led the author to conclude that the requirements and *actions* the order *imposed* on contractors were nothing more than an attempt to stimulate contractors to use up-to-date, objective personnel management methods—methods that should have been used by enlightened, progressive management in the first place, with no prodding from any outside group.

Many persons familiar with the state of personnel management methodologies in industry and in government are aware of the lack of progress in this important area in the management of human resources. The following examples are relevant:

• Many establishments have not prepared job specifications or position descriptions to guide their personnel decision making and related actions.
• Many employers do not have an objective understanding of the characteristics needed by their workers to perform specific jobs acceptably. Hence selection criteria are often fully or partially subjective.
• When promotional opportunities occur, someone working in or near the appointing officer's headquarters tends to be selected. It would be more equitable and rewarding to establish the duties and qualifications needed and to review all candidates possessing the potentials for successful performance.
• Many government employees (most of whom are required to qualify for promotions on the basis of Civil Service tests) say that they do not believe the examinations they take have sufficient connection with the job for which they are competing.
• Many critics report that if three counselors conducted a career exploration with the same individual, the counselee would receive suggestions con-

cerning three rather different career directions. Some counselors believe
that if such a person "thinks" he has been helped, the counseling process
has fulfilled its objectives. One wonders how a person can be counseled for
an occupation about which neither he nor the counselor knows anything,
and which cannot be addressed by any of the current interest or aptitude
instruments. Optimally, it shoud be possible to see one's capacities in relation to the entire occupational spectrum.

• A large company installed a numerical control machine that replaced
some 75 manual workers who had been laid off even though the company
was simultaneously hiring new people (at the same skill level) elsewhere in
its large establishment. It was assumed that the qualifications required for
the other jobs were unrelated to those required in the displaced job. More
important, the company did not believe that it should start with the *worker*
rather than the job requirements of the incumbent's job, to determine which
job in the establishment fitted each worker best. Instead it assumed that the
duties performed in the job to be terminated equally reflected the abilities of
all workers; therefore, all should be handled "en masse," either by transfer
to the same job or dismissal.

• The son of the executive officer of a large mercantile establishment (let's
call it Stacey's) wanted a job in the firm but did not want special consideration when he applied for it. He applied at the Personnel Department in-
cognito. He was turned down. The firm's officer later checked the records
and discovered that his son had been rejected because he was not the
"Stacey type."

• *The New York Times* carried a story on August 23, 1974, concerning
the recommendations of the transition team President Ford had appointed
to assist him in forming the new administration. The item stated "President
Ford's final decision on whether to accept the idea of the six advisors is dependent on the personalities of the men the President wants as his aides."

• Experience has indicated that some counselors are unable to relate a complete set of facts about a counselee to relevant areas in the world of work.
Instead, they rely too much on a stereotyped instrument (such as occupational tests) to assist them in identifying matching occupations for the
consideration of the client.

• Although there is much concern over supply-demand imbalances, most
economists agree that the present classification structures used to compile
and to present such data are seriously limited.

• A large organization interviews many candidates for each job as
vacancies occur. These records are not filed in a "retrieval" file arranged by
job title. When a new personnel requisition is received, the personnel office
is unable to find the records of qualified persons interviewed as recently as
the preceding day. Hence they recruit for the same job repeatedly, using

outside sources, because they are either unable or unwilling to devise a suitable job-seeker record file for the quick identification and retrieval of names of persons with requisite potentials. This situation might be partly attributable to the failure of the establishment to prepare position descriptions.

One can easily adduce many additional examples of inadequate personnel management practices. Isn't it possible that fewer problems would have emerged when Revised Order No. 4 was promulgated, if government contractors had a reasonably up-to-date personnel management system? Isn't it conceivable (if one agrees that innovation occurs only when crises emerge) that one of the important spinoffs of Revised Order No. 4 will be the forced development of improved personnel management methods and techniques? Isn't it also possible that many employers with inadequate personnel management practices would have opted for improvement if there had been less controversy about the validity of such measures, and if validity had been proved by successful experience in day-by-day operations?

In summary, it appears that full utilization of the nation's human resources has not occurred partly because of a paucity of personnel technique, and this condition might explain why personnel management continues to be unimaginative and fails to meet human and economic needs. If this assumption is correct, the development of a technology that would overcome many of these deficiencies would be in the public interest. Not only would it contribute to employer and national economic equilibrium, it would also set the stage for the development of a viable national manpower policy, which, among other things, would ensure that each person ready, willing, and able to work could secure meaningful work[3] to enable him to fulfill his vocational aspirations. A good manpower policy would synthesize social and legislative planning based on the integrated contributions of psychology, sociology, economics (fiscal and monetary policies), and public administration.

The identification or creation of the necessary manpower technology is complicated because much controversy exists within and among the disciplines that contribute to "manpower science." These contributions include vocational and industrial psychology, occupational sociology, economic forecasting, social and legislative planning, public administration, micro and macro economics, and other studies relating to the needs of the individual, the needs of employers, the needs of the community, and the national interest. Unfortunately each discipline and practitioner ordinarily limits attention to their respective narrow and specialized interest. It is clear that an integrated systems approach has been neither conceptualized nor implemented.

Having read the various orders leading to Revised Order No. 4, employers (hereafter termed "contractors") became concerned about the requirements of the revised order because the government agencies charged with enforcement failed to issue usable guidelines to assist those who sincerely wished to eliminate employment imbalances by developing and implementing Affirmative Action plans. It would have been helpful if such guidelines had specified the types of position description and counseling, for example, that were required by the order. Many consulting firms and nonprofit organizations have emerged to fill the breach, arranging conferences and workshops to help contractors understand the requirements of the order, thus to prepare adequate Affirmative Action plans. Some who paid to attend seminars and workshops returned more confused than ever, because they felt the discussions raised more question than were answered.

What are the issues and the problems? What specific factors have caused the confusion and the difficulty in developing operable Affirmative Action programs, policies, and procedures?

1. Difficulty in interpreting the requirements and intentions of specific provisions of the order. For example, it appears at first that contradictory provisions exist in the order: the Order requires setting "goals" for hiring minorities and women while simultaneously stipulating that there must be equal employment opportunity without reference to race, color, religion, national origin, or sex. This seems to make the creation of goals illegal if in meeting them, *preference* is to be given to minorities and women.

2. Technical difficulties in implementing specific provisions of Revised Order No. 4. Some of the problem areas are:

   (*a*) *statistical,* requiring the compilation of data that are difficult to obtain;

   (*b*) *qualitative,* requiring, for example, that "counseling" be provided to employees;

   (*c*) *"systems" factors,* requiring the development of methods for informing all workers and job seekers of job opportunities, and methods to ensure employer consideration of all employees and job seekers when promotional opportunities occur.

Several other issues are equally compelling. Problems in manpower planning by contractors to meet short- and long-term needs are complicated because "planning" (the amelioration of supply-demand imbalances) is best performed within the context of regional and national needs examined over various time frames. The resolution of some occupational imbalances, at least at the local level, may require shifting workers from occupations of oversupply to those of short supply, with minimal training, or training new workers who have the potentials for successful performance.

Since many of the necessary planning and implementing actions are beyond an individual contractor's control or ability to provide training, government financing is required. Depending on the statutory provision under which training is to be provided, it is currently approved and funded partially or entirely according to prescribed types of documentation and the fulfillment of preestablished criteria, which in the future should be largely based on a national manpower policy. Much progress has been made toward designing a national manpower policy since the passage of the Employment Act of 1946, but much of the necessary conceptualization is not yet on the drawing boards.

Another compelling issue is the inadequacy of today's personnel management technique, mentioned earlier. Many techniques (e.g., employment counseling, and selection of suitable candidates predicted to be successful on the job performers) are controversial and have not been fully validated. With employers, government, and the academic disciplines still groping toward a viable personnel theory and technology, attempts to achieve the full productive utilization of the nation's capacity fall short of what otherwise might be an achievable goal.

The human equation is perhaps the most important constraint, particularly if goals are to be implemented when promotional opportunities occur. A reasonable employee will not quarrel unduly when a more qualified candidate is hired to fill a job opportunity he has coveted for a long time. It is an altogether different matter when an employee sees a well-merited chance for promotion destroyed because the job is given to a minority candidate or to a woman, to fulfill a social purpose that is decidedly in the public interest. This problem is further compounded if the minority or female promotee is not immediately able to provide leadership to the disappointed employee. All this leads to charges of "reverse discrimination" (i.e., "illegal" preference given minorities and women).

Because of the many problems, one might well ask whether there is a technology available that might contribute to the resolution of the difficulties just named. If such a technology could fill both the conceptual and operational gaps, the issues would be reduced to manageable proportions. This book postulates that such a technology is available in the *Dictionary of Occupational Titles, Third Edition (DOT 3)*,[4] developed by the United States Department of Labor's Manpower Administration in 1965, and in the Manpower Administration's Job Analysis Formulation[5] on which *DOT 3* is based. *DOT 3* defines all jobs found in the economy and presents a conceptual structure that is, or can be made, useful in occupational classification, human resources diagnosis for selection (for hiring), career exploration, job restructuring, and other personnel management uses. The author used this tool in the development and early implementation of the Wagner

College Affirmative Action Plan during a 14-month period (May 1972–June 1973).

This book has several objectives. Its most direct aim is to describe the Wagner College Affirmative Action Plan and its underlying assumptions. This will indicate how one harried personnel director was able to resolve the major policy and procedural dilemmas encountered in attaining a greater penetration of minorities and women in a college nonfaculty workforce without violating the assumptions of equal employment opportunity for all. It is hoped that the Wagner Plan may serve as a model for replication, with or without adaptation, by other contractors.

However, an adequate description of the Wagner Plan necessitates further spinoffs, which form additional objectives of the book, for the Wagner College Affirmative Action Plan, as conceived, developed, and operated, represents what may well be the ultimate personnel management technique, described below. Affirmative Action, in its basic sense and in the highest tradition of the democratic ethic, can be construed to mean that every person who is ready, willing, and able to work, is entitled to a meaningful job that meets his aspiration levels and his latent and potential abilities to the extent that these can be realized in the labor market area of *his choice*. The operational assumption is that there exists a sophisticated personnel management technique that among other things, provides position descriptions for each job in the establishment, indicating the skills, knowledges, and abilities required of each incumbent. (Before applying for his first job, each incumbent should have received occupational counseling and assistance in career exploration consonant with his self-concept, aptitudes, and other characteristics, to assure the amount of growth and development he wants.) The position descriptions should comprise the basis for employer determination of objective "selection" (hiring) criteria and for developing performance standards and supervisory methodologies. Other assumptions follow. Promotion should be based on a "bidding" procedure (or a computerized retrieval system) that enables all interested employees to make a decision to bid on the basis of a thorough understanding of the tasks to be performed and the worker characteristics needed. This procedure would also provide counseling assistance to interested candidates, to help each one to determine how well his current and potential abilities relate to his present job and the job for which he is bidding and, if a discrepancy exists, to make the employee aware of other jobs that might better fit his needs. Moreover, this technique should allow the employer to group jobs on the basis of the same defined worker characteristics used in accomplishing the foregoing objectives, thereby facilitating the identification of incumbents in other positions requiring the same characteristics as the vacant job. This technique should also provide a more workable basis for job and position pricing (wage rates), job restructuring, and manpower planning. Finally, all this should be related to national manpower planning performed in the same terms of reference—those developed and utilized by the Manpower Administration's Job Analysis Formulation, and utilized and reflected in *DOT 3.*

The Wagner experience indicated to the personnel director of the college, to its nonfaculty workforce, and to the author, that the Manpower Administration's technology can function as planned. The author's review of the literature and the alternative available strategies, most of which represent minor variations from the Manpower Administration's formulations, suggests that *one* formulation is virtually mandatory for use by *all* interested groups, for the following reasons:

1.   A national manpower policy is essential for economic growth and stability. Such a policy must rely heavily on manpower projections, which in turn must be seen in terms of individual diagnostics related to career exploration, counseling for job adjustment, and use in many other aspects of personnel management. In other words, the manpower policy equation must take into account *workers'* needs and preferences and their adaptabilities, as well as the need for industry expansion, where most of the emphasis has been placed up to this time. For example, consider the viewpoint expressed in a *New York Times* editorial of August 11, 1974: "Specifically, the nation needs expanded programs for creating jobs, training and educating workers, providing needed health services, reforming the tax structure, and more fully distributing the tax burden."

This passage appears to be industry oriented: it seems to imply that the creation of jobs is the solution, on the assumption that workers will come forward to take any available job if the wage incentive is adequate. However, the jobs created should reflect the available workers' needs and preferences, and matching jobs should be created in the industries utilizing such occupations. This requires occupational inputs to match industrial input-output analysis,[6] which may well serve to identify the industries to be expanded.

2.   A common definitional frame of reference is needed to accomplish the purposes previously given. It should comprise building blocks or modules that can be used to determine the critical job and worker characteristics. Such a system of modules was utilized in creating the Manpower Administration's Job Analysis Formulation and its *Dictionary of Occupational Titles,* Third Edition.

3.   An enormous apparatus is needed to construct the *DOT,* to gather the data on an acceptable sampling basis, and to construct the 14,000 job definitions and the classification structure into which each definition is peg-

ged. It was decided to establish Occupational Analysis Field Centers in various locations throughout the country. Ten are currently in operation in New York, North Carolina, Florida, Michigan, Wisconsin, Missouri, Texas, Utah, California, and Washington (state). Each center has an assigned list of industries and a cadre of trained occupational analysts who study and follow up on jobs in representative establishments in each industry. The effort must be made under government auspices because of the heavy and continuing funding required, and also because this setup interacts with the staff of the 54 state employment security systems which include Puerto Rico, the Virgin Islands, the District of Columbia, and Guam. The local employment offices comprising that network constitute one of the chief users of the *DOT*, and the continuing feedback from these users to the *DOT* developers is critical.

4. Many organizations and academicians financed by government or private sources have conducted research in human and employer diagnostics. The author has reviewed many of them; most represent minor adaptations of the Manpower Administration's completed technology. Although perhaps some of the components should be changed, possibly by using factors developed through independent research, it is clear that there is no completed satisfactory alternative to the system developed by the Manpower Administration. The chances are that no other organization under private funding will ever produce a complete system that will compete with the Manpower Administration's findings and its *DOT*. It is contended elsewhere in this book that it is in the national interest for large organizations to use the current *DOT* and to report their statistics by its coding structure instead of according to theoretical modifications that have seen little experimentation and use. It is doubtful whether such organizations as the Bureau of Labor Statistics, the Bureau of the Census, and the state employment security agencies will use any privately developed alternative, either directly or through a conversion table, unless the plan has been completed and fully tested and is convertible to their classifications.[7] What is needed is a single standard occupational classification for presenting data by all users.[8] This is particularly necessary if the nation is ever to have a meaningful national manpower policy, including a means for stimulating the resolution of supply-demand imbalances.

A subsequent chapter indicates that a critical and significant part of the Wagner Plan is the counseling of incumbent workers, stimulating them to self-appraisal to show them where they are now and to suggest specific new career directions. For example, each incumbent at Wagner was given an hour-long interview during which his actual and potential skills, abilities, and interests were ascertained. These were related to the Worker Trait groupings in *DOT 3*, and the kinds of jobs requiring the same configuration of traits (whether available at Wagner or elsewhere) were discussed with the worker. Some dramatic results were noted. The supervisor of the Wagner College Reproduction Unit, for example, learned that she would doubtless be qualified to sell copying machines, to demonstrate them, or to train employees of customer firms.

The technology utilized at Wagner represents an adaptation of the *DOT* Worker Trait building blocks. The description and discussion of this part of the Wagner Plan will comprise a complete explanation, indicating among other things how the *DOT* can be used by counselors in relating worker characteristics to jobs and families of jobs. This is perhaps the most difficult aspect of current counseling methodologies. Without the *DOT*, most counselors rely on interest scales or aptitude profiles, or their own limited knowledge of jobs, to locate relevant fields of work. The *DOT* is a total systems approach wherein aptitudes, interests, temperaments, educational attainments, and other traits become interacting subsystems that can be related to job clusters requiring similar traits. The result is a number of options made known to counselees. This is a completely judgmental approach rather than a mechanical exercise, like certain computerized counseling approaches now being tested by their independent developers. Some systems require manual sorting of many variables; others utilize all or a few of the United States Employment Service (USES) Job Analysis elements for these purposes.

This entire book is developed in a systems mode and context. The matrix is Affirmative Action, which is regarded as synonymous with "updated, objective personnel management and manpower planning." Each of the ingredients used in the Wagner College Affirmative Action Plan is a subsystem: determining supply-demand and ethnic and male/female imbalances; developing position descriptions; clustering jobs, establishing selection and promotion criteria; providing occupational counseling to incumbents; creating a retrieval system of qualified or qualifiable incumbents or job seekers when promotional opportunities occur; performing job restructuring if needed; developing a bidding procedure. After completing the Wagner Plan and operating it, most of those concerned concluded that if the Manpower Administration's technology had not been available, it would have had to be invented!

BASIC ASSUMPTIONS

We make several basic assumptions in this book: one involves the USES Job Analysis formulation and *DOT 3*; others feature models of how people choose and find jobs, and also how manpower supply-demand imbalances might be resolved. We now review the assumptions based on the *DOT*, which itself was built on the elements of the Job Analysis Formulation.

The *Dictionary of Occupational Titles,* Third Edition, assumes that identified and defined "traits and factors" constitute a frame of reference in studying jobs and in establishing the qualification profile that workers should possess to be able to perform the job requirements successfully. In other words, the trait requirements represent situations to which a worker must adjust, even if he possesses higher levels of such traits.

The trait and factor theory and the *DOT* also postulate that a worker's needs and preferences can be identified by the same traits and factors used in studying jobs and job requirements. Hence the theory suggests that if the traits and factors so utilized are "correct," workers and jobs can be matched: a worker will be able to examine all job opportunities available and to choose the one that best accommodates his or her *needs.* This is possible since the DOT groups jobs by common traits and factors. This grouping also facilitates relating counselee facts to the entire occupational spectrum.

The trait and factor theory was developed in the early days of vocational guidance. The subject is covered more thoroughly in Chapter 2. Briefly, however, our theory is that no matter what technology or vocational choice theory is used by a counselor, a point is reached when counselor and counselee must determine appropriate career fields to meet the counselee's career needs. In the author's opinion, the optimum approach for society and counselee alike is to address the entire world of work to identify matching occupations. The only vehicle available for this purpose at this time is *DOT 3,* developed from the building blocks of the Job Analysis Formulation created by USES.

The Job Analysis Formulation

Job analysis was originally designed to improve efficiency under early scientific management theory. The USES approach expanded it to the worker as well as to the job. It represents an updated collection of traits and factors which implement one of the oldest theories of vocational guidance (see Chapter 2). Indeed it represents one type of implementation of the "trait and factor approach"; interest inventories represent another. The search for the ultimate traits and factors has occupied the attention of many researchers for a long time and is continuing, perhaps *at a more* accelerated pace. For example, a treatise prepared in 1943 states:

> Many [other] psychologists turned their attention to the improvement of instruments for measuring various human abilities and traits that might possibly prove to be important in helping a worker to be successful in his work. Mechanical abilities, clerical aptitudes, musical sensibilities, artistic judgment, and vocational interests were among the fields investigated. The development of better measures of human characteristics was taking place at the same time that

improvements were being made in statistical procedures for carrying on such research and in methods for determining the actual efficiency of workers on the job.[9]

With the advent of computer manpower matching,[10] the search has intensified, and these efforts will doubtless continue into the distant future.

Many workers in this field are looking for modules (the lowest common denominator) that in varying combinations reflect task and job requirements. These are "traits and factors" that describe workers and jobs. The trait and factor approach at first seems to be a "logical" apparatus to use in career decision making: determine the traits and factors that define all jobs; ascertain the degree to which counselees or job seekers possess such traits; then match the two. The objective is to identify the types of occupational areas that "fit" the counselee or job seeker. Many psychologists prefer to use constructs and methods other than this controversial theoretical approach, but the initial problem persists no matter what theoretical apparatus the counselor begins with. How does the counselor relate counselee facts to matching career fields to be presented to the client for his appraisal and approval? Unless this process results in a choice of career or in career clarifications, the counseling is of little immediate practical use. Moreover, to identify relevant occupations, the set of the "facts" identified for and with the counselee should be matched against the entire occupational spectrum, rather than against the limited range of occupations known to the counselee or the counselor. The problem is compounded when counselors begin assessment leading to career decision making too early in their training, without sufficient exposure to the world of work and without thorough understanding of the structure and content of industries and their constituent occupations. To be successful, occupational counselors must understand the critical factors that differentiate jobs. Effective occupational counseling must differ from psychoanalysis or psychotherapy, which seeks to provide patients with an apparatus for self-understanding that will enable them to adjust to living. Although occupational counseling should include assistance to the client in understanding his occupational assets and weaknesses, it must, on the other hand, lead ultimately to career decision making. To do less is to shun reality. Unless counseling results in a job, or at least in a career direction leading ultimately to a rather meaningful, firm career decision, it is unacceptable both to the individual and to society. Moreover, many manpower experts consider that counseling, including career exploration and decision making, should be an ongoing process, with several changes in career direction occurring during one's occupational lifetime, to pace individual growth and development as well as changes in technology and in the economy. The danger with traits and factors is the tendency of some practitioners to use an overmechanized approach, regarding too literally the preliminary findings obtained through tests and interest inventories. Findings so obtained must be recognized to be tentative, and they must be subjected by counselor and counselee to a searching, contextual reappraisal of all the client's needs and preferences. The context used during the Wagner College test was the USES Job Analysis Formulation and the *Dictionary of Occupational Titles* Worker Traits structure and its "groupings," mentioned previously. The objective was to determine how far these tools could be used to implement Affirmative Action. These tools were used and tested because no other sufficiently complete apparatus or instruments are now available for this purpose.

A review of the elements leading to the present state of the art in job analysis methodologies, in developing occupational definitions, and in designing classification structures, is beyond the purview of this book.[11] Suffice it to say that the present Job Analysis Formulation represents the apogee of these developments for two reasons: first, the authors of that formulation and *DOT 3* reviewed all previous developments and called on a committee of psychologists to assist them in developing the materials. Second, this approach has been used successfully in gathering information about the 14,000 basic jobs in our economy and in defining and classifying them in a structure that has been used to place millions of American job seekers. The present USES Job Analysis Formulation comprises a set of parameters or dimensions that purportedly can be used fully to describe any job in terms or descriptors that cut across the content of the jobs. These parameters[12] are:

- Work Fields (Methodologies–Technologies; Machines, Tools, Equipment, Work Aids (MTEWA)
- Materials, Products, Subject Matter, Service (MPSMS)
- Worker Functions (DATA, PEOPLE, THINGS, involvements)
- Worker Traits
     General Educational Development (GED—6 levels in three dimensions: Reasoning, Mathematical, Language Development)
     Specific Vocational Preparation (9 time frames)
     Aptitudes (11, scaled into 5 levels)
     Interests (5 bipolar pairs)
     Temperaments (12)
     Physical Factors (6)
- Working or Environmental Conditions

These traits and factors are represented in Chart 1. Each factor serves as a basis for structured observations and discussions with workers, foremen, and other informed persons to establish what is being done, as well as why and how; what the results are; and what skills, knowledges, and characteris-

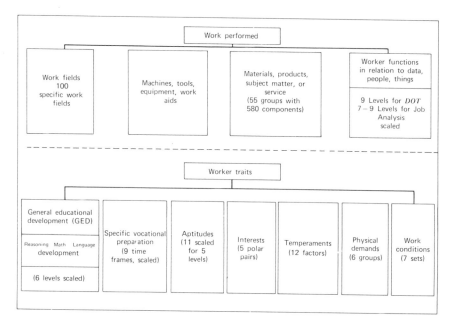

CHART 1 COMPONENTS OF JOB ANALYSIS AND *DOT* BUILDING BLOCKS

When referring to the various Appendices and Handbooks cited in the text, note that each term and level in the chart is defined as indicated. Some of the elements are "scaled" to indicate progressively higher "ordering." Any or all of the components are utilized to the extent each applies. Thus some jobs, (e.g., occupational analyst) have an important involvement with DATA and little significant involvement with PEOPLE or THINGS. The Worker Traits omit emotional factors not indigenous to job performance (e.g., need to "belong"). Slight differences will be found between the *DOT* and Job Analysis Formulation for Worker Function levels.

tics are required of average workers to meet intended standards. Each factor is used to the extent it is relevant. For example, a systems analyst may be involved with various machines and apparatus, including computers. Which? What model numbers? In what areas is competence required? At what level of complexity does the subject work with reference to DATA, PEOPLE, THINGS? What are the Worker Trait requirements? How much development in reasoning, mathematics, and language? How much training must the subject have? What specific aptitudes are needed to ensure successful performance? Which interests, which temperaments, what physical capacities? To which working conditions must the subject adjust? Regarding the Materials, Products, Subject Matter, or Service category, we must ask,

What office systems, dealing with what subject matter? Qualitatively or quantitatively oriented? With factory process flows, including numerical control machines? With offices to solve problems of payroll, records of transactions, manpower matching? Is there a preference?

The essence of this approach is to determine traits and factors that describe jobs in analytical modules, which can be used to relate jobs to one another. The relationships are based on trait commonalities. Jobs are related if they require the same or almost the same aptitudes, interests, temperaments, physical requirements, educational development, training time; the same relation to levels of complexity involving DATA, PEOPLE, THINGS; the same general technology to perform the work, and the same Materials, Products, Subject Matter, or Service. Differentiating among jobs in a cluster of those requiring the same traits are the *substantive* or experiential factors or tasks to be performed. For example, the following jobs require the same configuration of traits: academic dean, alumni secretary, director of admissions, community services and health education officer, labor relations officer, library director. Can persons experienced in any one of these be rotated to other jobs in this list? On what basis? With how much training? Is this more easily accomplished when the jobs are in the same environment, as in a college? The Job Analysis Formulation regards such transfer as a *possibility,* since all these jobs require the same traits. Theoretically, interested candidates would need specific training only in the new tasks to be performed and in other environmental and subject matter factors. It is claimed that such transfers would be expedited, because of the similarity in requirements for educational attainment, aptitudes, and so on.

Consider the Civil Service approach. A vacancy occurs in a government agency. Based on an analysis of the vacant job, a determination is made of jobs in the same "series" or in related "series" whose incumbents will be permitted to compete. A test is then given to help predict which candidates will perform acceptably in the job. Often, persons experienced in one area qualify for a job involving another subject matter because they pass the test (i.e., they predictably have the capacity to *learn* the *tasks* of the new job) and also because they have the related skills and experience to enable them to perform creditably. For example, an organization and methods analyst might advance to a middle manager in the personnel department, or in budget preparation. How much of such success is attributable to aptitudes, interests, and other traits common to these jobs? How much to knowing how to work with line and staff (as required in the former job)? How much to other unidentified traits and factors possessed by the successful promotee which might well override any other factor? Experience has shown that more often than not promotees so selected perform with reasonable competency.

In industry and in government, promotions are granted according to this general theory. Without too much scientific or analytical frameworks or fanfare, appointing officers select individuals, often citing a hunch or saying that the choice was intuitive. The chances are good that close analysis of this type of selection will indicate that the appointing officer used a set of criteria based on his long experience. Often such criteria are not even articulated. "John will be able to perform this job; Jim won't work out." How do they know? They do not know. They speculate, sometimes rightly, sometimes wrongly. Such approaches and the Job Analysis Formulation differ in that the latter is an organized means of using "scientifically" determined parameters, to replace the seemingly unstructured and limited criteria used by successful appointing officers who allegedly operate from the "seat of their pants."

But are the *DOT* elements the ultimate parameters? Have any been omitted? Are any superfluous? Since *DOT 3* was published in 1965, slight changes were made in Interest No. 6 (situations involving a preference for activities concerned with people and the communication of ideas—identified as 1b in the *Handbook for Analyzing Jobs*). Additionally, the *Handbook* has omitted two of the original Temperaments used in constructing *DOT 3* (namely, 6 "Working alone and apart in physical isolation from others" and 3, "Working only under specific instruction, allowing little or no room for independent judgment").

A substantial amount of research is needed to establish definitively the completeness of the traits and factors used, and to identify any other traits and factors that are needed. As stated previously, many academicians have explored these matters, and some innovations and additions have been reported in the literature. The author has related most of the traits and factors in one of these products to the existing USES Job Analysis structure (see Appendix H). Nonetheless, such developmental work is desirable and necessary. As stated in another chapter, however, such research findings should be reported to, and *evaluated* by, a central governmental occupational research unit if they are ever to be utilized on a scale broad enough to warrant their representation in the *DOT* and the national manpower planning effort.

It is also important to ensure that the USES Job Analysis Formulation focuses on the job seeker as well as on the job, since the same set of parameters can be used to describe both people and jobs. Thus it is clear that this approach should be used to assist the job seeker in clarifying job aims and in establishing job requirements and preferences when seeking work. Many placement interviewers tend to minimize the determination of the job seeker's preferences within his regular occupation. They assume the most critical factor to be the wage rate, even though this is often secondary. The determination of the job seeker's preferences and requirements should be just as important to the job seeker as it is to the employer.

OTHER ASSUMPTIONS

We know that little attention has been given to people's needs when problems occur in the economy. Reliance tends to be placed on the assumption that if jobs are created, the price mechanism will result in the absorbing of surpluses of idle workers; that is, if the price is right a worker will take any job, even if it does not meet his needs and abilities. Under this institutionalized approach, few remedial measures designed to correct manpower imbalances begin with an analysis of the kinds of workers who are unemployed, and the kinds of jobs that would best accommodate their needs.

In Chart 2, a model that recognizes the human factor in measures designed to attain supply-demand equilibrium, there are four dimensions: measures by the government, governmental agencies, and employers; the specific role and uses of *DOT 3*; the job seeker and his needs; and the role of institutionalized placement intermediaries. The objective of all foregoing sectors is to secure micro (individual) and macro (aggregate) equilibrium. This model shows the need for adequate social and legislative planning, the applicability of the *DOT* in personnel management, the process of individual vocational choice, and factors needed for adequate manpower matching (i.e., fulfilling the needs of employer and job seeker). Unless all function adequately in a total systems context, disequilibrium will occur, and there will be adverse effects on productivity and individual well-being, both monetarily and psychologically. In other words, Chart 2 indicates the merger of social planning, social legislation, public administration (of an adequate public manpower delivery system), and vocational choice. Additional clarification of the model follows.

Supply-demand imbalances are determined under government auspices using the *DOT 3* building blocks (in a matrix described in Chapter 3) and various studies by the Bureau of Labor Statistics, based on census data, input-output analysis, and other methodologies including job vacancy and other special studies. When the imbalances have been determined in occupational and industrial terms, remedial measures are developed. This leads to several types of inducement designed to resolve the identified imbalances—for example, authorizations by Congress for occupational training, including institutional as well as on-the-job programs; those provided under The Work Incentive program to stimulate employers to hire the disadvantaged; measures by occupational educators to provide the type of occupational training found necessary by input-output analysis; actions to be taken by employers, including changes in wage rates; job restructuring to provide a port of entry for the less experienced or new worker; and changes in the capital-labor mix on behalf of the employer, and ultimately the workers. All these steps point to newly trained persons who are ready to accept the jobs that had been shown to need additional personnel. The newly trained workers can obtain jobs with the employers who had expressed interest in such workers prior to training, or the workers can be placed through institutionalized placement agencies (e.g., the state employment services) or voluntary nonprofit placement agencies (e.g., the Urban League).

The role of the *DOT* is to contribute to the definition of supply-demand imbalances through statistical arrays of the unemployed, including individuals applying for unemployment insurance benefits. (This information is fed to government planning agencies, as discussed earlier.) In addition, the *DOT* and the Job Analysis Formulation are important tools in employer job design and redesign (restructuring), determining employer specifications and hiring criteria, and determining upgrading criteria; worker's qualifications would be set up using *DOT* as a primary diagnostic instrument, revealing current staffing patterns and predicting future needs. This cycle would produce a figure of the number of newly trained persons that should be hired.

The third element on Chart 2 relates to self-directed job seekers and the processes and steps leading to their initial job: appraisal, assisted by counselors and life experience, and the influences exerted by parents, friends, and relatives, including following in others' footsteps for lack of insight into one's own capacities, potentials, and needs. After career choice and hiring, the process is repeated, or the individual seeks institutionalized placement assistance.

The fourth element of Chart 2 describes the role of institutionalized placement intermediaries. The employer develops job specifications and hiring criteria. If workers are in short supply, the employer changes specifications or wage rates or redesigns the job. If the supply is satisfactory, the employer receives referrals from the placement agencies and hires.

The process starts with the job seeker: it is determined whether he is "job ready"; if he is, job opportunities are presented for his decision. If not, the job seeker is referred to remedial services including job counseling. After hire, the worker repeats the process if he is laid off or quits.

Additional detail for the micro or individual side of the equation is presented in Chart 3, which depicts the complicated interacting role of self-concept, self-knowledge, and aspiration level, arrayed against the pressures of influences of the school, parents, friends, and peers. Other influencing

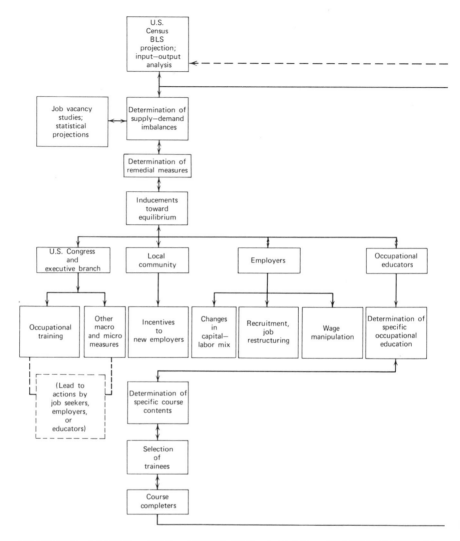

CHART 2 MODEL FOR ATTAINING LABOR SUPPLY—DEMAND EQUILIBRIUM

factors that retard or expedite the individual's vocational adjustment include institutional and noninstitutional factors, which in turn are critically affected by the capability of the people (agency staff) involved in hiring transactions and decision making, variables in the state of the economy, and the adequacy of available diagnostic tools and techniques.

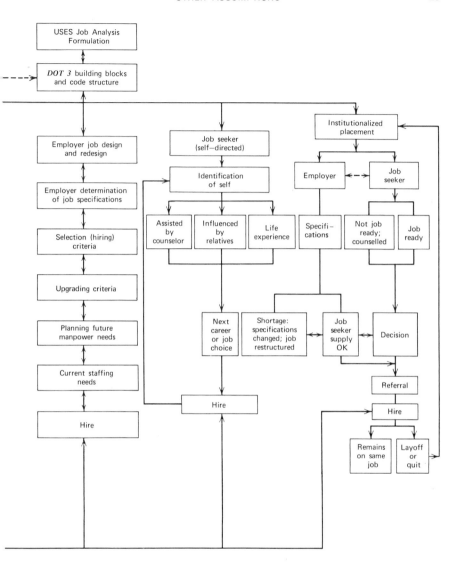

Initial career choices and the worker's movement from job to job
throughout his working lifetime are the product of many forces and
pressures. For many workers, few of the directions taken are deliberate, or
rational, or within the area of "choice." At the outset, the initial career "determination" is dependent on the individual's self-knowledge, self-concept,
aspiration level, and value system. These factors may be conditioned or
modified by parental influence and needs, or the judgments, values, and

Some micro factors in job search

Job seeker

Self—knowledge
Self—concept
Aspiration level

Knowledge of world of work
Role of school, parents,
friends, peers

Noninstitutional efforts

Institutional efforts

- Knowledge and availability
  of gate hire
- Friends, relatives
- Letter campaign
- Chance

- Union hiring halls
- Company recruiters
- Fee—charging agencies
- Classified ads
- College placement
- Placement through schools
- Public employment service
- CAP

Hire
(see personal factors, below)

Separation   Capability of agency
staff

State of the art in
placement technique

Tools and techniques ←→ Matching men and jobs ←→ Variables

- Clear—cut objectives
- Clear—cut standards
- Interviewing and
  counseling techniques
- State of the art
  — by academicians
  — in the serving agencies
- *Dictionary of Occupational
  Titles* — a new technique

Personal factors

- Job—seeker preferences as
  indicated by his GED
- Interests, temperaments,
  and psychosociological
  needs, including emotional
  factors

- State of the economy
- Level of wage rates
- Rate of unemployment
- Supply—demand relation—
  ships in specific
  occupations
- Existence of job
  opportunities in the
  locality
- Rigidity of employer
  specifications
- Length of job seeker's
  unemployment
- Worker's monetary situation
- Political factors
- Status factors
- Other sociological factors

Selection ←→ - Adequacy of manual
retrieval of applications
- Job bank
- Computer—assisted
  placement

Hire ←

- Informal groups
- Nature of the work
- Working conditions
- Promotional opportunities
- Theory $X-Y$ supervision
- Fringe benefits
- Growth and development

Separation

**CHART 3 AN "IDEAL" MODEL OF FACTORS INVOLVED IN JOB
SEARCH**

opinions of those with whom the job seeker interacts daily. Perhaps more important to some, the availability of suitable jobs within or near the geographical area of his choice may have a serious limiting effect. Another factor that may be critical is the availability of intermediaries to help the job seeker make the best possible juxtaposition of his discerned needs, the jobs that are open, and the means to find a job. The capabilities of such intermediaries, too, are conditioned by many interacting variables. Thus in the early 1960s the state employment services gave most attention to the deprived and the disadvantaged. Congressional funding did not always provide sufficient staff to meet the needs of all requesting service. Additionally, certain tools, techniques, and standards of the public employment service had to be reshaped and reconceptualized, and some lags occurred. Later, when employment service staff capability was achieved, the economy faltered, and counselees were unable to obtain the jobs that career exploration had led them to believe would meet their needs. Moreover, after hire, environmental factors and work experience may have a sharp impact, causing a need for redirection at any level or stage shown in Chart 3: new job choices, effective placement intermediaries, availability of government funded programs for occupational training, and so on.

Many findings of the Wagner College Plan and the author's experience indicate that rationality can be introduced into the job search–job adjustment process. For example, the *DOT* and the USES Job Analysis Formulation can assist the individual in determining the job or occupational area that best fits his needs and preferences, insofar as the individual, assisted by the counselor, is able to perceive them when the counseling takes place. The *DOT*, in other words, would assist the individual in actions leading to his first job. During his tenure on this (and subsequent) jobs, the individual would be subjected to various environmental influences shown in Chart 3: informal groups, the nature of the job, working conditions, the availability of promotional opportunities and the extent to which he could (and wanted to) obtain them, the kind of supervision (permissive or closely directed), and opportunities for growth and development. These factors would have an impact on the worker's self-concept, aspiration levels, expectations, and value system. Various decisions would be made because of the accumulated experience, including a decision to remain in the job or to leave it. If the worker leaves, the process shown in the chart would be repeated.

The remainder of this book is designed to bring these issues into focus and to describe and illustrate each contention made and each application developed and utilized. It should, therefore, be useful to personnel directors interested in updating their techniques and in constructing Affirmative Action Plans; to employment counselors and persons interested in self-appraisal using the building blocks of the *DOT*; and to anyone concerned with manpower planning. Finally, some of the directions needed to develop a national manpower policy are indicated.

Chapter 2 is an overview of the state of the art in (manpower) planning; we review the relevant literature dealing with the disciplines from which many personnel management techniques are derived.

An in-depth review of the *Dictionary of Occupational Titles* and the Job Analysis Formulation, Chapter 3 suggests how these tools can be applied in implementing Revised Order No. 4 and perfecting many of the necessary elements of personnel management.

Chapter 4 describes the Wagner College Affirmative Action Plan and tells how it meets the requirements of Revised Order No. 4. The findings about the operation of the Wagner Plan, including costs and benefits (Chapter 5) are discussed in the light of their implications, and the directions and dimensions of future research in human resources planning, in Chapters 6 and 7.

NOTES

1. Issued by the U.S. Department of Labor, December 4, 1971.

2. This convenient term represents members of the following ethnic groups: negroes, Hispanics (Spanish-speaking people), American Indians, and orientals.

3. This is envisioned in the Employment Act of 1946. What is needed is a set of programs to cover each facet of the problem. Many such programs have already been enacted and, after experience, revised.

4. U.S. Department of Labor, *Dictionary of Occupational Titles,* 3rd ed., (Washington, D.C., Government Printing Office, 1965).

5. U.S. Department of Labor, Manpower Administration, *Handbook for Analyzing Jobs* (Washington, D.C.: Government Printing Office, 1972).

6. After Leontief. Additional discussion on this aspect is presented in other sections.

7. Conversion is possible only if every job in one classification has been related to a job in another classification structure; the same data, therefore, can be presented by both. Many problems occur, however, in relating codes from one classification to the other. At best, such conversions are a compromise, and there are many omissions and adjustments. There is a conversion between *DOT 3* and the census classification.

8. Such a standard classification is being developed under government auspices. It will do for occupations what the Standard Industrial Classification (SIC) has made possible for industry.

9. William H. Stead and W. Earl Masincup, "The Occupational Research Program of the United States Employment Service," Public Administration Service, Chicago. The last sentence of the quotation relates to the research conducted by early pioneers of scientific management. Much of such research was aimed at determining the basic "movements" in work requiring physical effort as a basis for improving efficiency. (Frank and Lillian) Gilbreth were among the pioneers.

10. Matching job seekers with employment opportunities. Many such systems use the *DOT* or its building blocks in their system design (i.e., as the basis for the "match").

11. For a brief overview of the background prior to 1943, see "The Occupational Research Program of the United States Employment Service," cited in note 9.

12. For definitions of each, see *Handbook for Analyzing Jobs* (note 5). Worker Functions and Worker Traits are also defined in Appendices A and B.

CHAPTER 2

REVIEW OF
RELEVANT LITERATURE

THE GENESIS OF MANPOWER ISSUES

Issues and factors affecting manpower doubtless paralleled the emergence of intelligence in prehistoric times: the allocations of time for searching for food, the activities generated, and the specializations, supervisory relationships, and exchanges of roles which were involved. Many of the more proximate issues for our times emerged with the Industrial Revolution and, later, the beginnings of scientific management, the increased presence of agricultural migratory workers, the Employment Act of 1946 and its derivatives, and today's recognition of the need to identify and to resolve the requirements of the "disadvantaged" minorities.

That a piecemeal approach was used can be seen by reviewing the innovations designed to meet these needs and the problems encountered after implementation was well underway. Many of the devices created, whether legislative, conceptual, or administrative, were designed to assuage pressures from interested groups or from the outraged or concerned public. Many problems occurred because of the need to reorder priorities, with consequent alienation of those adversely affected. Many other problems stemmed from the lack of technique or of adequate tools, which the social sciences had been unable to generate with any degree of unanimity among the different schools of thought that developed.

GOVERNMENT SEARCH FOR SOLUTIONS

This unintegrated, undirected approach is reflected in major studies dealing with various aspects of manpower policy and its implementation. It is clear that most if not all the subsystems involved were characterized by confused objectives, unclear concepts, uncertainty in direction, and a paucity of technique. Several examples follow.

The Manpower Report of the President for 1972 states:

> As [this chapter] has indicated, there is hardly any aspect of government policy which does not have manpower implications and often far-reaching ones. These implications have been assessed so far on only a limited, piecemeal basis—in part because of the difficulties and uncertainties almost inevitably involved in efforts to foresee the repercussions of new program developments. Yet if this country is to move efficiently toward optimal growth with high employment levels for all groups and acceptable price trends, the manpower consequences of government action in all fields should be projected and appraised on a continuing basis and in a much more comprehensive, integrated manner. Advances in this direction would enhance the effectiveness of manpower policy and increase its contributions to achievement of the country's economic and social objectives.[1]

The *Manpower Report* goes on to develop the idea that manpower policies are important to shaping policies necessary for high employment and price stability. It further recognizes that the new manpower programs are yet to be tested and that it is necessary to explore them to determine "how they can be integrated most effectively with broader economic issues, to improve.... the effectiveness of fiscal and monetary policies to reduce unemployment without generating inflationary pressures."[2]

This section of the report concludes by emphasizing the importance of effective manpower delivery systems. It states:

> The linking of present manpower institutions into an effective system remains a challenge for the 1970s to which the Administration's legislative recommendations and administrative actions in the manpower field are specifically addressed.[3]

Another shift in emphasis is reflected in the 1973 report:

> While the Administration took further steps in 1973 toward a decentralized manpower system, the Congress renewed its efforts to achieve comprehensive manpower reform.... Near the end of the session, the bipartisan Comprehensive Employment and Training Act of 1973 was passed, ending several years of controversy over the basic design of the Nation's manpower efforts on behalf of the disadvantaged and unemployed.
>
> . . .
>
> The Comprehensive Employment and Training Act (CETA) makes nearly 500 cities, countries, and States eligible for direct grants of Federal manpower funds, effectively shifting the focus of activities away from Washington. Most categorical manpower programs will be eliminated in the course of the current year, to be replaced by locally devised mixes of manpower services suited to particular needs and circumstances.[4]

Another presidential concern, expressed in transmitting the *1972 Manpower Report* to Congress, was "to move toward a broader national manpower policy which will be an important adjunct of economic policy in achieving our Nation's economic and social objectives." The new legislation also addresses these goals through the establishment of the National Commission for Manpower Policy. The commission's broadly representative membership is responsible for identifying manpower goals and needs and assessing the impact on the present and potential labor force of various governmental programs and activities. With diligence and the cooperation of the many interests involved, the commission should help to move the nation closer to the "coherent, flexible, national manpower policy" sought by both the Administration and the Congress."[5]

RECOMMENDATIONS OF SOME CONSULTANTS

These expressions of intent and conceptualization in the *Manpower Report* reenforce E. Wight Bakke's views of some 9 years earlier. Bakke reviewed the entire spectrum of manpower services. He began by contrasting the British system (essentially social-work oriented) with the Swedish system, where "Employment and Manpower Services are fitting the requirements for a strong, stable, and growing economy." He emphasized *worker* needs as well as *employer* manpower *requirements*. Contrary to some authorities in the field, he urged that *all* client groups be served, to meet the needs of *all* employers. He examined the United States federal–state (employment service and manpower) relationship, relating the elements of his discussion to the need for an integrated national manpower policy and suggesting means to accomplish this objective. Thus Bakke's views and discussion center on an "active" or "positive manpower policy":

> A positive labor market policy implies that at the very heart of the nation's effort to make more productive, effective and just the operation of the economy and society, there is an agency or agencies which have the knowledge, the will, and the power to direct the dynamic development of the employment of the nation's manpower toward its maximum contribution to these ends and toward maximum self-realization in work of the individuals involved.[6]

In discussing the institutionalized means to achieve such a policy, Bakke noted both quantitative and qualitative aspects:

> Employment and Manpower Services are indispensable facilities for any public or private effort to plan for and achieve full employment, stability, and growth in the economy. They are indispensable to achieving, within the limits set and opportunities provided by that economy, a just, rewarding and satisfying distribution, among the workers of the country, of the chance to work and live by that work. The efficient and just functioning of a free economy requires that

manpower of the quantity and quality needed shall be developed, that it shall be fully and efficiently utilized, and that it be available when and where needed to make its maximum contribution. These are the tasks of the Employment and Manpower Services.[7]

Since Bakke considered the public employment services to be the chief manpower agency, it is appropriate to report the shifts in emphasis the state employment services found it necessary to take in response to emerging social, governmental, and societal imperatives.

The management consultants McKinsey & Company were retained by the New York State Employment Service (NYSES) in the early 1960s (while Bakke was preparing his book) to study the programs and operations of the NYSES. The first paragraph of their conclusions states:

> In an economy in which there is a large and increasing number of job moves of new entries and exits . . . there are consequent needs by workers, employers, unions, schools, industrial development councils, and other community agencies for minimizing the imbalances between labor demand and supply. There are needs for counseling and training of workers entering the job market for the first time and those forced by technological or other changes to make a move. There are needs by many institutions for information on the nature of the labor supply and the demand for labor. There are needs by employers for occupational analysis assistance and manpower planning so that they may utilize the workers available in coming years, including the youths, women, negroes, and the physically handicapped.
>
> But we must recognize that placement is the core process. . . . It is conclusive, however, that at present, the Employment Service makes its major impact in the placement area. The communities of New York State require more than that; they need a broadly conceived program of labor market assistance.[8]

Although McKinsey recognized that placement is the prime objective, they, like Bakke, emphasized the more comprehensive role that should be assumed by the employment service. (This role was accepted in subsequent years, as policy statements and new laws indicate.)

In any event, the McKinsey finding accurately defined the primary role of the employment service when the study was made—that is, to function as an employment exchange, to bring job seekers and employers together. Since the emphasis was on meeting employer needs, the diagnostic framework used was to identify and to locate job seekers with the requisite skills and abilities and to offer them job opportunities that would best meet *employer* production needs. Less attention was devoted to *job-seeker* preferences and to counseling. The broader objective was not used until 1969, when the Department of Labor promulgated a new model describing the employment service as "a comprehensive manpower agency."[9] The new direction was to require the employment service to reach out to the communities, to go directly to the socially, culturally, and economically deprived, and to offer them a series of "new programs."

The rapid proliferation of new programs, and the need to recruit, test, hire, and train staff, strained the capacity of the employment service to meet the legislative and administrative objectives. This situation was recognized by the Labor Department in the following release:

> The Federal–State employment service, as a primary manpower delivery system, has faced this challenge in the past and must meet it more squarely in the future. As a deliverer of manpower services to poverty-oriented programs such as CEP, WIN, Job Corps, N.Y.C., MDTA and NAB–JOBS, the employment service has been forced to redirect its efforts to the needs of the poor and disadvantaged. For the most part this has been achieved by add-ons of personnel and money and not by a fundamental redirection of basic resources.
>
> The consequences of the effort to develop alternative structures has been a proliferation and duplication of efforts and delivery systems, both within the Employment Service System itself and in community agencies, with related responsibilities in serving the poor and disadvantaged. From this proliferation, fragmentation and competition has emerged a demand by responsible community leadership for more orderly and effective delivery systems; in particular, a system which better plans coordinates, and directs job development contacts with employers.[10]

GOVERNMENTAL SHIFTS IN EMPHASIS

Following this mandate for an enlarged mission, the Employment Service placed heavy emphasis on serving the disadvantaged. In New York State some staff were additionally diverted from placement activities because a new law required welfare recipients to register at the Employment Service and to accept "any job in which they could engage." This may have diminished the ability of the state agency to meet the needs of some employers and some "job-ready" job seekers (i.e., persons who had performed acceptably in recent, prior employment and were ready for new jobs). Most large cities were required by the USES to install job banks in which all job opportunities available each day are listed and described in a job "bank book." In these cities, "job-ready" applicants were given a copy of the book and asked to identify any job for which they thought they were qualified. People who felt they could handle a given job were referred to the employer, sometimes after minimal screening.

The functioning of the job banks was complicated because although the Employment Service had to refer the disadvantaged as their first priority, employers were not obliged to hire these job seekers, whom, they often alleged, were marginally qualified. Only defense contractors were required to list their openings with the employment services under Executive Order

11598, now Public Law 52-940. A thorough review of this development is beyond the scope of this book; a few aspects are reviewed in succeeding chapters. Suffice it to say that in 1971 the Manpower Administration again shifted its emphasis. It began to stress the importance of *placement.* This new emphasis, however, was not intended to downgrade the importance of servicing the deprived. The "new" emphasis, however, supports Bakke's views that the Employment Service should serve all sectors of the community. Experience has shown that without employer cooperation in seeking new employees from the Employment Service, placement services to the disadvantaged fall short of meeting the need.

The reaction to the new direction was prompt. A few weeks after the new policy was announced, *The New York Times* printed a news item captioned "Job Bias Charged to Labor Agency."

Washington, April 10: The Department of Labor has been accused of discrimination for allegedly violating Federal mandates that it focus its employment service resources on the special needs of the poor and the disadvantaged.

The accusation was initially made in a class action lawsuit filed in a letter sent to James D. Hodgson, Secretary of Labor, last week by seven antipoverty and social action organizations.

The charges center on changes in "policy" governing the department's employment and training service (now the USES), a network of 2200 federally funded employment centers around the country that offer a variety of job counseling, placement and related training programs to the public.

In prior years, the Department of Labor has given priority to job training and placement of the disadvantaged, who include the hard-to-employ—those under 21 and over 45 with no skills and limited education.

But this year it has decided to shift its emphasis to making more job placements and developing more jobs.

Robert J. Brown, director of the employment service network, said in a recent interview that the service planned to increase job placements by 1.4 million over placements made in the 1971 fiscal year. This, he said, would mean increases in 314,700 placements for the disadvantaged, 510,000 for minorities—primarily blacks—and 468,100 for veterans and 110,500 in regular placements.

Mr. Brown said there was no disagreement that the spirit of the law gives priority to the disadvantaged. And that's exactly what we're doing, he said.

There are two parts to the equation, he said, and previously we have addressed only one part.[11]

SOME RESEARCH FINDINGS

Employers and other intermediaries involved in solving manpower issues are uncertain whether the needs of the disadvantaged should be set above those of the employer, and it is clear that an objective base is yet to be identified, accepted, and used by employers in formulating hiring specifications. For example, New York University's School of Commerce became interested in why employers reported recruitment difficulties in certain entry occupations for which many unemployed and underemployed minority group members seemed to qualify. This interest led to a federally funded study of hiring requirements to ascertain

> the role which employer hiring standards play in this labor market imbalance. Ten major entry and near-entry level occupations, where labor shortages were reported, were selected for study simultaneously in New York and St. Louis Standard Metropolitan Statistical Areas (SMSAs). The occupations included five white collar jobs (bank teller; cashier-checker; hotel clerk, salesperson, parts; and shipping and receiving clerk); four blue collar jobs (arc welder; press feeder, production-machine operator; and wire worker); and one service occupation (orderly).[12]

These occupations were studied as found in 14 industries.

The findings reported by the researchers (Professors Daniel E. Diamond and Hrach Bedrosian) included the following:

> The analysis indicated little or no relationship between hiring standards and job performance needs for all occupational groups in a significant percentage of the companies studies. Moreover the existence of considerable variability in minimum requirements and preferences among employers for the same occupation demonstrated that even the most objectively determined hiring standards may be influenced by subjective considerations.[13]

Additional evidence that many employers have not been able to identify the crucial criteria for successful job performance can be readily obtained. Apparently many employers are content to use intuitive, subjective criteria as a basis for hiring. During the NYU study one employer stated that he preferred high school graduates for low-level jobs, although the study indicated that this attribute was not relevant. The employer, however, justified his stand by stating that high school graduates were neater and better disciplined. Another employer wanted persons who were promotable to highest level positions; yet only a few high-level positions were ever available. During the depression of the 1930s some department stores on New York City's Fifth Avenue hired only very presentable female college graduates as elevator operators.

SOME SUGGESTED SOLUTIONS

Turning to a more general analysis of problems of manpower policy and related aspects of personnel management, Mary L. Tenopyr reports in *Personnel Psychology* that:

> The need for clear and concise description and clarification of actual work being performed has been recognized as underlying the whole field of personnel

management. Job analysis is a major function, yet it has been a relatively neglected field in personnel research. Considerable research time and effort have been devoted to personnel selection, motivation, and job satisfaction, all of which are tied in intrinsically to what people do at work. One can only speculate—as has been done in a comprehensive review of research findings on job analysis by Prien and Ronan ["Job Analysis: A Review of Research Findings." *Personnel Psychology.* Vol. 24 (November 3, 1971)]—why one of the most important aspects of personnel system has been subjected to so little research from which one can draw generalizations.[14]

In the *Harvard Business Review,* Lawrence L. Ferguson examines aspects of selection and criteria affecting promotion and "management development" within the context of what he terms "scientific personnel management." These developments, he says, were "completely impractical just a few years ago," and he attributes them to the following coinciding conditions:

1.   The development of highly effective flexible, time-shared real-time computer systems, with matching advances in analytical techniques for processing data.
2.   The increasingly significant progress that social scientists are making in providing insights into the management development and management process.

.   .   .

It is now possible to replace intuition with scientific analysis in the personnel area, just as intuition has successively given way to analysis in engineering, finance, production and marketing.[15]

He concludes by stating:

There is now sound evidence of the near-term practicality of a comprehensive simulation model of business careers that can given coherence and relevance to the various pieces of the selection, training, motivating and promotion processes. Such a model or system will also provide a rubric or matrix for examining the merits of different research and operating possibilities, and a perspective for planning and testing the means to improve important elements in the costly and relatively primitive process of manager development that is common today.[16]

A review of the recent literature has produced little to indicate that significant advances have occurred in this specific direction since Ferguson's article appeared in 1966.

Unfortunately, many other areas of "manpower" are characterized by confusion, disagreement, or disenchantment: Gifford writes that "job enlargement is a diffuse concept, which seems to be more an attitude or a strategy than an easily definable entity."[17]

Additionally he states

Assuming that theory "y" or theory "z" is a reasonable description of most modern workers, management must provide, through Horizontal and Vertical job enlargement:

1. Jobs which require a more complex utilization of cognitive and motor abilities possessed by the worker
2. Jobs bearing more freedom and responsibility in the performance of the assigned tasks
3. Jobs requiring a greater variety of knowledge and skill
4. Jobs involving an entire natural module of work whenever feasible.[18]

Several researchers conceive of the "task" as the basic module in research directed toward simplifying job analysis by constructing an inventory of tasks for groups of occupations.[19] For example, some investigators at Cornell University report in a recent study:

The functions–task theory avoids the job-title approach problems of varied tasks performed under the same job title and variations in job title for the same job. Problems of definitions of job titles, keeping job titles current and updating recruitment instruments resulting from technological change are also avoided. By focusing directly on tasks, the function–tasks theory avoids the intermediate step of defining competencies in terms of tasks. Using this theory as an approach also offers the opportunity for the identification of tasks common to the performance of functions in one or more occupations which may form the basis for the development of recruitment instruments and training programs with broad implications.[20]

This approach ignores sociopsychological traits thought by other researchers to be more significant than ability to perform sets of tasks. More specifically, considerable interest has developed in probing manpower problems in hospitals, doubtless as a result of recruitment and retention problems in such institutions. The New York State Governor's Advisory Council on Youth and Work conducted a study of manpower issues in the Buffalo Project on Health Manpower. Its 1970 report tells why the project was begun, describing in particular the new legislation, the methodology employed, and the council's recommendations.

In commenting on the heavy increase in manpower needed to implement the legislation, the report states

(1) . . . ideally, core curricula should be created to serve as the basis for training programs in several different occupations.
(2) . . . for the student taking the courses, core curricula would provide more opportunity for transfer from one occupation to another . . . If he is dissatisfied with his present job or course, he could transfer to another health field and thus not be lost to health services.

The duties already identified by the task force as being an integral part of the new job titles need to be developed into descriptions with the following identifying data:

Job definition
Job description
Educational level
Worker traits
Job-related traits[21]

Unlike the Cornell researchers, Fine finds it desirable to specify the "functional" and "content" skills in each task description. He identifies his job analysis approach as a system; this system was developed from the USES Job Analysis Formulation, and constitutes a further refinement of it. (See his monographs published by the W.E. Upjohn Institute.)

Gilpatrick, in her NYC Health Services Mobility Study (HSMS), determined that a more specific methodology than the USES Job Analysis Formulation was needed to meet HSMS objectives; these included the development of job-related education ladders, and performance evaluation. To fulfill these objectives, HSMS developed a more categorical definition of a task and rated each according to 16 *skill scales* (which can be grouped into six broad areas), a *knowledge scale* (for each knowledge identified through a Knowledge Classification System), and a *task frequency* scale.

In another dimension, Gilpatrick reported that:

The structure of the municipal hospital system makes efficient planning, development and use of health manpower extremely difficult. The structure of City government, the civil service, and especially City budgeting practices hamper efficient manpower administration in hospitals. They have hampered the development of an adequate manpower program. The lack of an adequate centralized personnel or manpower function makes overall planning almost impossible. . . .

(a) the relevance of job titles to job functions has been eroded by cumbersome Civil Service procedures and arbitrary budgeting requirements,
(b) the department of hospitals does not now collect or have access to adequate information on employment and vacancies by title . . .
(c) Promotional Civil Service lines function to provide pathways between jobs not requiring additional training; they do not aid in developing pathways between jobs requiring further education. . . .[22]

One of the authors' solutions is to make job analysis available:

Ideally, a job analysis method which identifies the skills and knowledge required to perform existing tasks (with existing technology) can result in a clustering of tasks into related skill and knowledge families. Jobs can be designed which are composed of tasks requiring related levels of skill and knowledge. From this, alternative job pathways can be designed.
Such a job analysis function can then handle changes in output and changes in

technology by rearranging job structures and selecting appropriate job populations for assignment to new or different functions. Information on staffing patterns, combined with the job family concept, can help avoid the creation of skill shortages.[23]

In her desire to establish a suitable data base, Gilpatrick found it necessary to make some adjustments in the *DOT 3* code structure. A fuller discussion of her modifications is available;[24] the book simply states:

> This occupational code[24] relies on the work already put into the third edition of the *Dictionary of Occupational Titles (DOT)* and actually supplements it. It is a three-digit occupational code system, in which the first two digits are a continuous variable. It eliminates industrial coding and is designed to be used with the Standard Industrial Classification (SIC) system. . . .

Occupational educators too have been aware of the need for updating concepts to meet the ever-emerging changes in occupational demands resulting from technological advances and economic imperatives. The authors of a recent study observe that "one solution to the problem may lie in the concept of occupational clustering where people would be trained not for a single position, but for a group of positions all having similar characteristics.[26] This approach apparently is intended to enable persons so trained to change from one job to another within the cluster with minimal additional training.

Riccobono and Cunningham describe the Position Analysis Questionnaire (PAQ) developed by McCormick, Jeanneret, and Meeham in 1969, which reportedly collects two different types of data—one concerned "worker-oriented" job dimensions, the other covering "human-attribute requirements ("aptitudes, temperaments, and interests").[27] The study also describes and reports on another instrument, the Occupational Analysis Inventory (OAI), designed to meet the following specifications:

> . . . a comprehensive set of quantitatively based work dimensions . . .
> 1. general enough for application to a wide variety jobs and occupations, yet specific and concrete enough to have curricular implications;
> 2. based upon current theories of behavior,
> 3. linked to established human dimensions for which there are standardized measures (i.e., tests in the cognitive, psychomotor, and affective domains; and
> 4. empirically supported.[28]

The study involved sophisticated statistical manipulations that resulted in the identification of 81 "work dimensions." In concluding, authors remark that the factors "must be considered tentative," that additional verification will be made through replicated studies, and that "exploratory analyses performed on data gathered subsequent to this study suggests there will be approximately 20–25 of these high order factors, . . . [which should prove to be more useful and should constitute a] "more manageable number."[29] One of these authors has also examined the other half of the equation (i.e., the human attributes).[30]

The studies, articles, and reports described above have underscored the need for conceptual clarification in many areas such as aggregate economics, personnel management, civil service systems, employer identification of realistic specifications, classification structures, criteria for determining clusters of related occupations, and identification of factors for the determination of career ladders. However, specific mention has not been made of what vocational guidance practitioners and theorists have termed "traits and factors:" that is, such "psychological" considerations as aptitudes and interest. The use of traits and factors is controversial. Thus Osipow observes that:

> Super and Bachrach (1957) have pointed out the futility of looking for personality traits in members of different occupations because too much overlap exists, and the occupations tolerate a wide range of personality differences among their members. It is likely to be more profitable to look for factors which influence the sequence of career decisions that people make, which seems to be precisely what the personality style approach, discussed earlier, seems to do. Until an extensive effort is made to analyze occupations functionally and to develop highly sophisticated tests of both personality and aptitude, no serious attempt to match people and job with a simplistic trait—factor method is likely to be highly successful.[31]

Divergence of opinion developed in the field of vocational guidance since its germination by Parson some 60 years ago and the following comments by some authorities demonstrate many of the current differences.

Calia, in his brief review of vocational guidance, reports:

> Vocational Guidance, or more specifically, the practice of disseminating occupational information in the school setting has fallen into considerable disrepute. It has been downgraded in importance (Ginzberg, Ginsburg, Axelrod, & Hema (1951), depicted as an essentially perceptual process (Rusalem, 1954), buried (Barry & Wolf 1962), deemed "destructive" (Lifton, 1963), and "junked" (Barry & Wolf, 1963).

> On the other hand, this Parsonian notion has been defended (Sayler, 1964), needed (Gaither, Hackman & Hay, 1963) and placed in its proper perspective (Borow, 1964, Calia, 1964; Tiedeman, 1963; Hackman, 1965). The issue, while complex, centers on the relative importance of occupational information in the guidance and counseling process.[32]

> Until persistent and concerted efforts are made to translate theory into practice, busy practitioners are likely to find the esoteric meanderings of the vocational theorists unfathomable, and will continue to subscribe to the familiar, if anachronistic, three-step Parsonian model.[33]

Osipow briefly describes controversial areas pointed out by some of the leading theorists. He identifies "four distinct approaches to thinking about career counseling. . . ."

Trait factor theories . . . assumes that a straightforward matching of an individual's abilities and interests with the world's vocational opportunities can be accomplished, and once accomplished, solves the problems of vocational choice for that individual.

Sociology and career choice . . . (provides) . . . that circumstances beyond the control of the individual contribute significantly to the career choices he makes and that the principal task confronting the youth (or older person, for that matter), is the development of techniques to cope effectively with his environment.

Self-concept theory . . . holds as its central thesis that (1) individuals develop more clearly defined self-concepts as they grow older although these vary to conform with changes in one's view of reality as correlated with aging; (2) people develop images of the occupational world which they compare with their self-image in trying to make career decisions; and (3) the adequacy of the eventual career decision is based on the similarity between an individual's self-concept and the vocational concept of the career be eventually chooses.

Vocational choice and personality theory generally hypothesize that . . . workers select their jobs because they see potential for the satisfaction of their needs.[34]

Osipow goes on to state that other approaches such as the psychoanalytic can be subsumed into the foregoing. In addition, he stresses the interdependence of these models: "For example, in the self-concept or developmental approach, part of the image of self-concept is based on tests which reflect the trait-factor approaches. . . ."[35]

In his "concluding suggestions" Osipow states:

Overall, the theories appear to be much too broad in scope and generally too skimpy in detail. What vocational psychology needs at the present time is a collection of miniature theories, each dealing with circumscribed, explicit segments of vocational behavior, to be woven into a broad theory after the smaller theories have been shaped by empirical findings. A miniature theory describing the decision-making process, a theory explaining job satisfaction, a theory explaining how career development is related to self concept implementation, could all be developed independently, and when the details are in order, connected by other theoreticians to a larger conception of how the human personality develops and functions.[36]

This seems to underscore the need for a total systems approach for vocational psychology. Osipow describes such an approach:

". . . the systems approach is in a position to take the most useful concepts of each theory of career development and apply them to the understanding of individual behavior. Elements of the social, personal, and economic situation within which individuals operate may be more explicity analyzed, and the relationship of the larger systems to one another may be more clearly understood than in the traditional approaches of behavior, which tend to emphasize only one major segment of either the individual or his environment.[37]

The following conclusions can be drawn from the foregoing review. (1) It is clear that most macro and micro aspects of manpower policy and technique are in critical need of reconceptualization, research, and development. (2) Most of the elements tend to be studied independently to meet the narrow concerns of each group. (3) The orientation and technology of the *DOT 3* systems approach may bring a much-needed analytical framework to bear to explore and resolve the manpower issues and problems described in Charts 2 and 3 of Chapter 1.

The need of Wagner College to design an Affirmative Action Plan provided an excellent opportunity to test the applicability of the *DOT* approach in resolving many of the issues previously enumerated. The Wagner College Plan provides that position descriptions be prepared for all nonfaculty jobs, using the job analysis formulation described in this chapter. Moreover, the building blocks of this formulation also are to be used as a diagnostic frame of reference in interviewing and counseling each worker and job candidate to help each to identify his or her career potentials and the opportunities for fulfilling them at Wagner College or outside it. The position descriptions are to expedite such exploration and decision making, as well as to provide a basis for effective supervision. In addition, the structure of the *DOT* is to act as a retrieval mechanism to locate qualified workers and job candidates (previously interviewed) when vacancies occur. Job restructuring and the construction of career ladders are to be initiated as needed. Finally, the development of a supply-demand matrix for Wagner and the surrounding area should facilitate planning and the identification of recruiting needs and resources.

We now describe the *DOT* and the USES Job Analysis Formulation on which it is based, since the implementation of the Wagner Plan was based on the utilization of these technologies.

NOTES

1. U.S. Department of Labor, *Manpower Report of the President* (Washington, D.C.: Government Printing Office), p. 23. Transmitted to the Congress March 1972.

2. Ibid., p. 19.

3. Ibid., p. 24.

4. U.S. Department of Labor, *Manpower Report of the President* (Washington D.C.: Government Printing Office), transmitted to the Congress April 1974, pp. 38, 3.

5. Ibid., p. 66.

6. E. Wight Bakke, *A Positive Labor Market Policy* (Columbus, Ohio: Charles E. Merill Books, 1963), p. 204.

7. Ibid. p. 204.

8. *A Study of the Programs of the New York State Employment Service,* McKinsey & Company, Inc., April 1963, pp. 2–20.

9. U.S. Department of Labor, Manpower Administration, *The Employment Service as a Comprehensive Manpower Agency,* June 25, 1969 (mimeographed copy).

10. Ibid., p. 1.

11. *New York Times,* April 11, 1972.

12. U.S. Department of Labor, Manpower Administration, *Hiring Standards and Job Performance,* Manpower Research Monograph #18 (Washington, D.C.: Government Printing Office, 1970), p. 1.

13. Ibid., p. 3.

14. Mary L. Tenopyr, "Research Roundup," *Personnel Administration,* January–February 1972, p. 52.

15. Lawrence L. Ferguson, "Better Management of Manager's Careers," *Harvard Business Review,* March–April 1966, p. 140.

16. Ibid., p. 152.

17. John B. Gifford, "Job Enlargement," *Personnel Administration,* January–February 1972, p. 42.

18. Ibid., p. 44.

19. U.S. Department of Labor, Manpower Administration. Task Analysis Inventories. (Washington, D.C.: Government Printing Office, 1973).

20. Arthur L. Berkey, William E. Drake, and James W. Legacy, "A Model For Task Analysis in Agri-Business" (Ithaca, N.Y.: *New York State College of Agriculture and Life Science,* June 1972), p. 5.

21. The Buffalo Project on Health Manpower Report prepared by the Governor's Advisory Council on Youth and Work, Albany, N.Y. (undated).

22. E. G. Gilpatrick and Paul K. Corliss, *The Occupational Structure of New York City Municipal Hospitals* (New York: Praeger Publishers, 1970), pp. 68–69.

23. Ibid., p. 144.

24. Eleanor Gilpatrick, "A Proposed System of Occupational Coding," *Monthly Labor Review,* Vol. 91, no. 10 (October 1968) pp. 47–53.

25. The Buffalo Project on Health Manpower Report prepared by the Governor's Advisory Council on Youth and Work, Albany, N.Y. (undated).

26. J. S. Riccobono and J. W. Cunningham, *Work Dimensions Derived Through Systematic Job Analysis; A Study of the Occupational Analysis Inventory* (Raleigh: Center For Occupational Education, North Carolina State University, 1971), Preface. See also Thomas C. Tuttle and J. W. Cunningham, *Affective Correlates of Systematically Derived Work Dimensions* (Raleigh: North Carolina State University Center for Occupational Education, 1972).

27. Ibid., p. 12.

28. Ibid., P. 15.

29. Ibid., p. 77.

30. R. W. Neeb, J. W. Cunningham, and J. J. Pass, *Human Attributes Requirements of Work Elements: Further Development of the Occupational Analysis Inventory* (Raleigh:

Center Research and Development Center for Occupational Education, North Carolina State University, Englewood Cliffs, N.J.:) Report No. 14. (1971).

31. Samuel H. Osipow. *Theories of Career Development.* Second edition, Englewood Cliffs, N.J.: Prentice-Hall, 1973, p. 226.

32. Calia Vincent F., "Vocational Guidance: After the Fall," *Personnel & Guidance Journal,* December, Vol. 45, No. 4 (1966), p. 320.

33. Calia, ibid., p. 326.

34. Osipow, ibid., pp. 9–11.

35. Ibid., p. 11.

36. Ibid., p. 307.

37. Ibid., p. 299.

CHAPTER 3

THE DICTIONARY OF OCCUPATIONAL TITLES, THIRD-EDITION: ITS STRUCTURE AND USES

The Dictionary of Occupational Titles, Third Edition (*DOT 3*) was issued in 1965. It defines the 14,000 basic jobs comprising the nation's economy and includes a classification structure. The latter was designed primarily to improve the placement process used by the 54 state employment services, all of which are affiliated with the United States Department of Labor's Manpower Administration. The local employment offices record pertinent facts about job seekers' experience, skills, knowledges, and abilities on application cards. These cards are coded and filed according to *DOT* codes, to be matched[1] against employer orders (job requisitions) when orders are received. The *DOT* classifications were based on and reflect elements of the Job Analysis Formulations to which we now turn.

THE ELEMENTS OF THE USES JOB ANALYSIS FORMULATION

The "building blocks" identified and fully defined in the Manpower Administration's *Handbook for Analyzing Jobs,*[2] comprise a standardized, structured frame of reference for all the parameters that describe jobs. Occupational analysts use this frame of reference when analyzing and defining jobs. The parameters are described in the following paragraphs.

A worker performs a task by using a specific methodology or technology: a clerk *RECORDS*, an author *WRITES*, a tailor *SEWS*, a weaver *WEAVES*, the worker involved in tending equipment that removes alcohol from beer, *DISTILLS*. Each of these occupations can be described respectively by the following *Work Fields*: ACCOUNTING—RECORDING;

WRITING; SEWING—TAILORING; WEAVING; DISTILLING. The *Handbook for Analyzing Jobs* identifies and defines 100 such Work Fields, which all together accommodate the 14,000 defined jobs found in the United States economy. It is possible to collect data on employment and unemployment by the 100 Work Fields because each *DOT* job title and code has been identified by its "parent" Work Field. When preparing the job analysis schedule following his observation of a job, the occupational analyst codes each job for its *DOT* code, its Work Field, and each of the other parameters or descriptors described below.

In performing these technologies or methodologies, the worker may use *Machines, Tools, Equipment,* or *Work Aids* (MTEWA). The analyst must ascertain which, if any, are employed to indicate the scope of the task being performed and the apparatus called for to perform it. Ability to use such apparatus may be a critical factor in the hiring process.

Another parameter—*Materials, Products, Subject Matter, or Service* (*MPSMS*) differentiates among jobs that involve the same Work Fields. Does a writer prepare *advertising copy* or *financial publications,* or is he a journalist preparing *news items* for *newspapers* or *magazines*? Does a sewing machine operator work on *ladies' garments, upholstery, canvas products, luggage,* or *ladies' handbags*? Does a molder work with *ferrous* or *nonferrous* metals? Is a given person a *mathematician* or *clinical* psychologist? Some workers may shift from one product or material or subject matter or service to another, but many frictions—perhaps involving union jurisdictions, trade traditions, or skill or knowledge considerations—seriously limit the possibility of such a shift. Thus a garment sleeve setter would seldom, if ever, shift to become a pocket setter.

In any event, all jobs can be classified into 55 groups that represent materials, products, subject matter, or service (MPSMS), and these are further classified into 580 items.[3]

Still another building block represents levels of complexity at which the worker performs. These *Worker Functions* can be classified in three ways: working with *DATA, PEOPLE,* or *THINGS.* Each is a defined term, and each comprises a number of levels of complexity: seven levels for DATA, nine for PEOPLE, and eight for THINGS. For example, the lowest DATA level is "Comparing," which is defined as "judging the readily observable functional, structural, or compositional characteristics (whether similar to or divergent from obvious standards) of data, people, or things."[4]

The highest level of complexity of DATA, "Synthesizing," is defined as: "integrating analyses of data to discover facts and/or develop knowledge concepts or interpretations."[5]

The complete array of the Worker Function structure is given in Chart 1.

CHART 1
WORKER FUNCTIONS

Data	People	Things
0 Synthesizing	0 Mentoring	0 Setting Up
1 Coordinating	1 Negotiating	1 Precision Working
2 Analyzing	2 Instructing	2 Operating-Controlling
3 Compiling	3 Supervising	3 Driving-Operating
4 Computing	4 Diverting	4 Manipulating
5 Copying	5 Persuading	5 Tending
6 Comparing	6 Speaking-Signaling	6 Feeding-Offbearing
	7 Serving	7 Handling
	8 Taking Instructions, Helping	

Each function is defined in the *Handbook for Analyzing Jobs*. A series of illustrations abstracted from job definitions is presented in the *Handbook* further to clarify the character, depth, and range of each term.

The elements listed in Chart 1 for DATA and THINGS comprise hierarchies: each level assumes that a worker who performs at that level can perform the tasks associated with each lower level, actually or potentially. Thus a worker who can function under the rubric "Analyzing" is assumed to be able to Compile, Compute, Copy, and Compare. The levels for PEOPLE are hierarchical only in a general sense: Mentoring (advising, counseling) is a higher function than Persuading or Negotiating and may or may not involve the other two. Instructing is not necessarily higher than Supervising, and therefore does not have a hierarchical relationship to it. Serving, however, is a lower level of complexity.

THE USE OF WORKER FUNCTIONS IN THE *DOT* CODE

All jobs in the universe can be characterized by the three levels of complexity. These levels also serve another purpose. With the addition of another concept, they comprise an important part of the *DOT* classification structure. When an assigned level of complexity is not considered significant, even though performance of it represents a high level of competence, it is identified as an "8" level, instead of the level assigned by the occupational analyst on the basis of the listing in Chart 1. For example, a musical instrumentalist is coded as .041 when his job is studied by an occupational analyst. This means that he or she functions at the Synthesizing level for DATA, the Diverting level for PEOPLE, and the Precision Working level for THINGS. Since the instrumentalist is essentially a creative entertainer, not a precision worker, the *DOT* code assigned is .048 (fourth, fifth, and sixth digits of the six-digit DOT code), the "eight" indicating that the involvement with THINGS is not significant in this case. When used for classification purposes the Worker Functions are listed in almost the same way, except that element "8" in the Worker Function listing for PEOPLE is eliminated, and lack of significance for a specific level is identified by "8." Note that DATA level 7 is used to indicate lack of significance for DATA, when THINGS levels 1 and 2 appear in the code (sixth digit). Level 8 is used for THINGS levels 3 through 8—thus .780, .781, .782, or .883. This was done to permit comparisons with data obtained under the *DOT 2* classification structure, which used "skilled, semi-skilled and unskilled" classifications, for non-white collar and outdoor jobs, all these categories being reflected in *DOT* codes in that edition. The Worker Function listing used to code jobs appears in Chart 2.

Each job in the universe can be translated into a six-digit code, having two

CHART 2

WORKER FUNCTION LEVELS IN DOT[a]

Data[b]	People[b]	Things[b]
0 Synthesizing	0 Mentoring	0 Setting Up
1 Coordinating	1 Negotiating	1 Precision Working
2 Analyzing	2 Instructing	2 Operating-Controlling
3 Compiling	3 Supervising	3 Driving-Operating
4 Computing	4 Diverting	4 Manipulating
5 Copying	5 Persuading	5 Tending
6 Comparing	6 Speaking-Signaling	6 Feeding-Offbearing
*7 Not significant	7 Serving	7 Handling
*8 Not significant	*8 Not significant	*8 Not significant

[a] For definitions see *Handbook for Analyzing Jobs*, or Appendices A and B.
[b] Asterisk represents change from Worker Functions listing used for job analysis.

sets of three digits each. The first set represents Work Fields; Materials, Products, Subject Matter, or Service; or an industry or activity (e.g., clerical).[6] The second set comprises the Worker Function levels in Chart 2. Each of the first three digits stands for something, beginning with "category," and there are nine of these. Each category is further refined into two digits, the "divisions." Each of the 84 divisions is subdivided into one or more three digit "code groups" (603 total). The position of each three-digit code group within its division (two digits) is numbered serially. The categories are:

0
1   Professional, technical, managerial occupations
2   Clerical and sales occupations
3   Service occupations
4   Farming, fishery, forestry, and related occupations
5   Processing occupations
6   Machine trades occupations
7   Bench work occupations
8   Structural work occupations
9   Miscellaneous occupations

Appendix C contains the full list of *DOT* two-digit divisions. One example is

15   Occupations in Entertainment and Recreation.

A relevant example of a three-digit code group is

152   Occupations in Music.

The codes assigned to represent the Worker Function levels comprise the second set of three digits. The three digits identifying the specific levels of complexity for DATA, PEOPLE, THINGS, respectively, are separated from the first three digits by a period. (When a job seeker is not fully qualified, an "X" is substituted for the period.) Thus since the first three digits represent the Work Field or the Material, Product, Subject Matter, or Service, the full code for instrumentalist is 152.048. An experienced user of the *DOT* can interpret the code at sight: the first digit tells him that the job is professional, technical, or managerial. He might know offhand what 15 represents, but a quick glance at Volume II of the *DOT*[7] will indicate that "15" stands for "Occupations in Entertainment and Recreation" and the third digit "2" means that the three-digit code group entitled "Occupations in Music" is the third code group listed for the two-digit division "15." When looking at the second set of three digits, a person trained in the use of

DOT knows at once that

"0"   represents the Synthesizing level for DATA
"4"   represents the Diverting level for PEOPLE
"8"   represents no significant relationship to THINGS

THE WORKER TRAIT PARAMETERS

The Worker Trait Factors

Implicit in the last three digits of a coded job is a representation of the Worker Traits, the characteristics required of the worker to perform the job acceptably. These traits comprise the remaining job analysis parameters used by occupational analysts in studying jobs and by placement interviewers and counselors in diagnosing job seekers and counselees. The Worker Traits comprise six discrete factors that become interrelated when job seekers or jobs are being diagnosed. The Worker Trait factors are:

General Educational Development   (6 defined levels)
Specific Vocational Preparation   (9 levels)
Aptitudes   (11 aptitudes, 5 levels each)
Interests   (5 bipolar pairs)
Temperaments   (12 in all)
Physical Factors   (6 groups)

This seemingly complicated structure is relatively simple to use in analyzing jobs and in placement and counseling operations. The definitions for each factor follow.

General Educational Development (GED) and Specific Vocational Preparation (SVP) together represent Training Time. This means that a job with a given GED requires a stated SVP (time period) for the average worker to acquire the specific skills, knowledges, and abilities to perform accpetably. Let us now consider GED, as defined:

General Educational Development: This embraces those aspects of education (formal and informal) which contribute to the worker's (*a*) reasoning development and ability to follow instructions, and (*b*) the acquisition of "tool" knowledges, such as language and mathematical skills. It is education of a general nature which does not have a recognized, fairly specific, occupational objective. Ordinarily, such education is obtained in elementary school, high school, or college. It also derives from experience and individual study.[8]

Thus General Educational Development represents the reasoning, language, and mathematical developmental levels actually required of a worker to perform acceptably. It should be distinguished from the "aptitude" for *intelligence*, which represents a potential or a capacity. (Thus a person who has a high degree of finger dexterity aptitude might become a typist if sufficiently motivated and trained. Aptitudes are described later.)

We know that each of the six GED levels has three elements: development in reasoning, mathematics, and language. Level 4, for example, is defined as follows:

Reasoning Development Apply principles of rational systems to solve practical problems and deal with a variety of concrete variables in situations where only limited standardization exists. Interpret a variety of instructions furnished in written, oral, diagrammatic, or schedule form.

Mathematical Development

Algebra: Deal with system of real numbers; linear, quadratic, rational, exponential, logarithmic, angle and circular functions, and inverse functions; related algebraic solution of equations and inequalities; limits and continuity, and probability and statistical inference.

Geometry: Deductive axiomatic geometry, plane and solid; and rectangular coordinates.

Shop Math: Practical application of fractions, percentages, ratio and proportion, mensuration, logarithms, slide rule, practical algebra, geometric construction, and essentials of trigonometry.

Language Development

Reading: Read novels, poems, newspapers, periodicals, journals, manuals, dictionaries, thesauruses, and encyclopedias.

Writing: Prepare business letters, expositions, summaries, and reports, using prescribed format and conforming to all rules of punctuation, grammar, diction, and style.

Speaking: Participate in panel discussions, dramatizations, and debates. Speak extemporaneously on a variety of subjects.[9]

From 1965 when *DOT 3* was issued until 1973, the *highest* GED level of the three components was used to represent the level for a given job. In 1973 the Manpower Administration directed occupational analysts to characterize each job by the appropriate level for *each* component—that is, by reasoning (R), mathematical (M), and language (L) development levels. This refinement gives far greater specificity to this critical trait. A new supplement to the *Dictionary*[10] assigns each of the RML levels and the highest of these three factors to each of the 14,000 defined job titles in the *DOT*.[11]

Specific vocational preparation (SVP) concerns the *specific* training or experience required to perform acceptably, given the GED level assigned to the job. Recall that General Educational Development is the attained level of reasoning, mathematics, and language skills in terms of generalized abilities; this means the ability to reason and to perform arithmetic and language activities without reference to the substantive aspects. SVP refers to the substantive elements. Thus a job analysis will indicate the specific GED level required for average performance. If a person wants to become a typist, he must possess the GED level already determined necessary. Persons with that (attained) GED level will require the specific substantive training necessary to become a typist. The length of time required for training has been identified by a "time frame," which is derived following the definition of SVP:

> The amount of time required to learn the techniques, acquire information, and develop the facility needed for average performance in a specific job–worker situation. This training may be acquired in a school, work, military, institutional, or avocational environment. It does not include orientation training required of every fully qualified worker to become accustomed to the special conditions of any new job. Specific vocational training includes training given in any of the following circumstances:
>
> 1. Vocational education (such as high school commercial or shop training, technical school, art school and that part of college training which is organized around a specific vocational objective);
> 2. Apprentice training (for apprenticeable jobs only);
> 3. In-plant training (given by an employer in the form of organized classroom study);
> 4. On-the-job training (serving as learner or trainee on the job under the instruction of a qualified worker);
> 5. Essential experience in other jobs (serving in less responsible jobs which lead to the higher grade job or serving in other jobs which qualify).[12]

Chart 3 explains the various levels of specific vocational preparation.

CHART 3
LEVELS OF VOCATIONAL PREPARATION

Level	Time	Level	Time
1	Short demonstration only	5	Over 6 months up to and including 1 year
2	Anything beyond short demonstration up to and including 30 days	6	Over 1 year up to and including 2 years
3	Over 30 days up to and including 3 months	7	Over 2 years up to and including 4 years
4	Over 3 months up to and including 6 months	8	Over 4 years up to and including 10 years
		9	Over 10 years

Aptitudes

Aptitudes represent tested capacities or potentials associated with given jobs. The theory of testing suggests that persons with the requisite level of the relevant aptitudes can learn the job duties more quickly and more easily than persons with lower test scores who have the will and motivation to overcome their limited potentials (as disclosed by the test). Persons without the will and motivation would be well advised to seek occupations for which they have greater capacities. The validity and value of testing is a controversial subject. Let us simply give the *DOT* definition of Aptitudes here.

Specific capacities and abilities required of an individual in order to learn or perform adequately a task or job duty.

G INTELLIGENCE: General learning ability. The ability to "catch on" or understand instructions and underlying principles. Ability to reason and make judgments. Closely related to doing well in school.

V VERBAL: Ability to understand meanings of words and ideas associated with them, and to use them effectively. To comprehend language, to understand relationships between words, and to understand meanings of whole sentences and paragraphs. To present information or ideas clearly.

N NUMERICAL: Ability to perform arithmetic operations quickly and accurately.

S SPATIAL: Ability to comprehend forms in space and understand relationships of plane and solid objects. May be used in such tasks as blueprint reading and in solving geometry problems. Frequently described as the ability to "visualize" objects of two or three dimensions, or to think visually of geometric forms.

P FORM PERCEPTION: Ability to perceive pertinent detail in objects or in pictorial or graphic material; to make visual comparisons and discriminations and see slight differences in shapes and shadings of figures and widths and lengths of lines.

Q CLERICAL PERCEPTION: Ability to perceive pertinent detail in verbal or tabular material. To observe differences in copy, to proofread words and numbers, and to avoid perceptual errors in arithmetic computation.

K MOTOR COORDINATION: Ability to coordinate eyes and hands or fingers rapidly and accurately in making precise movements with speed. Ability to make a movement response accurately and quickly.

F FINGER DEXTERITY: Ability to move the fingers and manipulate small objects with the fingers rapidly or accurately.

M MANUAL DEXTERITY: Ability to move the hands easily and skillfully. To work with the hands in placing and turning motions.

E EYE–HAND–FOOT COORDINATION: Ability to move the hand and foot coordinately with each other in accordance with visual stimuli.

C COLOR DISCRIMINATION: Ability to perceive or recognize similarities or differences in colors, or in shades or other values of the same color; to identify a particular color, or to recognize harmonious or contrasting color combinations, or to match colors accurately.[13]

Aptitude scores are generally established in relation to a standard of 100. By assigning a minimum "cutting score," we have an indication (i.e., a score of less than the minimum) of sufficient lack of the aptitude to warrant consideration by the client of occupations for which he has greater talent. In the *DOT* structure, the concept of an *average* degree of the aptitude rather than a *minimum* degree, was utilized. Moreover, unlike other structures giving only the *dominant* aptitudes called for, the required level is shown for *each* aptitude. This is reflected in the following quotation.

Explanation of Levels

The digits indicate how much of each aptitude the job requires for satisfactory (average) performance. The average requirements, rather than maximum or minimum, are cited. The amount required is expressed in terms of equivalent amounts possessed by segments of the general working population.

The following scale is used:

1   The top 10 percent of the population. This segment of the population possesses an extremely high degree of the aptitude.

2   The highest third exclusive of the top 10 percent of the population. This segment of the population possesses an above average or high degree of the aptitude.

3   The middle third of the population. This segment of the population possesses a medium degree of the aptitude, ranging from slightly below to slightly above average.

4   The lowest third exclusive of the bottom 10 percent of the population. This segment of the population possesses a below average or low degree of the aptitude.

5   The lowest 10 percent of the population. This segment of the population possesses a negligible degree of the aptitude.

Significant Aptitudes

Certain aptitudes appear in boldface type on the qualifications profiles for the worker trait groups. These aptitudes are considered to be occupationally significant for the specific group, i.e., essential for average successful job performance. All boldface aptitudes are not necessarily required of a worker for each individual job within a worker trait group, but some combination of them is essential in every case.[14]

The *DOT* lists the average required amount of each aptitude as stated in the definition. On the other hand, the General Aptitude Test Battery (GATB), an instrument used by all state employment service local offices, lists the scores required only for the aptitudes found to be "differentiators." For example, the GATB score would omit scores for the verbal aptitude for physicians, since all physicians in the test sample were found to be verbal.

In the *DOT,* each job is rated for each aptitude, regardless of whether it differentiated the successful from the marginal workers.[15]

INTERESTS

Many academic investigators have explored and performed substantial research with respect to vocational interests, particularly Kuder and Strong.[16] The authors of the *DOT* reviewed their findings exhaustively. However, the "interest formulation" adopted for *DOT* was the bipolar system developed by Cottle.[17] Studying jobs had revealed that an interest in one type of work is accompanied by a disinterest in another kind of work. "Those who like working with people generally prefer *not* to work with things, and vice versa."[18]

The interest factors as defined and described in *DOT 3* are shown in Chart 4.[19]

A closer examination of the interest factors will indicate that most relate to DATA, PEOPLE, THINGS. For example, interest 1 relates to things and objects (i.e., THINGS). Interests 2, 4, and 5 relate to PEOPLE. Interest 6 relates to PEOPLE and DATA. Interest 9 relates to THINGS. The worker function levels represent *abilities* required by a job, and an interest is *not* necessarily an ability. An interest may indicate capacity *after* training and experience. Finally, in assessing interests in people, the counselor must establish that an interest expressed by a client is vocationally significant. Thus a person may be "interested" in viewing various types of architecture, but his aptitude is vocationally significant only if he wants to become an architect.

TEMPERAMENTS

"Temperaments" as used in *DOT* differ from popular usage, which ordinarily associates the term with emotional responses. In *DOT,* temperaments are job and work conditions to which the worker must adjust. For example, some jobs require the worker to perform repetitive work "according to set procedures, sequence or pace."[20] Unless the worker can accommodate himself to this requirement, he will experience little job satisfaction and eventually may quit the job. The worker might quit because he prefers a job that requires "performing a variety of duties, often changing from one task to another of a different nature without loss of efficiency and composure."[21]

The *DOT* temperaments subsystem is as follows:

Temperaments constitute different types of occupational situations to which workers must adjust.

1 Situations involving a variety of duties often characterized by frequent change.

2 Situations involving repetitive or short cycle operations carried out according to set procedures or sequences.

CHART 4

INTEREST FACTORS[a]

Preferences for certain types of work activities or experiences, with accompanying rejection of contrary types of activities or experiences. Five pairs of interest factors are provided so that a positive preference for one factor of a pair also implies rejection of the other factor of that pair.

1 Situations involving a preference for activities dealing with things and objects.	vs. 6 Situations involving a preference for activities concerned with people and the communication of ideas.
2 Situations involving a preference for activities involving business contact with people.	vs. 7 Situations involving a preference for activities of a scientific and technical nature.
3 Situations involving a preference for activities of a routine, concrete, organized nature.	vs. 8 Situations involving a preference for activities of an abstract and creative nature.
4 Situations involving a preference for working for people for their presumed good, as in the social welfare sense, or for dealing with people and language in social situations.	vs. 9 Situations involving a preference for activities that are nonsocial in nature, and are carried on in relation to processes, machines and techniques.
5 Situations involving a preference for activities resulting in prestige or the esteem of others.	vs. 0 Situations involving a preference for activities resulting in tangible, productive satisfaction.

---

[a] U.S. Department of Labor, *Dictionary of Occupational Titles,* Vol 2, Occupational Classification, 3rd ed. Washington D.C.: Government Printing Office, 1965, p. 654.

3 Situations involving doing things only under specific instruction, allowing little or no room for independent action of judgment in working out job problems.

4 Situations involving the direction, control, and planning of an entire activity or the activities of others.

5 Situations involving the necessity of dealing with people in actual job duties beyond giving and receiving instructions.

6 Situations involving working alone and apart in physical isolation from others, although the activity may be integrated with that of others.

7 Situations involving influencing people in their opinions, attitudes, or judgments about ideas or things.

8 Situations involving performing adequately under stress when confronted with the critical or unexpected or when taking risks.

9 Situations involving the evaluation (arriving at generalizations, judgments, or decisions) of information against sensory or judgmental criteria.

0 Situations involving the evaluation (arriving at generalizations, judgments, or decisions) of information against measurable or verifiable criteria.

X Situations involving the interpretation of feelings, ideas, or facts in terms of personal viewpoint.

Y Situations involving the precise attainment of set limits, tolerances, or standards.[22]

Physical Factors

When physical factors are used to describe *job requirements*, they are termed physical *demands;* when the same factors characterize job seekers or *workers*, they are called physical *capacities*. The six elements comprising the physical factors are as follows:

1. The *Strength Factor* which is used to identify *sedentary, light, medium, heavy*, or *very heavy work*. In determining the presence of each factor, the following are considered:
a. Standing, walking, sitting
b. Lifting, carrying, pushing, pulling

Lifting, pushing, and *pulling* are expressed in terms of both intensity and duration. Judgments regarding intensity involve consideration of the weight handled, position of the worker's body or part of the worker's body used in handling weights, and aid given by helpers or by mechanical equipment.

Duration is the total time spent by the worker in carrying out these activities. *Carrying* is most often expressed in terms of duration, weight carried, and distance carried.

Care must be exercised in evaluating jobs in the strength categories, particularly in interpreting the force and the physical effort a person must exert. For instance, if the worker is in an awkward position while crouching, he may experience as much difficulty pushing a 5-pound force as he would exerting six times that force pushing at waist height.

Also, if he is required continuously to lift, push, and pull objects weighing 15 pounds or to carry these objects long distances, the worker may exert as much physical effort as he would in occasionally or even frequently lifting, pushing, and pulling objects twice as heavy, or in occasionally carrying these objects over short distances.[23]

2. Climbing and/or balancing
3. Stooping, kneeling, crouching, and/or crawling
4. Reaching, handling, fingering, and/or feeling
5. Talking and/or hearing
6. Seeing

Each of these factors is fully defined in the *Handbook for Analyzing Jobs,* and illustrative examples are supplied.

WORKING OR ENVIRONMENTAL CONDITIONS

Although working or environmental conditions are not traits as such, they are circumstances to which the worker must adjust, and they are usually included in discussions of worker traits. A full list follows.

1. Inside (work), outside, or both
2. Extreme cold, with or without temperature changes
3. Extreme heat with or without temperature changes
4. Wet and/or Humid Conditions
5. Noise and/or Vibration
6. Hazards
7. Atmospheric Conditions: Fumes, Odors, Dust, Mists, Gases, Poor Ventilation.[24]

Each is fully defined with illustrative situations in the *Handbook for Analyzing Jobs.*

In summary, worker traits (GED, SVP, aptitudes, interests, temperaments, and physical factors) indicate the kinds of traits the worker must possess to perform the duties of a given job with an average degree of acceptability. GED, SVP, and aptitudes are scaled, to indicate the relative amount of each trait required. Interests and temperaments are not scaled. Some of the physical factors are scaled. Working or environmental conditions represent situations to which the worker must adjust.

Each of the 14,000 jobs defined in the *DOT* was rated for these traits. These factors, however, were used as a frame of reference in preparing written job analysis schedules that define the job, list all the tasks performed, and provide a narrative statement to describe relevant processes, and the Machines, Tools, Equipment, and Work Aids utilized. Recall that each job is coded, in *DOT* and the first three digits represent the Work Fields (Methodology or Technology employed or involved), or the Materials, Products, Subject Matter, or Service (MPSMS) used or involved. The other three digits designate the levels of complexity required for DATA, PEOPLE, THINGS in terms of specific components arranged in hierarchies (except for PEOPLE). (See listing on p. 48). The hierarchies represent scalings, each level being higher than the lower level and accommodating all levels below it. The PEOPLE component is a hierarchy only in a general sense.

SAMPLE *DOT* DEFINITION

COUNSELOR (profess. & kin.) I. see Lawyer.—(profess. & kin.) II. 045.108. guidance counselor; vocational adviser; vocational counselor. Counsels individuals and provides group educational and vocational guidance services: Collects, organizes, and analyzes information about individuals through records, tests, interviews, and professional sources, to appraise their interests, aptitudes, abilities, and personality characteristics for vocational and educational planning. Compiles and studies occupational, educational, and economic information to aid counselees in making and carrying out vocational and educational objectives. Refers students to placement service. Assists individuals in understanding and overcoming social and emotional problems. Engages in research and follow-up activities to evaluate counseling techniques. May teach classes. May be designated according to area of activity as COUNSELOR, COLLEGE: COUNSELOR, SCHOOL.

Note how this definition reflects the *DOT* traits and factors.

WORKER TRAIT GROUPS

The Worker Traits are not represented in the *DOT* code number because this would require a large number of digits. More important, perhaps, it was determined that configurations of worker traits could be characterized by their generalized function levels (i.e., each set of relatively homogeneous traits represented occupations that generally or "modally" had the same worker function levels); thus it was not necessary to assign additional code numbers.[25] Jobs with the same worker traits were arranged into groups determined by the Worker Trait ratings of all 14,000 jobs until groupings were established empirically. Once that task had been completed, Worker Function levels of complexity were assigned to characterize each group as a whole. There were 114 Worker Trait Groups (WTGs) established in this manner (see, e.g., p. 77), and in 59 cases some of the Worker Function levels had to be used to describe more than one group. This "doubling up" occurred because groups of homogeneous jobs (jobs having the same Worker Traits) bear the same relationship to DATA, PEOPLE, THINGS, even though the trait patterns are different. For example, the WTG covering jobs in "Administration" has the same relationship to DATA, PEOPLE, THINGS (.168) as Legal and Related Work, and Flight and Related Training. However, the Worker Trait configurations differ for each of the three groups—all identified as .168 for DATA, PEOPLE, THINGS.

An example of a Worker Trait Group appears on page 000. Briefly, a WTG describes in narrative terms the *work performed,* the *worker requirements* for jobs in the group, *clues for relating applicants and requirements, training, and methods of entry.* A qualification profile reflects the specific traits described in narrative terms in the section on worker requirements. In addition, *related classifications* (worker trait groups) appear on the lower left of the page. Finally, the next page(s) list job titles (six digits plus title) that belong to this group. A review of the *work performed* section indicates the tasks exemplifying all the jobs in this Worker Trait Group. The *worker requirements* section gives all the Worker Trait factors involved in all the occupations under the group; these are stated in coded terms in the qualifications profile. The codes for GED, SVP, aptitudes, interests, temperament, physical demands, and working conditions are listed and defined in Appendix B of *DOT*, Volume II, reproduced in this book as Appendix B also. All the other factors are self-explanatory.

The 114 Worker Trait Groups have been further grouped into 22 uncoded areas of work (see p. 214 of *DOT*, Volume II, and in Appendix D of this book). A full list of the WTGs within the areas of work appear in Appendix E.

During the counseling process it may be revealed that a worker or job seeker "fits" into a Worker Trait Group. If appraising a job seeker's profile and checking it against the profile for a given WTG does indicate a "fit," it is necessary to determine which of the occupational options listed on the page(s) following the WTG description is best for the job seeker in the labor market area (city) of his choice. The listing is by the full six-digit code, the first three digits reflecting the Work Field, or the MPSMS, or activity. Hence the counselor must ask the job seeker, which subject matter or activity he prefers. For example, suppose a Manpower Research and Planning Director (050.118) has lost his job. Which of the following divisions (first two digits) of the Worker Trait Group entitled "Administration," would appeal to him and would require minimal retraining? Each division lists the six-digit job titles that fall within this WTG:

07   Medicine and Health
09   Education
10   Museum, Library, and Archival Work
15   Entertainment and Recreation
16   Administrative Specialties[26]

Of the ones preferred, which specific occupation (six digits) is his best target? If there is none, the interviewer/counselor could explore the related Worker Trait Groups listed to the left of the qualifications profile, since all jobs in a WTG require the same basic configuration of Worker Traits and the same level(s) of complexity for DATA, PEOPLE, THINGS. For the Worker Trait Group "Administration," the Worker Function levels are .118 and .168, shown at the top of the first page (refer again to the example on pp. 77–79).

Ordinarily, a single qualifications profile is assigned to a given occupation—that is, one Worker Function level; one GED; one SVP; all relevant aptitudes, with one level designation for each; two interests; two temperaments; and one set of physical demands. A range of Worker Traits may be needed to represent all jobs in a Worker Trait Group. The first item in a qualifications profile for a group, therefore, indicates that most occupations in the group require that characteristic; the additional Worker Traits are listed to show their order of incidence for other occupations in the group. Thus for Administation most occupations require GED 5, SVP 8, the first line of aptitudes shown, the first two interests, the first two temperaments, and physical demands S and 5. Similarly, most of the occupations that appear have the .118 relationship to DATA, PEOPLE, THINGS.

Additional explanations of the use of Worker Trait Groups is presented following the section on occupational counseling.

THE *DOT* Classification Structure

The preceding discussion has indicated that data on employment and unemployment can be presented in certain groupings. These are:

| *ITEM* | *BASIS* |

1. *DOT* code, which comprises six digits: 9 broad groups, represent the first digit, 84 less broad groups comprise the first two digits, and there are 603 groups of the first three digits taken together. Hence data can be presented by the first, by the first and second, or by all three digits in the first set of three digits of the full *DOT* code.

2. By Work Fields (methodologies or technologies). By MPSMS, also.

3. By the full six-digit *DOT* code, whose first three digits represent Work Fields, or MPSMS, or Activities. The last three digits represent defined levels of complexity for DATA, PEOPLE, THINGS and a configuration of Worker Trait factors.

1. This is possible because this structure and its definitions are used by all local employment offices in the nationwide employment security system, to code job seekers, including those seeking unemployment insurance benefits. The resulting data are made available to the interested public periodically.

2. This is possible because each *DOT* code and title has been coded for Work Fields and MPSMS by Occupational Analysts. Each Work Field is defined.[27] Work Field codes appear on internal records only and have not been published.

3. This is possible because each job, after analysis, is defined and coded by occupational analysts.

After each job was analyzed in the field according to the procedure just outlined, it was "rated" for Work Fields, MPSMS, Worker Functions, and Worker Traits by occupational analysts working in the field under the aegis and functional supervision of the Manpower Administration. Then the definitions were completed, and coded. Before coding was initiated, however, the classification structure had to be determined. In other words, the Job Analysis Formulation comprised a frame of reference to ensure that the information gathered through observations of the job and discussions with the worker, the foreman, the personnel office, and other informed people was complete. Observing the job through the Job Analysis Formulation, the analyst asked: What tasks did the worker perform? What was their relation to DATA, PEOPLE, THINGS? At what level of complexity (Worker Function levels)? What methods and techniques (Work Fields) did the worker use, with which, if any, machines, tools, equipment, or work aids (MTEWA)? Which specific materials did he or she use? What products resulted or were involved? Did the worker provide any type of service, or was there any involvement with a particular subject matter (MPSMS)? What were the traits required of the worker who performed with average competency: how much reasoning, mathematical, or language development (GED)? How much training time did the worker require to obtain the necessary skills, knowledges, and abilities (SVP)? Which specific aptitudes were required to ensure that the worker would profit from the training and become an average performer? Which interests and temperaments, and physical demands were called for, and to what degree? What environmental conditions and situations would have to be adjusted to if the worker was to be successful? (A sample Job Analysis Schedule is given in Appendix F.)

To determine the classification structure, we have to know its objective. Is it to be used primarily to provide input to economists to enable them to present data on employment and unemployment? This requires heavy emphasis on an industrial basis for classification, since data are most easily obtained by industry particularly data from employing establishments concerning projected expansions and contractions. Or is the primary purpose to expedite the placement processes in local employment offices in the state employment security system? In this case the classification structure must ensure that jobs requiring the same skills, knowledges, and abilities are grouped together, to expedite locating job seeker records that matches employer job openings received. Since many of the same jobs are found in different industries, however, an industrial base presents serious limitations. Moreover, if a job seeker with the precise *DOT* code is not available, the classification structure should make it easy to retrieve the names of job seekers with related skills, to expedite substitutions.

Another objective involves counseling of job seekers who have not made a firm occupational choice and need assistance in exploring occupations that match their potentials in terms of GED, aptitudes, interests, temperaments, and physical factors.

If training is to be undertaken, it is essential to locate persons with the potential for successful performance after training. If the classification is to be used primarily for presenting data on employment and unemployment, it must have a structure compatible with input concerning the projected expansions and contractions of employing establishments. As stated previously, such data are most easily developed in terms of products manufactured or services supplied—that is, on the basis of "industrial" rather than occupational components.

The issues raised in the search for an appropriate structure present a formidable technical problem that has baffled manpower technicians in the past. For example, the census classification has serious limitations if used in placement work (i.e., classifying job seekers, and filing and retrieving their records for matching against job openings) and in counseling. It is simple to classify professional, technical, managerial, clerical, sales, or service jobs, or those involved in agriculture, forestry, and fishery. The problem occurs in classifying all the others. If an industrial basis is selected, how can we handle jobs that cut across industrial lines—for example, machine shop workers who fabricate products employed in many industries, each one being treated as a separate product line in an *industrial* classification. This is an acute problem in placement work and in counseling. For these purposes clustering should be based on *occupational* homogeneities. The straight industrial basis is, of course, more acceptable to economists because it is easier to predict expansions and contractions by industry than by occupation.

The structure developed in *DOT 3* represents a compromise. The occupational area for professional, technical, managerial, sales, service, farming, fishery, and forestry is essentially similar to the census classification structure. The significant change was with respect to occupations in manufacturing, construction, transportation, graphic arts, and other nonmanufacturing, blue collar occupations. It was decided to use a functional approach that recognized the need to classify in the broader categories jobs that cut across industrial lines. The structure now used for this and the "white collar" segments of the occupational structure follows:

0
1 Professional, technical, and managerial occupations
2 Clerical and sales occupations
3 Service occupations
4 Farming, fishery, forestry, and related occupations

> 5   Processing occupations
> 6   Machine trades occupations
> 7   Bench work occupations
> 8   Structural work occupations
> 9   Miscellaneous

Categories 5, 6, 7, 8, and 9 represent the innovative solution made. Why? Because these groupings are based on Work Fields and Materials, Products, Subject Matter, and Service, as indicated in the Introduction to *DOT*, Volume I (pp. XVII–XVIII). A close review of the occupational divisions (first two digits), which represent subgroupings of the foregoing categories, shows the solution in another dimension. For example, note the following excerpt from the full array of occupational divisions in *DOT*, Volume II (pp. 1–2; also presented as Appendix C in this volume).

> 5   Processing Occupations
> 50   Occupations in processing *metal*
> 6   Machine Trades Occupations
> 60   *Metal* Working Occupations
> 7   Bench Work Occupations
> 70   Occupations in the fabrication, assembly
>   and repair of *metal* products, n.e.c.
> 8   Structural Work Occupations
> 80   Occupations in *metal* fabricating, n.e.c.

Similar distributions were made among other materials and products. For given products, a review of the occupational divisions in the occupational group arrangement will indicate the distribution of all their constituent jobs into

> Processing occupations
> Machine trade occupations
> Bench work occupations

For example, occupations involving *wood* and *wood products* are distributed as follows:

> 56   Occupations in processing *wood* and *wood* products
> 66   *Wood* machining occupations
> 76   Occupations in fabrication and repair of *wood* products.

In some instances the second digit could not be used consistently to indicate the relationship to the material or product. For example,

> 52   Occupations in processing *food, tobacco,* and *related* products

has no counterpart in Machine Trades Occupations or in Bench Work Occupations. Machining and Bench Work are not involved in food and tobacco industries. Another example is

> 55 Occupations in processing of chemicals, *plastics synthetics, rubber,* paint, and related products.

There is no counterpart in Machine Trades Occupations, but there is a counterpart in Bench Work Occupations:

> 75 Occupations in fabrication and repair of *plastics, synthetics, rubber,* and related products. (Note the deletion of occupations in chemicals and paint since these have no occupations in Bench Work.)

It is clear, therefore, that occupations found in many industries have been functionally classified. Jobs were grouped according to whether they were Processing, Machine Trades, or Bench Work occupations. To accomplish this, industries were subdivided into segments that represent Processing, Machine Trades, or Bench Work: each occupation in those industries was assigned to *one* of the foregoing segments only; that is, each of the 14,000 defined *DOT* titles was assigned to only *one* two-digit division representing segments of industries. Let us take wood and wood products for an example. The three-digit subdivisions are shown in Chart 5.

Still another category (first digit) applies to the wood trades found in construction:

> 8   *Structural Work Occupations*
> 86   Construction occupations, n.e.c.
> 860 Carpenters and related occupations

Thus each of the 14,000 occupations defined in the *DOT* was related to a Work Field and either to a *material, product, subject matter,* or *service* (MPSMS), to an activity (e.g., clerical) or to a *generic term* (welder, tailor, etc.). These groupings were then structured into the first three digits of the code as explained in the Introduction to Volume I of the *DOT* (p. XVII, ff). This brought together all jobs having the named *factors* in *common.*

Workers are designated in the next set of three digits, representing occupations grouped on the basis of *trait* commonalities (i.e., GED, SVP, aptitudes, interests, temperaments, physical factors). Next the groups were related to and identified by the Worker Function levels of complexity—that is, their involvement with DATA, PEOPLE, THINGS.

This leads to a discussion of three additional uses of the *DOT:* the use of Worker Traits and Worker Trait Groups in placement and in counseling, the use of Worker Traits and Worker Functions in job restructuring, and the use of the six-digit code groups as an *occupational matrix* for presenting data about supply-demand imbalances and for making manpower projec-

CHART 5
THREE-DIGIT SUBDIVISIONS

5	*Processing Occupations*
56	Occupations in processing of wood and wood products
560	Mixing and related occupations
561	Wood preserving and related occupations
562	Saturating, coating and related occupations
563	Drying, seasoning, and related occupations
569	Occupations in processing of wood and wood products, n.e.c.
6	*Machine Trades Occupations*
66	Wood Machining Occupations
660	Cabinetmakers
661	Patternmakers
662	Sanding occupations
663	Shearing and shaving occupations
664	Turning occupations
665	Milling and planing occupations
666	Boring occupations
667	Sawing occupations
668	Chipping occupations
669	Wood machining occupations, n.e.c.
7	*Bench Work Occupations*
76	Occupations in the fabrication and repair of wood
760	Bench carpenters and related occupations
761	Occupations in laying out, cutting, carving, shaping, and sanding wood products, n.e.c.
762	Occupations in assembling wood products, n.e.c.
763	Occupations in the fabrication and repair of furniture, n.e.c.
764	Cooperage occupations
769	Occupations in the fabrication and repair of wood products, n.e.c.

tions, an indispensable element in the implementation of a national manpower policy.

USE OF THE *DOT* IN PLACEMENT TRANSACTIONS

The *DOT* and its building blocks can be used diagnostically in placement transactions involving the determining of a job seeker's skills, knowledges, and abilities, which are coded to facilitate the retrieval of matching job requisitions received from employers.

We have already indicated how the *DOT* elements can be used as a frame of reference in a diagnostic mode. The job seeker's work and educational history is elicited and explored to obtain enough data to establish the person's qualifications profile as needed in a given case. The information obtained often confirms that the job seeker's last job (occupation) is appropriate, since it accommodates his trait needs and preferences. In such instances the interviewer informs the job seeker of opportunities in his regular occupation that meet his interest, temperament, and subject matter preferences. For example, a person who is basically happy with his government occupation as employment interviewer might prefer interviewing candidates for admission to a college, conducting market research interviewing, or doing placement interviews in the personnel department of a large retail corporation. Similarly, he might prefer a different type of noncommercial environment such as a hospital or educational institution. Moreover, he might be happier in a position requiring a wide area of discretion and the exercise of judgment, particularly in an establishment that places a heavy premium on innovation. If, however, it appears that the job seeker would now prefer to change his *occupation*, rather than his assignment in that occupation, he is referred to the counseling staff for the process described in the next section. In any event, the job seeker is assigned a *DOT* code to signal the kind of a job opportunity he would consider.

A job order is diagnosed in a similar fashion. The *DOT* elements are used as a frame of reference to the extent necessary to elicit all the relevant information: the methods and techniques used, the machines, tools, equipment, or work aids, the MPSMS, the ability required with respect to DATA, PEOPLE, THINGS levels, and the relevant traits, particularly interests and temperaments. The experienced order taker ascertains all these factors, starting with the tasks to be performed, and asks for the additional information needed to determine type of worker wanted, degree of supervision to be exercised, area of discretion for judgment, and so on. As a rule, the interviewer can establish the other factors (such as worker function levels, interests) with little or no additional questioning. The order taker then codes the job order by its *DOT* code.

Job-seeker and order files can be arranged by six-digit *DOT* codes or by Worker Trait Groups. The latter would be particularly valuable to make substitutions possible when filling job orders. Orders matching the code might not be available, for a given applicant, but since orders with the same qualifications profile are filed together, orders in other related codes can be examined. Similarly, if no job seekers with the matching code for a given order are available, others with the same qualifications profile can be found in the same WTG file, under other six-digit codes.[28] It should be noted that related Worker Trait Group files should also be searched as needed; these related WTG are listed on each page in *DOT*, Volume II, which describes a WTG.

Computers can accomplish such matching, and some of the state employment services have been experimenting with this approach, funded by recent manpower enactments. Some of the systems place heaviest initial reliance on the nine-digit *DOT* code; that is, the full six-digit code with a standard three-digit "suffix" to represent the title as listed in a supplement to *DOT 3*. Additional descriptors are used for salary, location, educational level, and so on. Other systems use some of the elements of the Job Analysis Formulation instead of the code, such as Work Fields, MPSMS, aptitudes, interests, and temperaments. Still other systems use additional vocabularies related to tasks. In addition, some of the states search order files (data banks) for job openings to match job-seeker descriptors that have been identified on a "search request," which becomes the input. Ordinarily five of the *most relevant* opportunities are printed out. In other applications bidirectional search is possible—matching orders against the job-seeker data bank, and conversely, matching job seekers against the job-order data bank. Undoubtedly over time such searches will utilize both the *DOT* code and any one of a few alternative "vocabularies" for given job opportunity and job seeker types.

USE OF THE *DOT* IN OCCUPATIONAL COUNSELING

Let us look at counseling as a three-step process: obtaining the relevant facts; relating them to the entire occupational spectrum, to identify occupations that seem to accommodate the counselee's needs and preferences; and discussing with the client his or her strengths and weaknesses in relation to the possible occupations. The end product should be a career decision that will enable the counselee to fulfill discerned potentials, and ideally, expectancies consistent with aspiration levels. In this section we reveal how the *DOT* building blocks can facilitate the achievement of these processes.

Obtaining the Facts

During the usual fact-finding stage, the counselor should endeavor to obtain a complete set of facts to identify the counselee's needs and preferences. Articulate counselees may supply the information during an unstructured, free-flowing interview in which they themselves touch all necessary bases. Such individuals require little or no assistance in coming up with the relevant facts; indeed, they can furnish as much information as a skilled counselor could obtain using a more structured approach. Problems occur with less articulate, less self-assured clients, and the *DOT* frame of reference is most useful here. In such instances the counselor should first elicit the client's work history, if any, and his leisure pursuits. He should then probe for additional details, using the work history or leisure pursuits as a reference base, to identify as specifically as possible the worker's relation to DATA, PEOPLE, THINGS: the methodologies and technologies used in former jobs or leisure pursuits; the machines, tools, equipment, and work aids, if any; the client's GED levels, his aptitudinal strengths (in so far as these can be determined, either by tests or by the counselee's self-appraisal); and the client's interests, temperaments, and physical factors. Since the counselor needs sufficient data to establish the client's qualifications profile, he should try to obtain information concerning the client's current abilities, potentials, and preferences, particularly with respect to DATA, PEOPLE, THINGS levels, GED levels, interests, temperaments, and physical factors. In addition, the counselor should begin to identify possible Work Fields and ultimately the client's preferences with respect to specific materials, products, subject matters, or service.

Relating the Facts to Worker Trait Groups

The simplest and most desirable method for determining relevant career fields is for the counselor to review the list of the 22 areas of work (see Appendix D)[29] and select from it the one that seems most relevant. He then reviews the Worker Trait Groups within that area of work (see Appendix E)[30] to identify one that apparently accommodates the counselee facts. The next step is to see how well the client's qualifications profile matches the WTG qualifications profile. The counselor then discusses with the client the types of work included in the Worker Trait Group and its trait requirements, aiming to stimulate self-appraisal. The client is also encouraged to compare his preferences against the type of work performed and the characteristics required for the occupations comprising that Worker Trait Group and listed in it. This involves the determination of the counselee's preferences for particular work fields (methodology–technology) and for working with specific materials, products, subject matter, or service, as the case may be. It then becomes possible to pinpoint which of the occupations in the Worker Trait Group is most relevant, since the first three digits of each *DOT* code (listed for each WTG) designate Work Fields and/or MPSMS.

Assisting Client in Appraisal

The sifting process should never be mechanical, although the temptation is great because the counselor is matching two sets of facts, each one being identified by code numbers for Worker Traits. However, the counselor must never forget that each fact represents a judgment, and these facts must be used interactively. As the counseling dialogue unfolds, the counselor indicates and emphasizes critical issues, assisting the client as much as possible to interpret and to delimit his own characteristics. For example, a client may think he likes "business contact with people," but there are some contacts he might enjoy and others he might dislike. Thus an interviewer might like to conduct placement interviews but dislike interviews leading to determinations of entitlement and eligibility for unemployment insurance beneficiaries: in the first case the interviewer is *helping* the client; in the second, he might be *taking* something away. In other words, a counselee may prefer "helping" people to limiting his involvement and decision making to the fulfillment of legal requirements. Yet both tasks can be called "working with people."

Other methods for determining relevant career areas may tend to become even more mechanical and less judgmental, at least initially. There are three principal methods.

1.   The counselor can establish the client's actual or potential Worker Function levels (DATA, PEOPLE, THINGS) and review these against a numerically arranged listing of the combinations (.018, .028, .038, etc.), indicating the Work Traits Group that accommodates them. (The counselor must create this listing, since it does not appear in any government manual or brochure.) In using this method, the counselor has to adjust the levels for the *significance* factor—that is, to convert a level to an "8" when the actual level is not significant. For example, Musical Instrumentalist, .041, represents the synthesizing level for DATA, the Diverting level for PEOPLE, and the Precision Working level for THINGS. This is converted to .048, since a musician is an "entertainer" rather than a "precision worker" (THINGS, level 1), even though "precision" is necessary to produce the music.

2.   A related method for counselors in the public employment service is to use the Occupational Ability Patterns (OAP) constructed from test scores achieved on the General Aptitude Test Battery (GATB) used by all state employment services. Or, the client can prepare the Interest Checklist, also used by state employment services, which gives the counselee an opportunity to indicate his attitude (like, dislike, uncertain) toward many job–worker situations. Both these instruments have been related to the *DOT* Worker Trait Groups and are available to Employment Service staff for these purposes.

3.   Having constructed the client's qualifications profile, it is possible to develop various indices for relating a client's trait configuration to the Worker Trait Groups. Many such devices have been developed and are being used experimentally. On a more practical basis, it is possible to obtain "packages" prepared by commercial firms and publishers active in this area. A typical package consists of a box containing a card for each of the

114 Worker Trait Groups, printed with the definition for that group. Each card is prepunched for the Worker Trait factors. The client develops his own profile and manipulates "knitting needles" for each of his trait factors successively, or in combinations of factors, until he locates the WTG that seems to fit the client's characteristics. Considerable experimentation and developmental work is in progress, much of it under grants from the Manpower Administration, which has funded developmental work by several state employment security agencies in computerized manpower matching systems. Many systems use the *DOT* building blocks as descriptors: once the relevant "descriptors" have been identified, a "search" request form is prepared and fed into the computer, which prints out the most relevant job opportunities filed in the data bank. It is likely that these techniques will be extended to the counseling area, using the same general approach.

It is the author's opinion that counselors in the relatively near future will use the computer routinely to identify occupational groups or occupations matching a client's configurations of traits. The machine can be programmed to print out a list of such occupations and the matching occupational descriptions or monographs, enabling the counselor to assist in appraising the counselee's strengths and weaknesses against the occupational computer outputs. This process should increase the importance of the counselor's role rather than diminish it.

Counseling can be provided to individuals who have worked for some time in one occupation and must choose another occupation, or to young people who must make an initial career decision. The following example of counseling to a young person includes (1) presenting a set of facts about the client, (2) relating this set of facts to relevant occupational (Worker Trait) groups, and (3) making a career decision or arriving at a "career direction," as well as outlining the successive steps to be taken to fulfill it.

The Facts

The counselor elicited the following facts about his client, Robert T.

2/5/73

FACT SHEET

The Case of Robert T.

Robert T., born in a city of 25,000 population in the New York suburbs, was the third child of middle-class parents who were able to send all their children to college by denying themselves the more luxurious amenities. In high school he was one of the best students; his best subjects were English composition, literature, history. He was involved in nonathletic extracurricular activities and won an award for "contributing most to his school." Robert was in the Boy Scouts. He enjoyed the outdoor activities and the association with the others. When he was appointed patrol leader, he was delighted. He would have felt "hurt" had he not been selected.

He followed the same academic pattern in college, excelling in English composition, literature, history, and also in psychology. He performed creditably in all the social sciences. Although he received high grades in math, he found that he had to work harder to do so; he avoided the physical and biological sciences because he was not interested in the categorical detail of the subject matter. He realized that he liked to relate subjects to each other, to view the "big picture," to make analyses and to interpret; however, he preferred interpretation to analysis as the end product; that is, he liked analysis as a vehicle leading to interpretation.

Robert worked each summer in various jobs to earn pin money, to buy a bicycle, and to pay for two weeks' board at the Boy Scout camp. While attending college he worked as a waiter in a summer resort hotel. The following summer, he was selected to be head waiter supervising 14 college student waiters. Since the resort served weekenders primarily, considerable planning was essential. Robert found that he enjoyed doing this and also dealing with the clientele—seating them and seeing to it that they were satisfied with the dining room arrangements. He also assisted the owner in ordering staple food supplies, a task he found to be not onerous but not as rewarding as his other duties.

While in college he tried to "figure out" his long-term career. He knew he liked people and liked to help them, but he did not perceive himself as a doctor or teacher. He considered law and advertising but felt that he would like something more socially useful and less commercial. His friends told him that he was very articulate and personable. He realized that his difficulty in making a career decision was lack of knowledge about the occupations that utilized his abilities.

After obtaining these facts, the counselor tentatively developed the possible qualifications profiles for Robert T., shown on page 73. Having developed these possible levels, the counselor was able to arrive at the following possible fourth-, fifth-, and six-digit *DOT* codes: .028, .038, .068, .128, .138, .168, .208, .238, .268. The next step was to determine the GED level.

GED Level   After reviewing Robert's set of facts, the counselor estimated a GED level of "5." Level 5 is defined as follows: "Persons with GED 5 apply logical principles to define problems, collect data, draw valid conclusions, interpret technical instructions. Deal with several abstracts and

Potential Worker Function Levels

Data	People	Things
0	0	
1		
2	2	
	3	
	6	
		8

Where DATA	0	level refers to Synthesizing
	1	level refers to Coordinating
	2	level refers to Analyzing
PEOPLE	0	level refers to Mentoring
	2	level refers to Instructing
	3	level refers to Supervising
	6	level refers to Speaking-Signaling (interacting with people)
THINGS	8	no significant relationship

concrete variables." Robert then estimated his strongest aptitudes. Robert believed he had the following capacities:

G	V	N	S	P	Q
1	1	2	4	1	2

where G = Intelligence
V = Verbal
N = Numerical
S = Spatial Perception
P = Form Perception
Q = Clerical Perception

The most critical, however, in Robert's view were G, V, N. Definitions of each follow:

G General learning ability. The ability to "catch on" or understand instructions and underlying principles. Ability to reason and make judgments. Closely related to doing well in school.

V Ability to understand meanings of words and ideas associated with them and to use them effectively. To comprehend language, to understand relationships between words, and to understand meanings of whole sentences and paragraphs. To present information or ideas clearly.

N   Ability to perform arithmetic operations quickly and accurately.

S   Ability to comprehend forms in space and to understand relationships of plane and solid objects. May be used in such tasks as blueprint reading and solving geometry problems. Frequently described as the ability to "visualize" objects of two or three dimensions, or to think visually of geometric forms.

P   Ability to perceive pertinent detail in objects or in pictorial or graphic material, to make visual comparisons and discriminations and see slight differences in shapes and shadings of figures and widths and lengths of lines.

Q   Ability to perceive pertinent detail in verbal or tabular material. To observe differences in copy, to proofread words and numbers, and to avoid perceptual errors in arithmetic computation.

The levels shown mean
1   The top 10% of the population
2   The next $23\frac{1}{3}$% of the population
4   The lowest 10% of the population

Interests: The counselor estimated that Robert had the following possibly relevant interests:
2   Business contact with people
4   Working for people for their presumed good
5   Activities resulting in prestige or esteem of others; includes leadership, need to dominate.
6   Dealing with people and the communication of ideas
0   Activities resulting in tangible, productive satisfaction

Temperaments: Robert T. seemed to have the following:
1   Work situations requiring variety and frequent change
4   Directing, planning, and controlling an entire activity or the activity of others
5   Dealing and interacting with people in actual job duties
7   Influencing people in their opinions, attitudes, and judgments
9   Arriving at generalizations, judgments, or decisions against sensory or judgmental criteria

Since Robert T. appeared to be in good physical condition and had neither the need nor desire to be involved in unusual physical activities, this factor was not given particular consideration; neither were working conditions.

During the counseling process, the counselor and Robert agreed to the following additional facts:

1.   Although Robert was a good student, he was not particularly

interested in becoming a scholar. For example, he wrote very well but was bored by grammar and did not wish to master every rule.

2. He confused interest in "theory" with interest in creativeness. Thus he first thought that he was a theorist and that this was important in certain types of problem solving which he enjoyed. Yet in college he had avoided courses in philosophy, and he very much preferred labor economics to economic theory, particularly the highly abstract theories that involved mathematical symbols. He agreed with the counselor that he preferred the specific, or concrete, to the theoretical. Most of all he liked to analyze and to synthesize concrete issues and facts. He had been confused because he had thought that projections involving "synthesis" invariably required theoretical rather than imaginative frames of reference.

3. He liked to conceptualize. Although able to work out details, he preferred to establish broad concepts. Having established the concepts, he liked to have someone cope with the details, to test them and to feed back findings to enable Robert to reshape the concepts, tailored to fit the experiential facts.

It became clear that Robert could handle detail oriented toward designing solutions for complicated problems, but routine, repetitive detail in itself, even on a quasi-professional level, did not suit him.

On the basis of all the foregoing material, the counselor and Robert agreed to explore the following Work Fields. The tentative degree of relevance is reflected in the order of listing.[31]

Administering	(295)
Information giving	(282)
Researching	(251)
Teaching	(296)
Writing	(261)

MPSMS The counselor and Robert determined that the following subject matters were possibly relevant to Robert's needs and preferences:

Social Sciences
    Economics (practical aspects)
    History and political science
    Psychology
    Sociology
Miscellaneous Arts and Sciences (n.e.c.)
    Journalism
    Literature
Business Services and Administration
    Advertising and public relations

Miscellaneous Professional Services
Educational
Social, Employment and Spiritual Service
Guidance and advisory
Employment
Government

Having established the foregoing traits and factors as reference points, the Counselor explored appropriate Worker Trait groups.

Procedure to Determine Relevant Work Trait Group   After scanning the list of the 22 areas of work (see Appendix D), the counselor tentatively decided to review

Business Relations
Counseling Guidance and Social Work
Education and Training
Writing

Scanning the list of worker trait groups within areas of work (see Appendix E), the counselor tentatively identified the following as worthy of consideration:

Business Relations
.118
.168   Administration [p. 237, *DOT* Volume II]
.168
.268   Consultative and Business Services [p. 248, *DOT* Volume II]
.168
.268   Interviewing; Information Giving and Related Work [p. 250, *DOT* Volume II]

(It will be recalled that the codes in the first column represent the fourth, fifth, and sixth digits of the *DOT* codes, which respectively indicate the involvements with DATA, PEOPLE, and THINGS).

Counseling Guidance and Social Work
.108
.208   Guidance and Counseling [p. 296, *DOT* Volume II]

Education and Training
.228   High School, College, University, and Related Education [p. 341 *DOT* Volume II]

Writing
.088
.018   Creative Writing [p. 514 *DOT* Volume II]

The review was beginning to present issues. How strong was Robert's desire to teach, to write, to provide counseling, or to administer? Which fields would best utilize Robert's need to innovate and to create? Which minimized long-term involvement with scholarship and detail?

The list of Worker Trait Groups indicates that Robert has the potential to meet the requirements of the *levels* shown for DATA, PEOPLE, THINGS, but additional information is clearly needed with respect to the character of each WTG and to Robert's attitudes and abilities, actual and potential. For these reasons, the counselor asked Robert to read the material about the Worker Trait Group entitled "Administration," which appears in *DOT* Volume II, pages 237–238.

ADMINISTRATION

.118; .168

Work Performed

Work activities in this group primarily involve formulating and carrying out administrative principles, practices, and techniques in an organization or establishment. These activities typically entail program planning, allocation of responsibilities to organizational components, monitoring the internal activities of these components, and coordinating their achievements in a manner that will insure success of the overall objective.

Worker Requirements

An occupationally significant combination of: Organizational ability to plan, formulate, and execute policies and programs; capacity to acquire knowledge of various administrative concepts and practices and successfully apply them to different organizational environments; verbal facility to deal effectively with persons at all levels; facility with numbers to prepare and review various financial and material reports; ability to relate to people in a manner to win their confidence and establish rapport; flexibility to adjust to changing conditions; and an analytical mind to solve complex problems.

Clues for Relating Applicants and Requirements

Successful achievement and advancement in lower level jobs in similar or related fields.

Educational background that includes business or governmental administration coursework.

Extracurricular or leisure-time activities and positions held that have afforded opportunities to acquire organizational skills, such as serving as community chairman of charity drives and production manager of amateur plays.

Training and Methods of Entry

Entry into this type of work may be accomplished in a variety of ways. Applicants frequently enter after years of experience, working up from lower level positions in which they have become familiar with the policies and operations of an organization or activity and have impressed others with their efficiency, initiative, judgment, and organizational ability.

Many organizations have established administrative training programs. They hire promising college graduates, usually those with a degree in business administration, and funnel them through a training program designed to familiarize them with the functions of all phases of the organizational network and thereby prepare them to step into administrative positions.

RELATED CLASSIFICATIONS

Accounting, Auditing, and Related Work (.188; .288) p. 252

Business Training (.228) p. 241
Consultative and Business Services (.168; .268) p. 248
Contract Negotiating and Related Work (.118; .168) p. 239
Managerial Work (.168) p. 245

QUALIFICATIONS PROFILE

GED:	5	6				
SVP:	8	9				
Apt:	G V N	S P Q	K F M	E C		
	1 1 2	4 4 4	4 4 4	5 5		
	2 2 3	3 3 3		4		
Int: 5	2	6				
Temp: 4	5	1	9			
Phys. Dem: S	L	5				

04	LIFE SCIENCES
045.	Psychology
045.118	DIRECTOR OF GUIDANCE IN PUBLIC SCHOOLS (education)
05	SOCIAL SCIENCES
050.	Economics
050.118	MANPOWER RESEARCH AND PLANNING DIRECTOR (gov. ser.)
052.	History
052.168	DIRECTOR, RESEARCH (motion pic.)
07	MEDICINE AND HEALTH
075.	Nursing
075.118	CONSULTANT, EDUCATIONAL, STATE BOARD OF NURSING (gov. ser.)
	DIRECTOR, EDUCATIONAL, PUBLIC-HEALTH NURSING (medical ser.)
	DIRECTOR, NURSING SERVICE (medical ser.)
	DIRECTOR, OCCUPATIONAL HEALTH NURSING (medical ser.)
	DIRECTOR, PUBLIC-HEALTH NURSING (medical ser.)
	DIRECTOR, SCHOOL OF NURSING (medical ser.)
	EXECUTIVE DIRECTOR, NURSES' ASSOCIATION (medical ser.)
077.	Dietetic Work
077.118	DIETITIAN, CHIEF (profess. & kin.)
079.	Medicine and Health, n.c.c.
079.118	PUBLIC HEALTH EDUCATOR (profes. & kin.)
	SANITARIAN (profess. & kin.)

079.168	COMMUNITY SERVICES AND HEALTH EDUCATION OFFICER (gov. ser.)
09	EDUCATION
090.	College and University Education
090.118	ACADEMIC DEAN (education)
	ALUMNI SECRETARY (education)
	DEAN OF STUDENTS (education)
	DIRECTOR, EXTENSION WORK (education)
	FINANCIAL-AIDS OFFICER (education)
	PRESIDENT, EDUCATIONAL INSTITUTION (education)
090.168	DIRECTOR OF ADMISSIONS (education)
	DIRECTOR OF STUDENT AFFAIRS (education)
	DIRECTOR, SUMMER SESSIONS (education)
	REGISTRAR, COLLEGE OR UNIVERSITY (education)
091.	Secondary School Education
091.118	PRINCIPAL (education)
	HEADMASTER (education)
	SUPERINTENDENT, SCHOOLS (education)
094.	Education of the Handicapped
094.118	DIRECTOR, COMMISSION FOR THE BLIND (gov. ser.)
	DIRECTOR, SPECIAL EDUCATION (education)
097.	Vocational Education, n.e.c.
097.118	DIRECTOR, VOCATIONAL TRAINING (education)

099.	**Education, n.e.c.**
099.118	DIRECTOR, EDUCATIONAL PROGRAM (education)
	EDUCATIONAL SUPERVISOR, PENAL INSTITUTION (education)
	SUPERVISOR, EDUCATION (education)
099.168	AUDIOVISUAL SPECIALIST (education)
	EDUCATIONAL SPECIALIST (education)
	SCHOOL EXAMINER (education)
10	**MUSEUM, LIBRARY, AND ARCHIVAL SCIENCES**
100.	**Library Work**
100.118	LIBRARY DIRECTOR (library)
102.	**Museum and Related Work**
102.118	CURATOR (museum)
109.	**Museum, Library, and Archival Sciences, n.e.c.**
109.118	SUPERVISOR, HISTORIC SITES (gov. ser.)
15	**ENTERTAINMENT AND RECREATION**
153.	**Athletics and Sports**
153.118	SUPERVISOR, HISTORIC SITES (gov. ser.)
15	**ENTERTAINMENT AND RECREATION**
153.	**Athletics and Sports**
153.118	DIRECTOR, ATHLETIC (education)
	MANAGER, ATHLETIC TEAM (amuse. & rec.)
	STEWARD, RACETRACK (amuse. & rec.)
159.	**Entertainment and Recreation, n.e.c.**
159.118	PRODUCER (radio & tv broad.)
16	**ADMINISTRATIVE SPECIALTIES**
159.118	PRODUCER (radio & tv broad.)
16	**ADMINISTRATIVE SPECIALTIES**
160.	**Accounting and Auditing**
160.168	CHIEF EXAMINER (gov. ser.)
161.	**Budget and Management Analysis**
161.118	BUDGET OFFICER (gov. ser.)
161.118	DIRECTOR, JOINT FINANCING (nonprofit organ.)
Con.	TREASURER (any ind.)
	UNION TIMESTUDY MAN (clerical)
162.	**Purchasing Management**
162.118	ADMINISTRATOR, CONTRACT AND ORDER (any ind.)
	RESEARCH-CONTRACTS SUPERVISOR (gov. ser.)
	CONTRACT SPECIALIST (gov. ser.)
163.	**Sales and Distribution Management**
163.118	MANAGER, CONTRACTS (petrol. production; petrol. refin.; pipe lines)
	MANAGER, EXPORT (any ind.)
	MANAGER, PROMOTION (hotel & rest.)
	MANAGER, SALES (any ind.)
	MANAGER, CIRCULATION (print. & pub.)
164.	**Advertising Management**
164.118	DIRECTOR, ADVERTISING (print. & pub.)

	MANAGER, ADVERTISING (any ind.)
	MANAGER, ADVERTISING AGENCY (bus. ser.)
166.	**Personnel and Training Administration**
166.118	DIRECTOR, EDUCATIONAL (education)
	DIRECTOR, SAFETY (education)
	DIRECTOR, INDUSTRIAL RELATIONS (profess. & kin.)
	MANAGER, PERSONNEL (profess. & kin.) I
166.168	DIRECTOR, INDUSTRIES AND MAINTENANCE (gov. ser.)
169.	**Administrative Specialities, n.e.c.**
169.118	ADMINISTRATIVE OFFICE, STATE BOARD OF NURSING (gov. ser.)
	CONCILLATOR (profess. & kin.)
	DEFENSE COORDINATOR (profess. & kin)
	LABOR -RELATIONS SPECIALIST (profess. & kin.)
	SALARY AND WAGE ADMINISTRATOR (profess. & kin.)
	STEWARD, PORT (water trans.)
169.168	CIVIL DEFENSE TRAINING OFFICER (gov. ser.)
18	**MANAGERIAL WORK, N.E.C.**
181.	**Mining Management**
181.118	MANAGER, BULK PLANT (petrol. refin.: ret. tr.)
	MINE SUPERINTENDENT (mining & quarrying)
183.	**Manufacturing Industry, Management**
183.118	MANAGER, BRANCH (any ind.)
	PRODUCTION SUPERINTENDENT (any ind.)
184.	**Transportation, Communication, and Utilities Management**
184.118	DIRECTOR, PUBLIC SERVICE (radio & tv broad.)
	DIRECTOR, TRANSPORTATION (motor trans.)
	MANAGER, HARBOR DEPARTMENT (water trans.)
	MANAGER, INDUSTRIAL DEVELOPMENT (r.r. trans.)
	MANAGER, AREA DEVELOPMENT (light, heat, & power)
	MANAGER, IRRIGATION DISTRICT (waterworks)
	MANAGER, OPERATIONS air trans.: motor trans.; r.r. trans.; water trans.)
	MANAGER, REGIONAL (motor trans.)
	MANAGER, STATION (radio & tv broad.)
	DIRECTOR, INTERNATIONAL BROADCASTING (radio & tv broad.)
	OPERATIONS MANAGER (tel. & tel.)
	REVENUE-SETTLEMENTS ADMINISTRATOR (tel. & tel.)
	SUPERINTENDENT, AIRPORT (air trans.)

CHIEF, FISHERY DIVISION (gov. ser.)
CIVIL DEFENSE OFFICER (gov. ser.)
COMMISSIONER, CONSERVATION OF RESOURCES (gov. ser.)
COMMISSIONER OF CONCILIATION (gov. ser.)
COMMISSIONER, PUBLIC WORKS (gov. ser.)
ROADS SUPERVISOR (gov. ser.)
CUSTOMS COLLECTOR (gov. ser.)
DIRECTOR, AERONAUTICS COMMISSION (gov. ser.)
DIRECTOR, COUNCIL ON AGING (gov. ser.)
DIRECTOR, FIELD REPRESENTATIVES (gov. ser.)
DIRECTOR, MEDICAL FACILITIES SECTION (gov. ser.)
FOREIGN-SERVICE OFFICER (gov. ser.)
GENERAL SERVICES OFFICER (gov. ser.)
HOUSING-MANAGEMENT OFFICER (gov. ser.)
INDUSTRIAL PLANNING ADMINISTRATOR (gov. ser.)
MANAGER, CITY (gov. ser.)
POLICE COMMISSIONER (gov. ser.) I
WELFARE DIRECTOR (gov. ser.)
DIRECTOR, BUREAU OF PUBLIC ASSISTANCE (gov. ser.)

188.168   DIRECTOR OF VITAL STATISTICS (gov. ser.)
DIRECTOR, SAFETY COUNCIL (gov. ser.)
TRAFFIC-SAFETY ADMINISTRATOR (gov. ser.)
RELOCATION COMMISSIONER (gov. ser.)
SECRETARY OF STATE (gov. ser.)

189.   **Miscellaneous Managerial World, n.e.c.**
189.118   ASSOCIATION EXECUTIVE (profess. & kin.)
DIRECTOR, RESEARCH AND DEVELOPMENT (any ind.)
MANAGER, INDUSTRIAL ORGANIZATION (any ind.)
PRESIDENT (any ind.)
VICE PRESIDENT (any ind.)

19   **MISCELLANEOUS PROFESSIONAL, TECHNICAL, AND MANAGERIAL WORK**
195.   **Social and Welfare Work**
195.118   ADMINISTRATOR, SOCIAL WELFARE (profess. & kin.)
DIRECTOR, WELFARE (profess. & kin.)

199.   **Miscellaneous Professional, Technical, and Managerial Work, n.e.c.**
199.168   URBAN PLANNER (profess. & kit.)
37   **PROTECTIVE SERVICES**
373.   **Fire Protection Service**
373.118   FIRE CHIEF (gov. ser.)

373.168   BATTALION CHIEF (gov. ser.)
375.   **Police and Related Work, Public Service**
375.118   POLICE CHIEF (gov. ser.) II
375.168   HARBOR MASTER (gov. ser.)
SUPERINTENDENT, COMMUNICATIONS (tel. & tel.)
185.   **Wholesale and Retail Trade Management**
185.168   SUPERVISOR, LIQUOR STORES AND AGENCIES (gov. ser.)
186.   **Finance, Insurance, and Real Estate Management**
186.118   BUSINESS MANAGER, COLLEGE OR UNIVERSITY (education)
CONTROLLER (profess. & kin.)
DEPUTY INSURANCE COMMISSIONER (gov. ser.)
MANAGER, INSURANCE (any ind.)
MANAGER, FINANCIAL INSTITUTION (banking; finan. inst.)
MANAGER, LEASING (petrol. production)
PROPERTY LEASING (petrol. production)
PROPERTY MANAGER (gov. ser.)
REAL-ESTATE AGENT (r.r. trans.)
TRUST OFFICER (banking)
186.118   VICE-PRESIDENT, BANK (banking)
186.168   BANK CASHIER (banking)
187.   **Service Industry Management**
187.118   BUSINESS AGENT, LABOR UNION (profes. & kin.)
DIRECTOR, COMMUNITY ORGANIZATION (nonprofit organ.)
DISTRICT ADVISER (nonprofit organ.)
EXECUTIVE VICE PRESIDENT, CHAMBER OF COMMERCE (nonprofit organ.)
MANAGER, DEPARTMENT, CHAMBER OF COMMERCE (nonprofit organ.)
MANAGER, WORLD TRADE (nonprofit organ.)
MANAGER, HOTEL (hotel & rest.) I
MANAGER, MOTEL (hotel & rest.) II
PUBLIC HEALTH SERVICE OFFICER (gov. ser.)
RECREATION SUPERVISOR (profess. & kin.)
RECREATION SUPERVISOR, SPECIAL ACTIVITY (profess. & kin.)
SUPERINTENDENT, CIRCUS (amuse. & rec.)
SUPERINTENDENT, INSTITUTION (any ind.)
SUPERINTENDENT, HOSPITAL (medical ser.)
SUPERINTENDENT, RECREATION (gov. ser.)
188.   **Public Administration Management**
188.118   APPRENTICE-TRAINING REPRESENTATIVE, FIELD (gov. ser.)

Robert and his counselor were impressed with the degree of relevance: the match for the Worker Function levels, and the Worker Trait factors was great. Occupations in this Worker Trait Group required ability in planning; conceptualizing programs, missions, and goals; ability to execute policies and programs; ability to read reports; ability to win support; and flexibility. It was immediately apparent, however, that although such occupations appealed strongly to Robert, he could not qualify for any of them with his current abilities. Instead he would have to start at a lower level and advance to one of the jobs represented in the group. On reviewing the list, a large number of options emerged which involved specific subject matters: health, counseling and guidance, education, museum library, and archival sciences, and so on. Part of Robert's initial occupational decisions, the counselor pointed out, would result from chance (e.g., obtaining a position at an entry level in the geographic area of Robert's choice would lead to greater insights and decisions). Thus the first job accepted would depend on availability of such work and the type and number of competing candidates; other important constraints would be the management climate and growth and promotional opportunities. The counselor also pointed out that Robert could partially control his options by aiming at a specific subject area. For example, if he aspired to be a college dean, teaching experience in a college was a virtual requirement. It was also possible that Robert would be able to identify other subject matters that interested him once he became involved in a job situation.

Next the counselor reviewed the other Worker Trait Groups shown earlier. For example, he checked out Consultative and Business Services (*DOT* Volume II, p. 248). Many of the Worker Trait and Worker Function levels matched, but a high degree of clerical aptitude was required, and Robert lacked this. In addition, the jobs called for a substantial degree of attention to detail and research—precisely the areas in which Robert felt that he was least interested and least capable. Robert also discounted his preference for the "Creative Writing" Worker Trait Group (*DOT* Volume II, p. 524) because these activities included "writing poetry, fiction, criticism, lyrics, advertising copy, and plays." Robert believed that he could write advertising copy (he had had a college course in this subject), but he felt that most of the jobs would be too commercial and insufficiently oriented toward the welfare of people. Moreover, he thought the work might not provide sufficient scope for program conceptualizations and the other types of synthesizing he preferred.

The counselor then reviewed the WTG for "High School, College, University, and Related Education." The qualifications profile matched Robert's closely, as did the qualifications profile for Counseling and Guidance (*DOT* Volume II, p. 296). After considerable thought, Robert came to an important realization—namely, that over the *long term,* the Worker Trait Group that best fitted his needs was Administration. He thought that his preferred subject area would be college administration. He also realized that one method of entry would be to start as a teacher, next to become a counselor, and as experience provided further insight, to shape and reshape his goals accordingly. Another obvious port of entry was through the college series of examinations given by the federal and many state governments; passing such examinations creditably could result in government jobs in personnel management, industrial relations, budgetary work, staff training, or management systems. Robert thought that this might ultimately lead to jobs in the educational area or other "helping people" areas. He did not reach final career decision at the time of his last counseling interview, but he felt that he had achieved a high degree of career clarification and was ready to get his first job: he would seek a teaching job, take the college examination series (both federal and in his home state), and apply for entry-professional level jobs in personnel at some of the nearby colleges and universities. In the meantime, he decided to consult college catalogs for courses in the field of organization and management, and personnel. He would decide on the courses after obtaining his first job, either in teaching or personnel.

Chart 6 is a tabulation of Robert's profile and the profiles of the Worker Trait Groups reviewed. Clearly the profiles for most of the groups shown match Robert's. Robert's decision must heavily be weighted by his preferences for specific tasks, the degree of detail and research, and character and degree of working with people. The social values, the subject matter, and the work field—that is, administering, teaching, or writing—were also important in making his choice. Each factor comprises a subsystem that must be judged in the context of a total matrix. The matrix, of course, is Robert's needs and values, as he perceives them now and as he predicts they will emerge changed or not over time. Many of the contingencies will depend on chance, but would it not be better to utilize the more rational approach possible under the *DOT* system? This approach seems to be particularly necessary to select the job that will qualify for the next rung in one's "planned" career progression over his working lifetime, when one of several alternative job opportunities must be followed to achieve specific experience, or when alternative occupational training opportunities are available.

The tabulation of Robert T.'s Worker Traits seems to illustrate how this system interacts, underscoring that some factors have greater weight than others, at least from time to time. For example, all the six groups have at least one *interest* in common, four have the same two in common. Similarly, all have at least one *temperament* in common, and four have the

CHART 6

Worker Trait Group	Page Number in DOT 3, Vol. II	Worker Function Levels	GED	Aptitudes						Interests					Temperaments					
				G	V	N	S	P	Q	2	4	5	6	9	1	4	5	7	9	0
Administration	237	.118, .168	5, 6	1 2	1 2	2 3	4 3	4 3	4 3	x					x	x	x	x	x	x
Consultative and Business Service	248	.166, .268	5	2 2	2 2	1 2	3 3	4 4	1 2			x	x		x	x	x			x
Social Science, Psychological, and Related Research	294	.088	5, 6	1 2	1 2	2 1	3 3	4 4	2 3				x		x			x	x	
Guidance and Counseling	296	.108, .208	5, 6	1 2	1 2	3 3	4 4	4 4	4 4		x	x	x		x	x	x		x	
High School, College, University, and Related	341	.228	4, 5, 6	1 2	1 2	1 2	3 4	3 4	3 4		x	x	x		x	x	x	x	x	x
Creative Writing	524	.088	6, 5	1 2	1 4	4 4	4 4	4 4	3 3			x	x	x			x	x		
Robert's Profile	xxx	Any of the above	5	1	1	2	4	1	2	x	x	x	x	x	x	x	x	x	x	x

same three. This suggests that interests and temperaments are better modifiers than they are differentiators. The same point might be made for aptitudes (in this case), though less conclusively. Robert's most significant aptitudes are *GVN*. Two of the groups have the same pattern as Robert's; all but one have the same level for *G* and *V*, which are the most relevant; five have levels that represent a one-step variance. Worker Function differences constitute a more interesting and perhaps a more critical factor. For DATA, a one-step differential prevails, if the benchmark is level 1. The variance here is significant. Assuming that Robert has the potentials to attain the top level, what are his aspiration levels? Synthesizing? Coordinating? Analyzing? With respect to PEOPLE, does he prefer to advise (Mentor), level "0," to Instruct (level "2"), or to work with people (Speaking-Signaling, level "6")? Each combination relates to differing job types and the kind of goal to be established.

It may be even more significant to learn which of the Work Fields are most important to Robert—Administering, Information Giving, Researching, Instructing, or Writing. (The subject matter also becomes critical at the last stage of Robert's decision, i.e., when he decides which of the available jobs to accept.) Would Robert elect to prepare himself to teach in high school and become an administrator in the secondary schools, or would he rather set his sights on college administration, which did not involve teaching, as personnel director or admissions director? The latter goals might stimulate him to teach, enhancing and enlarging his interest and focus.

It is one thing to settle on teaching as a total career. It is an altogether different matter to accept teaching as a stepping stone to a career in, say, educational administration. In the second case, the incumbent would begin to relate each job experience to the long-term career goal, which in this case is administration. Such a goal should tend to make the teaching three-dimensional; that is Robert would see his daily job as a teacher, as a pedagogical theorist, and as an administrator. This would subordinate some of Robert's interests and temperaments to others, perhaps only for the short term, to gain the related and necessary experience and insights. For example, if he disliked "theory" and a knowledge of "theory" was necessary for his long-term goal, he should be able to accept the study of theory in the context of his major goal. Yet in so doing he might begin to like certain aspects, uses, and implications of "theory." Finally, one might well ask whether Robert's decision would be affected by other less occupationally oriented factors: length of training time required, costs, availability of job and educational opportunities in the geographical areas of interest, and Robert's willingness to move to sites at which these were available.

The case of Robert T. indicates how and why the *DOT* building blocks are useful in counseling and in career decision making. There is no question of their value for Robert. Greater complications and problems would doubtless be encountered with persons who were less articulate and had never perceived themselves as career decision makers. Many young people never look at themselves in career terms because they believe that their limited educational and job opportunities mean that they will never have career choices to make. To remedy this, many authorities have concluded that children should be stimulated in the secondary schools to think about the world of work and their place in it. And the experts are beginning to develop techniques and apparatus for these purposes. Interestingly, most developments are based on the *DOT* building blocks, either in their original form or with minor adaptations.

JOB RESTRUCTURING

Job restructuring represents yet another application of the Job Analysis Formulation, which provides a technique for subdividing an existing job into, say, two jobs. The first would retain the more skilled components, thereby enriching the work. The second would comprise the less skilled tasks, thereby providing a port of entry for the disadvantaged, or other persons without experience or other necessary credentials. Subdividing is also used when it is not possible to meet recruiting needs, modifications in technology in certain industries, changed economic conditions, or the needs of valued employees who become physically limited. The Rehabilitation Act of 1973 requires employers holding government contracts for $2500 or more to provide equal opportunity to the handicapped, and compliance with the law often necessitates job restructuring.

Job restructuring is accomplished by identifying the tasks to be performed in sufficient depth and detail to permit rating each task as if it were a complete job. The factors used vary with the type of occupation. In one recent study it was found that Worker Function levels and GED were most useful. In other instances the addition of SVP ratings for each task provided further differentiation. In still others, aptitudes were chosen to narrow the field.

After analysis of the ratings for each task, the tasks are regrouped on the basis of the commonalities ascertained into two or more jobs, that is "new" and residual jobs.[32] The new jobs may include many of the tasks of the initial job, as well as tasks from other jobs in the establishment. The residual job consists of the tasks that remain after some of the tasks in the original job have been assigned to other jobs. The residual jobs may thus be enriched because less complex tasks have been transferred to other existing jobs or to new jobs. The regrouping of tasks is constrained by such factors as production process requirements; whether the tasks comprising the new job require, say, 8 hours daily (and in such instances, possible combinations of the new jobs with other jobs having some homogeneous elements); traditions in the industry or in given establishments; legal requirements (licensure, etc.); the traits of workers already employed; requirements stipulated in union contracts; and the availability of new workers for the new jobs. Restructured jobs often comprise a skill ladder; that is the new jobs created might well be qualifying for the restructured residual jobs. An example of job restructuring is shown on pages 88–93. The first set of tasks represents the original job. The next three sets represent three new jobs developed from two core groups of tasks.

JOB LADDERS

Job ladders or lattices represent progressions for jobs generally, for jobs within an establishment, or for a given individual. The term "job ladder" generally is limited to upward progressions. The term "job lattice" implies lateral or diagonal movement. Most often, progressions are upward, lateral, *and* diagonal.

Consider the merit system. The announcement for an examination for a moderately high-level job states the types of prior experience that will be accepted as qualifying. Extensive studies have not been made in this area, but it seems evident that many criteria are brought to bear in such determinations, including the opinions of the appointing officers, the number of possibly interested candidates, the desire to appoint a particularly meritorious candidate (which might suggest that the field of competition be limited), and the experience and knowledge of the merit system technicians. In any event, the progression represents an empirical career ladder based on opinion rather than scientifically determined criteria.

Similarly, some job evaluation systems contain the rudiments of job ladder construction, since jobs are ranked for purposes of setting progressively higher job prices (wages) and salaries, which are related to preestablished criteria including degrees of skills, knowledge, abilities, responsibilities, and judgments.

The Job Analysis Formulation is potentially useful in the largely intuitive area of promotions because some of its components are scaled: Worker Functions (DATA, PEOPLE, THINGS) GED, SVP, Aptitudes. The word "potentially" is used because insufficient research has been devoted to this area by the *DOT* developers. The methods used for determining job ladders through the *DOT* follow.

The occupational group arrangement of the *DOT* (Volume II, p. 33 ff) lists all six-digit codes in numerical sequence. It will be recalled that the first three digits represent a Work Field, or Material, Product, Subject Matter, Service, or Activity. The second three digits represents the levels of complexity for DATA, PEOPLE, THINGS, each combination of which indicates, for a given Worker Trait Group, the specific worker traits required for the occupations clustered in that group. For a given set of first three digits, therefore, a ladder can be discerned by reference to the Worker Function levels, arranged in descending order. For example, code 209 (first three digits) covers Stenography, Typing, Filing, and Related Occupations. (Hence 209 represents a Work Field).[33] It comprises the following six-digit codes:

209.138
209.368
209.382
209.388
209.488
209.584
209.587
209.588
209.687
209.688

Each of these code numbers contains one or more base or related job titles. Following is a small sample of all titles shown in the *Dictionary* for first three digits "209."

209.138   Stenographic Pool Supervisor (Clerical)
209.382   Justowriter Operator
209.388   Clerk-Typist (Clerical)
209.488   Invoice Control Clerk (Clerical)
209.588   Clerk, General
           Credit Card Clerk (ret. tr.)
           Price Clerk (Clerical)
209.687   Address Plate Inserter (Clerical)
209.688   Sorter (Clerical)

In the *DOT* system, a person in the lowest rung for a given first-three-digit combination might be able to progress from .688 to .138 (in this example) if he has the ability and aspirations to make the climb; the

Original Job

JOB RESTRUCTURING WORKSHEET

Establishment Job Title Electronics Assembler DOT Title and Code _____ No. Employed __39__ Date _____

Department __Assembly__ Supervisor __John R. Doe__ Title __Foreman__ Analyst __S. W. Brown__

| Task description | Time (minutes) | Functions | | | GED | Important aptitudes | Other pertinent worker traits | Comments |
		D	P	T				
1. Reviews production order and requisitions appropriate parts from stockroom -------	30	3	6	7	3	V-3, N-3, Q-4	Near acuity	
2. Assembles numbered panels to form apparatus cabinet, using hand and power tools -------	60	6	8	7	2	S-4, K-4, M-4		
3. Attaches components such as motors, heaters, and cooling units to cabinets, using hand and power tools -------	90	6	8	4	3	S-3, K-3, F-3, M-3		
4. Connects and alines electronic parts such as photocells and relays, using handtools, test equipment, and diagrams ----	60	3	8	1	3	S-3, P-3, F-3	Near acuity	
5. Attaches terminals, plugs, rheostats, dials, and knobs, using handtools -------	15	6	8	4	3	K-3, F-3, M-3		

88

6. Solders wires to components and controls, using soldering iron and wiring diagrams ------	30	6	8	4	3	P-4, K-3, F-3, M-3	Near acuity
7. Attaches resistors, transistors, and diodes to printed circuit board, using handtools, soldering iron, and diagram.	30	6	8	4	3	P-3, K-3, F-3, M-3	Near acuity
8. Cleans cabinet and components, using cleaning solution and air hose ------	60	6	8	7	1	M-3	
9. Connects glass and plastic tubing and attaches valves, using handtools ------	15	6	8	4	2	S-4, K-3, F-3, M-3	
10. Attaches operating instructions and caution decals to unit, using water and squeegee ------	30	6	8	7	1	M-3	
11. Secures serial number plate to cabinet, using screwdriver, and records number on production order ------	15	6	8	7	1	K-4, F-4, M-4	
12. Tests and adjusts electronic parts and mechanisms to specified tolerances, using electronic and mechanical test, equipment, and handtools ------	45	3	8	1	4	G-3, N-3, S-3, P-3	Near acuity

Job developed from tasks in core group I

JOB RESTRUCTURING WORKSHEET

Establishment Job Title __Electronics Assembler I__ DOT Title and Code _____ No. Employed _____ Date _____

Department __Assembly__ Supervisor _____ John R. Doe __Title__ __Foreman__ Analyst __S. W. Brown__

Task description	Time (minutes)	Functions				Other Important apitudes	pertinent worker traits	Comments
		D	P	T	GED			
2. Assembles numbered panels to form apparatus cabinet, using hand and power tools -------	240	6	8	7	2	S-4, K-4, M-4		
8. Cleans cabinet and compo-nents, using cleaning solution and air hose -------	90	6	8	7	1	M-3		
10. Attaches operating instructions and caution decals to unit, us-ing water and squeegee -------	60	6	8	7	1	M-3		
11. Secures serial number plate to cabinet, using screwdriver, and records number on production order -------	90	6	8	7	1	K-4, F-4, M-4		

New job created from revision of
job developed from core group II

JOB RESTRUCTURING WORKSHEET

Establishment Job Title __Electronics Inspector__ DOT Title and Code _____ No. Employed ____ Date ____

Department __Assembly__ Supervisor __John R. Doe__ Title __Foreman__ Analyst __S. W. Brown__

Task description	Time (minutes)	Functions D	P	T	GED	Important aptitudes	Other pertinent worker traits	Comments
1. Reviews production order and requisitions appropriate parts from stockroom ----	180	3	6	7	3	V-3, N-3, Q-4	Near acuity	
12. Tests and adjusts electronic parts and mechanisms to specified tolerances, using electronic and mechanical test, equipment, and handtools ----	300	3	8	1	4 3	G-3, N-3, S-3, P-	Near acuity	

Revision of job developed from tasks in core group II

JOB RESTRUCTURING WORKSHEET

Establishment Job Title Electronics Assembler II DOT Title and Code No. Employed _____ Date

Department Assembly Supervisor John R. Doe Title Foreman Analyst S. W. Brown

Task description	Time (minutes)	Function s			GED	Important aptitudes	Other pertinent worker traits	Comments
		D	P	T				
3. Attaches components such as motors, heaters, and cooling units to cabinets, using hand and power tools -------	180	6	8	4	3	S-3, K-3, F-3, M-3		
4. Connects and alines electronic parts such as photocells and relays, using handtools, test equipment, and diagrams -----	120	3	8	1	3	S-3, P-3, F-3	Near acuity	
5. Attaches terminals; plugs, rheostats, dials, and knobs, using handtools -------	30	6	8	4	3	K-3, F-3, M-3		

92

6. Solders wires to components and controls, using soldering iron and wiring diagrams -----	60	6	8	4	3	P-4, K-3, F-3, M-3	Near acuity
7. Attaches resistors, transistors, and diodes to printed circuit board, using handtools, soldering iron, and diagram -------	60	6	8	4	3	P-3, K-3, F-3, M-3	Near acuity
9. Connects glass and plastic tubing and attaches valves, using handtools -----------------	30	6	8	4	2	S-4, K-3, F-3, M-3	

[a] U.S. Department of Labor, Manpower Administration. A Handbook for Job Restructuring. Washington, D.C.: U.S. Government Printing Office; 1970 pp. 17–22.

necessary potential GED, aptitudes, interests, temperaments, and physical capacities; and is willing to undertake the additional training needed (SVP). The theory rests on the fact that this progression requires the *same* Work Fields, MPSMS, Worker Functions, and Worker Traits. This, however, is not the case, with respect to first three digits 209, which fall into the following Worker Trait Groups as shown by the *DOT*, Volume II:

Six-Digit Code	Page Number in *DOT 3*, Volume II	Worker Trait Group
209.138	p. 243	Supervisory Work (Clerical, Sales & Rel.)
209.368	p. 258	Information Gathering, Dispensing, Verifying, and Related
209.382	p. 274	Typesetting, Reproducing & Rel. Mach. Work
209.388	p. 276	Classifying, Filing, and Related Work
	p. 256	Corresponding and Related Work
209.488	p. 280	Computing and Related Recording
209.584	p. 282	Sorting, Inspecting, Measuring, & Rel.
209.587	p. 282	Sorting, Inspecting, Measuring, & Rel.
209.588	p. 287	Typing and Related Recording
	p. 289	Routine Checking and Recording
209.687	p. 282	Sorting, Inspecting, Measuring, & Rel.
209.688	p. 289	Routine Checking and Recording

This example serves to illustrate once again the importance of all *DOT* and Job Analysis components and how they interact. For purposes of *job ladders* therefore, the approach just described is subject to one overriding consideration. In constructing a job ladder through these means, one must ascertain that the Worker Trait patterns are the *same* or almost the same for all codes in the ladder. Inspection of the foregoing tabulation indicates that this may not be the case for some of the titles in the progression. Thus we must examine each job title and either prepare the Worker Trait ratings or obtain them from the Worker Trait Groups in which each appears,[34] then making the necessary adjustments in the job ladder.

It should be noted that in some instances job titles in a six-digit code group have been "split" among different Worker Trait Groups. This does not destroy the usefulness of the system, however, because it has occurred in only 87 instances of the 14,000 job titles. The splits did not occur within categories 5, 6, 7, and 8.

The identification of *career* ladders for given *individuals* necessitates a different methodology. For the individual, the present and the potential qualifications profile must be ascertained. One should not identify a job ladder for an individual on the basis of the person's last job, which may not have been the job he preferred and may not have offered optimum utilization of his Worker Traits. Since in real life so many variables occur unpredictably, it is obviously necessary for one to review his job goals constantly and to make adjustments within his *generally* perceived career direction. The possible variables are shown in Chart 3 of Chapter 1. It is the opinion of the author that a measure of control can be exercised despite the presence of uncontrolled or uncontrollable variables, if the worker is able to use the body of knowledge and technology contained in the *DOT,* in making adjustments after each change in his occupational fortunes.

THE OCCUPATIONAL MATRIX

One of the chief ingredients of a national manpower policy is data describing the current national manpower balance sheet and its imbalances. Such data should lead to corrective measures, both immediately and for the future.

For example, in the face of rising employment toward the fall of 1974, *The New York Times* reported (August 11): "Specifically, the nation needs expanded programs for creating jobs, training and educating workers, finding needed health services, reforming the tax structure, and more fairly distributing the tax burden."

An issue implicit in this view is the need to decide what kinds of program should be established for *what kinds of people.* Attention is seldom focused on the latter—the jobs needed to absorb the unemployed. One might well suppose that future determinations of this type will stem from input-output analysis,[35] to indicate which industries should be expanded (and the rippling impact on the other industries), leading to the creation of additional jobs. Such determinations doubtless rest on the "old religion"—that is, the tenet that workers will come forward to accept the jobs if the wage is satisfactory, even though many will find themselves in work they do not like, which is at variance with their occupational talents and needs. Eventually, of course, such workers will quit if and when they can find jobs they prefer.

Much friction will occur even with the most careful determination of worker skills and needs and the industries that can absorb them: facilities might not be available locally; sufficient numbers of the type of workers called for may not be available where needed; or government opportunities that are to be expanded under the Public Service Employment Program,[36] may not be available in sufficient numbers in the right localities. In addition, other constraining factors may arise, affecting labor and management. Nonetheless, is not the development of a suitable methodology for these purposes worthy of exploration? Surely it is time to add worker analysis to input-output analysis to achieve the best possible compromise and accommodation.

Input-output analysis concerns *industrial* expansion. Its occupational counterpart is the Bureau of Labor Statistics (BLS) Occupational Matrix, which determines the percentage of occupations in the matrix that will come from each industry in the matrix. This is particularly important for occupations that recur in many industries (machine shop worker, electronics worker, etc.). The difficulty is that the same occupation may be found in the fabrication of various articles representing different industries. Once these ratios are determined, manpower projections are expedited. If projections are by industry, determining the total number of workers needed in a given occupation for that industry requires application of the previously determined percentage that occupation bore to that industry in the latest study.

Two pitfalls are associated with this approach; one concerns the number of occupations included and the second concerns the well-known limitations of the census data. The Bureau of Labor Statistics Occupational Matrix includes only 190 items, which do not adequately cover the detail of the entire occupational spectrum. With respect to the second limitation, data to be used in classifying workers are obtained either during an interview with the census enumerator or by questionnaire, supposedly prepared by the worker. Often, however, the data are provided by the worker's spouse or child, who may have only a slight idea of the duties performed by husband or father. Mistaken notions of what the worker does, or the lack of specificity in the data obtained by the census enumerator, necessarily lead to inaccuracy.[37]

An alternative approach is to use the type of matrix developed by the author from the two segments of the *DOT* code: the entire occupational spectrum is covered, and the data can be obtained as often as needed from the files of the employment security system, which requires all local employment offices to register and classify for employment (by *DOT* code) all persons seeking jobs or unemployment insurance benefits. Such job seekers and benefit claimants do not constitute the entire roster of the unemployed, but they form the greatest sample available.

In the *DOT* occupational matrix the first three digits represent the demand or employer side of the manpower equation, and the second set of three digits stands for the supply or human side of the equation. The first three digits represent a *material, product, subject matter,* or *service* (MPSMS), or a methodology or technology (Work Field) needed to produce an MPSMS. Such activities are carried out by industry or commerce. The quantities needed can be predicted and reported. The second set of three digits (kind of worker needed to perform at the required levels of complexity for DATA, PEOPLE, THINGS) designates the Worker Trait capacities and abilities needed to perform at these levels of complexity. Hence the second set of three digits describes the kind of worker needed. The BLS matrix reflects *job* rather than *worker* requirements.

The foregoing concepts are further described in Chart 7. Employers require workers to enable them to fulfill their missions and objectives. Such workers use methods, techniques, and activities (Work Fields) to produce materials, products, subject matter, or service (MPSMS), thereby fulfilling employer objectives or societal needs. On the other side of the equation, the

CHART 7

GENERAL MODEL INDICATING HOW JOB ANALYSIS DIMENSIONS CAN BE
USED IN MANPOWER PLANNING

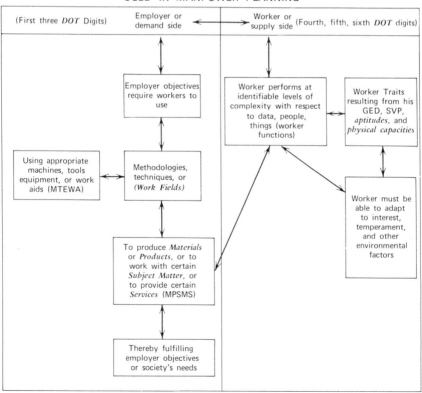

worker performs at defined levels of complexity to produce the materials, products, subject matter, or service. To do this, he must bring to a job the necessary level of General Educational Development (in reasoning, mathematics, and language), the substantive skills and knowledges obtained through relevant training courses (SVP), specified capacities or aptitudes, specified interests and temperaments that will enable him to adjust to the job–worker situation, as well as specified physical capacities and the ability to adjust to the environmental conditions. Chart 8 illustrates the matrix.

The Worker Trait Groups represent one axis of the matrix (supply). (The format uses the WTG title, or *DOT* Volume II page numbers, rather than the Worker Function level, since as stated elsewhere 59 WTGs carry one set of Worker Function levels. The remaining 55 WTGs carry more than one combination of Worker Function levels. The use of the page number or title overcomes this factor.)

The other axis uses the first two or first three digits of the *DOT* code. The sample format and the Wagner study revealed that the first two digits (of which there are 84) were adequate. Detail for the 603 first-three-digit code groups can be obtained if that much detail is needed. Moreover, the first two- or three-digit columns can be subdivided to show additional data. For the Wagner College Affirmative Action Plan each first-two-digit cell was subdivided to show data for negroes, Spanish-speaking, female, and all other minority groups (i.e., American Indians and orientals, which did not reach 2% of the total; when the percentage is 2% or higher, separate data are required for such minority groups, including women). For the public employment service, subdivisions can be used to show "workers registered" and "job openings" available; see Chart 9.

Since the same Worker Traits are required for a given line in Chart 9, substitutions are possible to correct imbalances appearing in the detail for each industry. For example, *DOT,* Volume II, page 282, contains the

CHART 8

Worker Trait Groups	First Two Digits of *DOT*					
——— ——— ———						
						Total
Total						

CHART 9[a]

WTG page number	First Two Digits									
	07		21		37		52		Total	
	JS	JO	SS	JO	JS	JO	JS	JO	JS	JO
282	5	10	15	2	3	14	45	64	68	90
289	15	12	5	14	12	5	30	49	62	80
Totals	20	22	20	16	15	19	75	113	130	170

[a] JS = job seekers; JO = job openings.

Worker Trait Group for Sorting, Inspecting, Measuring, and Related Work. Some of the first-two-digit codes found in this group are 07, 10, 21, 37, 52, 67, 72, 86, and 97. In the study of a file for a given local employment service office, job seekers, and openings were found, say, only in the first two digits 07 (Medicine and Health); 21 (Computing and Account Recording); 37 (Protective Services); and 52 (Processing Food and Related Products). These data represent the supply-demand situation for each two-digit group. Where supply-demand imbalances exist for a single two-digit group, substitutions may be possible [see note 28] by recruiting or shifting opportunities and/or workers from one group to another, provided the workers are willing to undertake the training, and the employers to accept the substitution. In theory, such substitutions will be successful because the trait patterns for all jobs and workers for a given line are the same. Moreover, the total supply-demand situation for a given WTG may indicate either that new workers must be trained to meet the total demand or that more jobs are needed to utilize the total supply. The second line represents data for another Worker Trait Group (i.e., Routine Checking and Recording, p. 289).

The "total" line at the foot of the chart indicates imbalances by two-digit groups, whereas the totals in the last column are totals for each WTG.

The next chapter describes the use of this matrix at Wagner; there are additional uses for it in the public employment service in planning promotional (obtaining additional job orders) and recruiting campaigns (finding additional workers). More important, each local office prepares its annual plan of service, which specifies the manpower imbalances in the communities served and the corrective measures to be taken. Since the matrix represents a community supply-demand balance sheet, thereby identifying specific imbalances, it should prove to be indispensable in planning.

ANOTHER LOOK AT THE WORKER TRAITS GROUPS

Some experts believe that the chief contribution of *DOT 3* to occupational classification theory lies in the Worker Traits approach and the Worker Trait Groups. However, the present classification structure can serve in some applications without the Worker Trait Groups. Why, then, were these included? What is their objective? Since the Worker Traits constitute a controversial subject area, is their continued use justified?

The Worker Trait Groups appear to have three primary uses:

• They make possible the resolution of manpower shortages when persons with the precise experience and ability are not available.

• They improve and facilitate that part of the counseling process which leads to career decision making.

• They provide an improved means for determining and resolving supply-demand imbalances. More important, they provide a means to represent worker capabilities and potentials in the supply-demand equation.

The third objective (use as a matrix) was developed by the author; the first two objectives, on the other hand, were intended by the creators of *DOT 3.*

The Use of Worker Trait Groups in Placement

The Worker Trait Groups represent clusters of occupations sharing the same nonsubstantive traits and factors. Data on interests and temperaments tell about attitudes and attributes and the capacity to adjust. General Educational Development indexes attained capacities in reasoning and in mathematical and language development. Aptitudes constitute potential abilities that can be realized, given substantive training in the task to be performed or the subject matter. The differentiating factors among the occupations in a Worker Trait Group, therefore, are the *subject matters.* It is implicit in the Worker Trait Group theory that all occupations in a group have the same psychoneurological base (assuming that some aptitudes are neurological), which enables persons in these occupations to learn any subject matter characteristic of the occupations *in that group* more expeditiously than persons who do not have the same configuration of traits. In some instances (say, SVP 1 and 2) the substantive factor is so slight that employers will hire anyone belonging to that group.

For example, an employer would readily hire a former *material handler* to fill a vacancy for *yard laborer,* since minimal training is required. Or if a college required a *dean of students,* might it not consider a candidate who had been a director of *student affairs?* In other instances, interchangeability is not feasible because several years may be required to learn the new subject matters required for different occupations in the same group. If an organization needed a *labor economist* and none was available, would it consider an *industrial economist,* a *political scientist,* a *social psychologist,* an *anthropologist,* a *job analyst?* All are in the same Worker Trait Group. From the placement point of view, this clustering has only partial value; that is, substitutions might be possible depending on the other qualifications of given *individuals,* rather than because the occupations required the same basic traits and attributes. As a further illustration, note that *physicists, geologists, biochemists,* and *research nutritionists* are in the same Worker Trait Group. Under what conditions are transfers among such occupations possible?

Clearly, substitutions among occupations in a Worker Traits Group are most readily possible in the 40 WTGs of lower levels of complexity, listed in Appendix G.

The use of Worker Trait Groups in Counseling

What is the rationale for clustering occupations with higher levels of complexity? A partial answer lies in the use of Worker Trait Groups in counseling; in addition, these groups can be helpful in manpower economics (discussed in the next section).

When all the relevant facts are obtained about a counselee, the counselor begins to relate them to the world of work. The American economy comprises 14,000 defined occupations; another 8,500 job titles represent specializations of these defined titles. In the *DOT,* defined titles are known as "base" or "defined related titles" (titles related to the parent base title; "undefined related titles" are specializations of a base or defined related title).

When the 22,500 titles are listed alphabetically by job title, they are merely a disorganized mass of information. Much order and organization are introduced when they are listed by code number, because the arrangement is based on a *Work Field,* a material, product, subject matter, or service (MPSMS), activity (e.g., clerical), or generic term (e.g. welders, tailors). Even this organization however, cannot be easily related to types of people, with different degrees of GED, SVP, and aptitudes, and different interests and temperaments. Clustering by such factors is therefore needed, if *people* are to be related to occupations that match their abilities, needs, and preferences, and made aware of options.

The criteria for clustering occupations for *counseling* purposes differ from the criteria for clustering for *placement* purposes; for the latter, substitutability among occupations in the cluster is most important. For counseling, however, similarity in kinds of activity is the principal criterion; thus if a person fits a cluster, it remains to determine which *one* in the cluster is best for him or her. Thus one of the earlier examples (material handler to substitute for yard laborer) was taken from the Worker Trait Group "Handling"; here the code of .887 denotes the lowest levels of complexity (GED 1 or 2). The dean of students/director of student affairs example was taken from the Worker Trait Group "Administration" (GED 5 or 6; code .118 or .168). Although the latter is not a low level of complexity, a moderate drgree of transferability is possible among some occupations in that group. The labor economist example was from Worker Trait Group "*Scientific Research.*" In the counseling process, the counselor indicates the various types of jobs requiring such research by looking at the detail in that Worker Trait Group (p. 466, *DOT* Volume II). If relevant information is turned up, the counselor describes the different types of *subject matter* and technology involved in the occupations for the client's appraisal and ultimate decision.

The Use of Worker Trait Groups in Manpower Economics

In this presentation, the term "manpower economics" means (*a*) quantitative data on current supply and demand, and (*b*) projections of supply and demand in the near and foreseeable future. As stated previously, manpower statistics can be presented by *DOT* codes as follows:

- first digit (9 categories)
- first two digits (84 divisions)
- first three digits (603 code groups)
- six digits (3,000 six-digit codes)
- six digits and job title (14,000 titles)
- the Worker Trait Groups (114)
- Work Fields (100)
- MPSMS (55 groups; 580 items)

Data can be obtained from information supplied by state employment services. If data is to be obtained from census figures or by special surveys (e.g., by the BLS), conversions will be necessary to the *DOT* system. This step is possible only with substantial technical adjustments; therefore, much of the data would not be convertible readily, if at all, to the last five items just listed.

A more critical issue, however, is the need to obtain statistics reflecting job seekers' needs and preferences. Such data can be obtained only from agencies that interview job seekers diagnostically and record their needs and preferences by the code number. Obviously, the greatest producers of such data are the state employment services. At the six-digit level, need-preference data can be displayed in matrix format as explained in preceding sections: the fourth, fifth, and sixth digit *when reported by Worker Trait Group,* therefore, designate the *kinds* of job seekers; the *first three* digits tell the kinds of activity (industry) in which job seekers want to be hired.

This matrix differs from the BLS matrix in that the BLS reflects supply-demand in terms of *industry requirements,* whereas the *DOT* matrix provides such data in terms of *people requirements.* The implications of this difference are significant for counseling and for manpower planning. For example, when a community loses a large employer, and attempts are made to attract more jobs to the area, would it not be desirable to focus promotional efforts on firms that require the *kinds* of workers already available?

The implications of the matrix for national manpower planning and policy formulation are even more important. Over time, such data would be important in fashioning legislation to meet indicated supply-demand contingencies (as in Sweden), and in another direction, in estimating the future capital-labor mix for certain industries.

CHAPTER SUMMARY

This chapter described the *DOT* and the Job Analysis Formulation on which it rests, discussing the various applications of both instruments in identifying and solving supply-demand imbalances in human resources. These applications included the use of the *DOT* as a diagnostic instrument for obtaining information about job seekers and employer needs and matching them; the use of *DOT* in occupational counseling; and the use of the *DOT* and Job Analysis Formulation in job restructuring, constructing job ladders, and preparing the occupational matrix.

NOTES

1. Among the new methods now in use in larger offices are the job bank, previously mentioned (a computerized listing of all job orders on hand) and computerized manpower matching systems now in experimental use in a dozen states.
2. U.S. Department of Labor, Manpower Administration, *Handbook for Analyzing Jobs* (Washington D.C.: Government Printing Office, 1972).
3. Ibid., p. 166 ff.
4. Ibid., p. 76.
5. Ibid., p. 73 ff.
6. For a complete indication of which parts of the coding were based on Work Fields, MPSMS, Activities, and so on, see *DOT 3,* Vol. I, pp. XVII–XVIII.
7. The Occupational Group Arrangement, p. 33 ff.
8. *Handbook for Analyzing Jobs,* p. 209.
9. *Handbook for Analyzing Jobs,* pp. 210–211. The definitions and detail for GED levels appear in *DOT 3* (Appendix B), in the *Handbook for Analyzing Jobs,* and in a brochure entitled, "Relating GED to Career Planning." The descriptive material in the *Handbook* presents many illustrative examples for each level. The brochure also presents the curricula needed to attain each level. Examples of "principles of rational systems" mentioned under Reasoning Development are bookkeeping, internal combustion engines, electric wiring systems, house building, nursing, farm management, and ship sailing."

10. U.S. Department of Labor, Manpower Administration Contract #373 0708 004 "Estimated Requirements of Occupations: Educational Development, Specific Vocational Preparation, Physical Demands and Working Conditions." Center for Occupational Education, North Carolina State University, Raleigh, January 1974.

11. A new test entitled "Basic Occupational Literacy Test" (BOLT) was issued by the Manpower Administration in 1973. It tests individuals for the first four GED levels for mathematical and language development, among other things.

12. U. S. Department of Labor, *Dictionary of Occupational Titles*, Vol. II, Occupational Classification, 3rd ed., Washington, D.C.: Government Printing Office, 1965, p. 652.

13. *DOT 3*, Vol. II, p. 653.

14. U. S. Department of Labor, *Dictionary of Occupational Titles*, Vol. II, Occupational Classifications, 3rd ed., Washington D.C.: Government Printing Office, 1965, p. 653.

15. An excellent discussion of the differences between GATB and *DOT* aptitude scoring appears in: U.S. Department of Labor, Bureau of Employment Security, *Counselor's Handbook*, (Washington, D.C.: Government Printing Office, 1967). Distribution of this brochure has been suspended until further notice.

16. G. F. Kuder, *Revised Manual for the Kuder Preference Record* (Chicago: Science Research Associates, Inc., August 1960); E. K. Strong, Jr., *Vocational Interests of Men and Women* (Stanford, Calif.: Stanford University Press, 1934).

17. William C. Cottle, "A Factorial Study of the Multiphasic, Strong-Kuder, and Bell Inventories Using a Population of Adult Males," *Psychometrika*, Vol. 15 (March 1950), pp. 25–47.

18. *Handbook for Analyzing Jobs*, p. 317.

19. In page 317, of the *Handbook for Analyzing Jobs*, the Interest Factors are numbered in bipolar sequence (i.e., Interest 1a vs. 1b, rather than 1 vs. 6, as in *DOT 3*).

20. *Handbook for Analyzing Jobs*, p. 305.

21. *Handbook for Analyzing Jobs*, p. 309–310.

22. In *Handbook for Analyzing Jobs*, the codes for temperaments are letters, and temperaments 3 and 6 have been omitted, p. 295.

23. Ibid., pp. 325–330.

24. *Handbook for Analyzing Jobs*, pp. 331–336. Brief definitions appear in Appendix B.

25. Many of the interests and aptitudes relate to the Worker Function components of DATA, PEOPLE, THINGS. The latter represent abilities. Interests represent preferences for these types of activity, not abilities. Aptitudes represent capabilities, which can become abilities after training.

26. The following subdivisions may be most relevant for this job seeker: Budget and Management Analysis; Advertising Management. For all other possibilities, see *DOT*, Volume II, p. 237.

27. See *Handbook for Analyzing Jobs*, p. 87 ff. For a list of MPSMS, see p. 166 ff.

28. Such substitutions are most possible for WTGs of lower levels of complexity. Forty such groups are listed in Appendix G. For the other groups, substantial training might be needed if workers wish to transfer among occupations in the same group.

29. Also listed in *DOT 3*, Vol. II, p. 214.

30. Also listed in *DOT 3*, Vol. II, p. 217 ff.

31. For definitions of Work Fields, see *Handbook for Analyzing Jobs*, pp. 87–148. The numbers in parentheses are working identifiers for sorting use and have no relation to *DOT* codes.

32. For a more complete and detailed discussion of objectives and techniques see U.S. Department of Labor, Manpower Administration *A Handbook for Job Restructuring,* (Washington, D.C.: Government Printing Office, 1970).

33. The Work Field identification for these activities are 231 and 232. See *Handbook for Analyzing Jobs,* pp. 134–135.

34. The first Supplement of the *DOT* indicates the Worker Trait Group for each of the 14,000 defined job titles. See U.S. Department Of Labor, Manpower Administration, *Selected Characteristics of Occupations, a Supplement to the Dictionary of Occupational Titles,* 3rd ed. (Washington, D.C.: Government Printing Office, 1966).

35. See Wassily Leontief, *Input-Output Economics* (New York: Oxford University Press, 1966).

36. Several bills regarding public service employment were before Congress in September 1974. For an interesting summary, see the article by Eileen Shanahan, *The New York Times,* September 29, 1974, Section 4, The Week in Review, p. 3.

37. See U.S. Department of Labor, Bureau of Labor Statistics Bulletin No. 1737 (Government Printing Office, Washington, D.C., 1971), for the methodology, and additional sources used to construct the matrix.

CHAPTER 4

THE WAGNER COLLEGE
AFFIRMATIVE ACTION PLAN

Previous chapters served to sharpen the focus of Affirmative Action by reviewing its chief requirements and implications, citing the relevant manpower literature, and describing the structure and uses of the *DOT*. It has been proposed that the *DOT* and its building blocks can contribute to the fulfillment of the legislative and administrative mandate of Revised Order No. 4 to establish equal employment opportunity through affirmative action. This chapter describes the elements of the Wagner College Plan and the pertinent sections of Revised Order No. 4 that each element implements. Areas in which the Wagner Plan exceeds the requirements are indicated. The discussion of each element includes the implementing and testing methodology.

Wagner College is located in Staten Island, New York, a 30-minute ferryboat ride from downtown New York City. The college has a student enrollment of 3,300, a nonfaculty work force of 148 employed in 116 positions represented by 55 occupations, a permanent faculty of 126, and more than 108 lecturers as needed. The campus is small and closely knit. Many of the employees are local residents who prefer to work at Wagner for lower wages than they could earn in Manhattan (about $1\frac{1}{2}$ hours' travel by bus or train, ferry, and subway), because it is close to home and because employees' children receive tuition-free education. Although many employees have formed close associations in their work group and with others working on campus, some are irritated by their perception that the college administration provides little recognition of their efforts. Others believe there are entirely too few opportunities for promotion. The installation of the Affirmative Action plan and policy was, therefore, a potentially sensitive campus issue.

SCOPE OF REVISED ORDER NO. 4

The chief issue in designing the Wagner Plan was its scope. Was the main thrust of Revised Order No. 4 the increased employment of minority workers and women? Did it apply to all workers, with greatest priority to minorities and women? Or did it intend that equal employment opportunity be extended to all under any conditions, with Affirmative Action to be initiated when preestablished criteria exist? These ambiguities were reduced somewhat by reference to subpart B of Executive Order No. 11246, which implements the Civil Rights Act of 1964:

(1) The contractor will not discriminate against any employee or applicant for employment because of race, color, religion, sex or national origin. The contractor will take *affirmative action* to ensure that applicants are employed and that employees are treated during employment, without regard to their race, color, creed or national origin. . . .[1]

Further information concerning affirmative action appears in Revised Order No. 4 (issued December 4, 1971)[2] pursuant to Sec. 201 of Executive Order 11246 which states:

An Affirmative Action program is a set of specific and result-oriented procedures to which a contractor commits himself to apply every good faith effort. The objective of those procedures plus such efforts is equal employment opportunity . . . an acceptable *affirmative action* program must include an analysis of areas within which the contractor is deficient in the utilization of minority groups and women and further, goals and timetables to which the contractor's good faith efforts must be directed to correct the deficiencies and thus to increase materially the utilization of minorities and women, at all levels in all segments of his work force where deficiencies exist.[3]

This provision seems to require that where deficiencies have been noted, the contractor must increase the utilization of minorities and women on a priority basis. Subsequent provisions, however, seem to deny that "preference" is required and instead affirm that the overriding requirement *is* "equal employment opportunity."

Thus Section 60-2.20,[4] which deals with the "development or reaffirmation of the equal opportunity policy," states:

(*a*) The contractor's policy statement should . . . include but not be limited to (1) recruit, hire, train, and promote persons in all job classifications, without regard to race, color, religion, sex, or national origin, except where sex is a bona fide occupational qualification. (2) Base decisions on employment so as to further the principle of equal employment opportunity by imposing only valid requirements for promotional opportunities . . . (4) Insure that all personnel actions such as compensation, benefits, transfers, lay-off, company sponsored training, education, tuition assistance, social and recreation programs, will be administered without regard to race, color, religion, sex or national origin. . . .

Finally, under "Responsibility for implementation," Section 60-2.20 stipulates

(*b*) Line responsibilities should include, but not be limited to the following. . . . (5) Review of the qualifications of all employees to insure that minorities and women are given full opportunities for transfer and promotion. (6) Career counseling for all employees. . . .

It is difficult to reconcile these seemingly contradictory provisions; apparently it is desired to provide equal opportunity while attempting to increase "the utilization of minorities and women," perhaps to the detriment of the nondisadvantaged, thereby denying "equal employment opportunity" to all.

A basic guideline for the Wagner College Affirmative Action Plan was developed in an attempt to ensure compliance with the ambiguously worded order. Thus the Wagner guideline stipulated that when vacancies occur, each individual in the pool of apparently qualified candidates be interviewed; minorities and women are to be given "greatest consideration" after the qualifications of all candidates have been reviewed. Once the contractor has resolved the initial imbalances, all employees and candidates are to be afforded "equal consideration" in all *subsequent* personnel transactions. The rationale was that unless "preference" is provided initially and until deficiencies have been corrected, minorities and women will not be able to gain the necessary experience and training to make them truly eligible for equal employment opportunities in a given establishment. Thus in the short term minorities and women in a pool of qualified candidates are to be given "greatest consideration"; however, "greater consideration" should not be necessary for such employees where a full objective personnel management system is in effect.

The principle of "greatest consideration" rests on the reality of the hiring process. If an employer interviews five apparently qualified applicants for a single vacancy, his decision may rest on any of a number of possible criteria. He may select the most complacent, the most aggressive, the one who seems to have the same characteristics as a previously successful employee, the one who seems to think and act as the employer does, or the most attractive individual. The Wagner College Plan stipulates that unless other critical factors apply, the person hired will be a member of a minority group or a woman. This is no more discrimination than hiring the most attractive candidate.

The Wagner Affirmative Action Plan was designed within the framework outlined and is in operation. Thus its basic premises were derived from a broad interpretation of the letter and spirit of Revised Order No. 4. It provides that all employees and job seekers are to be given objective consideration in hiring and in promotion. This is to be accomplished by matching the qualifications of each applicant against written, verified job specifications based on observation and interview for all nonfaculty jobs at Wagner and using the methodology of the USES Job Analysis Formulation. Every effort is to be made to increase the employment of minorities and women where people in these categories are underrepresented, consistent with the availability of qualified or *qualifiable* minorities and women. In addition, the Wagner Plan provides that all workers and job seekers be interviewed and counseled, to make them aware of their capacities and potentials for career growth and development at Wagner *or outside it*. All employees are encouraged to "bid" at any time for any job they think they are qualified or qualifiable for. These "bids" are placed in an "Opportunity File" for subsequent consideration when vacancies occur. The proponents of the Wagner Plan contemplated that these methods would put the aims of the legislation into constructive perspective. It was also expected that such a rational approach would reduce the feelings of hostility of nonminorities and males whose opportunities for promotion were "given" to minority candidates or women, who were perceived to be less qualified. Many government employees who have been adversely affected consider that this aspect of equal opportunity has received insufficient attention in the past and tends to weaken the acceptance and implementation of this apparently desirable social goal.

We now turn to a review of the specific requirements of Revised Order No. 4. These may be grouped into two categories: quantitative factors and qualitative factors.

The *quantitative factors* concern (*a*) setting quantitative goals for Affirmative Action, and (*b*) measuring the extent to which the contractor (Wagner) extended good faith efforts to achieve Affirmative Action (i.e., took steps to provide more jobs to minorities and to women, to meet goals).

The *qualitative factors* concern informing employees of the objectives of Affirmative Action and the *methodology* to be used to fulfill the objectives. These are: (*a*)preparing job specifications or position descriptions detailing the tasks to be performed and the skills, knowledge, abilities, and traits required for successful average performance; (*b*) conducting counseling interviews to make employees aware of their occupational abilities, to stimulate them to "bid" for other jobs at Wagner College or to consider more appropriate jobs outside it consistent with their interests, abilities, and aspiration levels; (c) initiating equal employment opportunity actions to fill vacancies through recruitment and promotion.

Chart 1 is a model of objectives cited; it specifies for each qualitative and quantitative factor the sections in Revised Order No. 4 that requires it.

QUANTITATIVE FACTORS

Quantitative data required by Revised Order No. 4 are summarized in Chart 3.

Section 2.11 specifies that "the contractor shall direct special attention in his analysis and goal setting . . . to the following categories of jobs, since these are groups in which experience has been shown that minorities and women . . . are most likely to be underutilized." The contractor is required to conduct the analysis by the categories[5] listed in Chart 2 to ascertain if minorities and women are being underutilized—that is, "having fewer minorities or women in a particular job classification than would be reasonably expected by their availability." Separate data are required for women and minorities with slight, but somewhat significant differences in respect to minorities as compared with women, as shown in Chart 2. The objective is to determine "underutilization" in *any job classification.*[4]

Thus contractors are required to maintain two classes of data: data describing their work force and data concerning the availability of workers in their area (with or without the appropriate skills). Two issues are implicit in these requirements: (a) the depth of the detail needed, and (b) ways and means to obtain such data.

The problem of obtaining the data in the requisite detail is compounded because neither Revised Order No. 4 nor Regulation 14[6] delineates the proper level of classification. The regulation says that the major classifications (official/manager, professional, etc., listed in Chart 2) "would be subdivided into groupings of common job classifications, earnings ranges or common skill groups for each category" (p. 5). Section 2.11 of Revised Order No. 4 defines job classification as "one or a group of jobs having similar content, wage rates, and opportunities." [The same language also appears in Regulation 14 (B), Work Force Analysis. See, however, note 4.]

The problem associated with obtaining the data is recognized in Regulation 14, which states

> . . . to aid in the analysis, much material is available and continuously being developed by the Bureau of the Census, Bureau of Labor Statistics, Bureau of Employment Security, Chamber of Commerce, and many other resources which should be part of a reference library in all contract compliance offices.

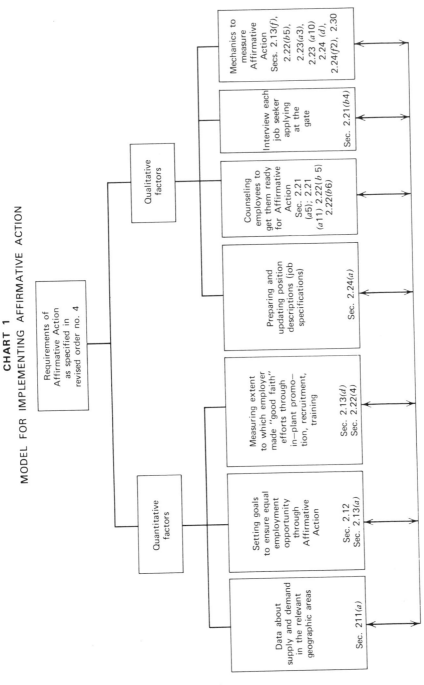

CHART 1

MODEL FOR IMPLEMENTING AFFIRMATIVE ACTION

Requirements of Affirmative Action as specified in revised order no. 4

Quantitative factors

Qualitative factors

Data about supply and demand in the relevant geographic areas

Sec. 211(*a*)

Setting goals to ensure equal employment opportunity through Affirmative Action

Sec. 2.12
Sec. 2.13(*a*)

Measuring extent to which employer made "good faith" efforts through in—plant promotion, recruitment, training

Sec. 2.13(*d*)
Sec. 2.22(4)

Preparing and updating position descriptions (job specifications)

Sec. 2.24(*a*)

Counseling employees to get them ready for Affirmative Action

Sec. 2.21 (*a*5); 2.21 (*a*11) 2.22(*b* 5) 2.22(*b*6)

Interview each job seeker applying at the gate

Sec. 2.21(*b*4)

Mechanics to measure Affirmative Action

Secs. 2.13(*f*), 2.22(*b*5), 2.23(*a*3), 2.23 (*a*10) 2.24 (*d*), 2.24(*f*2), 2.30

CHART 2
CATEGORIES OF JOBS

For Minorities	For Women
Officials and managers	Officials and managers
Professionals	Professionals
Technicians	Technicians
Sales workers	Sales workers (except over-the-counter
Office and clerical	sales in certain retail establishments)
Craftsmen (skilled)	Craftsmen (skilled and semiskilled)

The wording reflects the fact that the U.S. Employment Service (and its affiliated State Employment Services), now in the Manpower Administration, was formerly part of the Bureau of Employment Security. Data are indeed "continuously being developed" in many instances, but as a rule the required detail must be compiled specifically either by or for the contractor. The New York State Department of Labor's Research and Statistics Office rose to this occasion by publishing "Minority Manpower Statistics, with Special Reference to Their Application in Affirmation Action Compliance Programs, July 1971." An updated edition entitled "Labor Force Statistics, Information Useful for Affirmative Action Compliance Programs in New York State," was issued in August 1973. This brochure contains

1. Data for census classifications, since much of it was compiled from the 1970 enumeration.

2. Data from the files of job seekers registered at the State Employment Service—namely, totals by SMSA[7] and county without occupational breakdown.

3. Projected available manpower figures by total and minority groups, by region, SMSA, and county; these are totals only, without occupational breakdown.

4. Minority group "employment as a percent of total employment by occupation for selected industries in standard metropolitan statistical areas of New York State." This is based on a study prepared in 1966.[8] The New York brochure states that the data is limited, although "it includes three-fourths of the workers in manufacturing; more than one-half in mining and finance, insurance and real estate; about one-third in trade and service; and one-sixth in construction." The detail is by eight census categories only.

Perhaps the most critical data element needed is "persons with requisite skills," since this would doubtless be required initially by the compliance officers to establish the employer's good faith efforts in Affirmative Action.

(When vacancies occurred, did he recruit available minorities and women with requisite skills?) The single best and most complete source for such data are the state employment services, whose files are coded to delineate the requisite skills possessed by job seekers for each job classification. All state employment services use the *Dictionary of Occupational Titles*; none uses the census classifications. Although there is a conversion, it is not one-to-one, and to use it requires adjustments beyond the scope of the current program of the state employment service local offices.[9]

For this and other reasons detailed in other sections of this chapter, the *DOT* was used herein as the primary "carrier" of the data needed for Affirmative Action within Wagner; however, the data were related and grouped by the major classifications, in accordance with Revised Order No. 4 and Regulation 14.

CHART 3
FACTORS TO BE ANALYZED

For Minorities	For Women
1. Minority population in *surrounding* labor areas[a]	Not applicable
2. Size of the minority unemployed in *surrounding* labor area	Same for women
3. Percentage of minority work force to total work force in the *immediate* labor area	Not applicable
4. General availability of minorities having requisite skills in *immediate* labor area	Same for women
5. Availability of minorities having requisite skills in an *area* "in which contractor can reasonably recruit"	Availability of women seeking employment in the *labor or recruitment area* of the contractor
6. Availability of promotable and transferable minorities in-house	Same for women
7. Existence of training institutions capable of training persons in the requisite skills	Same for women
8. Extent to which contractor can train to make all jobs available to minorities	Same for women

[a] Because Staten Island, the site of Wagner College, is small and is viewed by many of its residents as a self-contained community, it was considered to comprise the "surrounding," "immediate" area in which the contractor can "reasonably recruit."

Methodology

The following methodology was used to compile data for Staten Island, where Wagner is located.

1. Basic census data were compiled from the New York State brochure ("Labor Force Statistics").

2. The writer and his staff prepared a special matrix representing supply and demand for workers with requisite skills.[10] Demand is represented by job vacancies (orders for workers) on file in New York State Employment Service office in Staten Island. Supply is represented by unemployed job seekers registered in the same office. Supply is subdivided into the following categories: female, negro, Spanish-speaking, and other (including American Indians and orientals; specific data for any group may be omitted if less than 2% of the total). The source of the concept of the matrix is illustrated in Chart 7 of Chapter 3, which has a section explaining the matrix.

3. A list was established of all nonfaculty jobs at Wagner related to the groupings required by Section 2.11 of Revised Order No. 4.

4. All nonfaculty jobs related to the supply-demand matrix were tabulated, indicating the possible availability of persons *with requisite* skills registered in the Staten Island office of the NYSES.

5. A chart of the distribution of Wagner jobs and positions by Worker Trait Groups was made, to be reviewed in conjunction with the matrix.

6. Special forms for projecting vacancies were ready, with an indication of possible availability of persons with requisite skills, or persons who are considered to be trainable. For the latter, a special survey will be required. The completed forms provided all the data needed.

Input for all the items listed, together with an analysis of the facts, costs, and benefits, are presented in the next chapter. The data are used in determining compliance and in establishing goals for the more equitable employment of minorities and women.

QUALITATIVE FACTORS OF REVISED ORDER NO. 4

To implement Revised Order No. 4, it was necessary to prepare position descriptions, conduct counseling interviews, and to fill vacancies through recruitment and promotion. A description of each of these qualitative factors and the methodology employed follows.

Position Descriptions

Section 2.24 of the order requires the contractor to prepare position descriptions[11] based on detailed analysis. In addition, he is to

(*b*) validate worker specifications by division, department location or other organizational unit by job category using job performance criteria. Special attention should be given to academic, experience and skill requirements to ensure that the requirements in themselves do not constitute inadvertent discrimination. Specifications should be consistent for the same job title in all locations and should be free from bias as regards to race, color, religion, sex or national origin except where sex is a bona fide occupational qualification.

We must briefly digress to point out some important differences in terminology. Compare, for example, "job category" as used in the preceding quotation from Revised Order No. 4 with "job classification," defined in note 4, and with "job specification," defined below. Several terms that appear in this chapter do not have standardized definitions, hence have been used interchangeably by some practitioners. The terms are: occupational analysis, job analysis, job specification, position description, qualitative standard, duty statement, and delegation of authority.

Delegation of Authority is a written statement prepared by a supervisor and specifying to a subordinate the duties that employee is to perform, how he is to perform them, and his area of discretion (i.e., the kinds of decisions he may make, or the tasks he may perform without prior approval).

Duty Statement is a written statement of the tasks an employee is required to perform. Ordinarily it neither tells how he is to perform such duties nor delimits the area of discretion.

Position Description is a written description of the tasks a given *individual* is assigned to perform in a given job in a specific establishment, as well as the competencies (skills, knowledges, abilities) needed to perform the tasks. Competencies may be reflected in the tasks or they may be listed separately. The characteristics or traits required of the worker may also be included. A separate position description is prepared when the tasks to be performed differ slightly and different worker traits are required to handle the variations. Additional specific qualifications are included. See also "job analysis."

Job Analysis is a study of a job as performed in a given establishment by all workers who do the same or closely related duties in that establishment, regardless of whether the Worker Traits in some of the positions differ slightly. Thus if eight people perform the same set of tasks, with slight variations requiring different Worker Traits, and five of the eight perform precisely the same tasks requiring the same Worker Traits, four *position descriptions* would be prepared: one for the five workers, and one each for the remaining three workers. However, *one job analysis* would be developed covering the eight positions. The job analysis would describe the core job and all the *variables* that may or may not be assigned from time to time to the individual positions. Job analysis also includes a more detailed description of the tasks, an explanation of the processes, a listing of the machines, tools, equipment, and work aids (with explanations, if necessary), a glossary of terms, and relevant comments. See also "occupational analysis."

Job Specification lists the core tasks to be performed in a given job, and the variables and competencies required. An important feature is the description of the qualifications, which aids in recruitment and selection (hiring).

Occupational Analysis is the study of a job as it typically exists in *many* establishments engaged in activities found in one or more industries. If the study results in a written statement, the detail is derived from many job analyses, each one pertaining to the *same* job (as performed by several incumbents) in *one* establishment. The definition that emerges represents the core job and all the variations found in all the participating establishments. In addition, the written statement may include a description of the processes involved in the performance of the job, the specific machines, tools, equipment, and work aids, a glossary of terms, and any pertinent comments.

Qualitative Standards indicate what constitutes satisfactory performance, generally stressing end products. Usually standards are restricted to a statement of the activities necessary to fulfill an organization's objectives, goals, and mission. Example: the training of subordinates might be a duty, but it is not a standard when performed by a person responsible for operations. Standards for such a person should indicate the qualitative factors relating to the end product or mission that will satisfy the organizational goals.

It was determined that the scope and depth of the position description concept would best implement the requirements of Section 2.24 (a)–(c) of Revised Order No. 4.

A position description, unlike a job specification, describes the tasks to be performed by an *incumbent* in a specific assignment, that is, by the person responsible for the collection of tasks needed to accomplish the same or closely related work in a *given* establishment. An occupation is the duties performed by persons in the same or closely related job in *many* establishments. The position description may be limited to a recital of the tasks performed, or it may indicate the competencies required (skills, knowledges, abilities, responsibilities). Such position descriptions may be prepared either by the incumbent, his supervisor, the staff of the personnel office, or other qualified individuals.

The USES Job Analysis Formulation provides an excellent structured framework for preparing any type of job description, including position and occupational descriptions and specifications. Each job is observed and studied within the context of the elements of the Job Analysis Formulation, using each to the extent it is relevant: Work Fields, MPSMS, Worker Functions, and the constituent Worker Trait factors. This approach assures a degree of objectivity so necessary for equitable personnel management.

In the Wagner College Plan, position descriptions were intended to provide an objective statement of assigned tasks to enable the employer, the incumbent worker, and the job seeker to understand fully, almost visually, the work to be done, how it was to be done, the competencies required, and the Worker Trait requirements and experience and training needed. The objectives were as follows:

1. To establish a basis for objective recruitment and assignment after hire.

2. To provide a basis for the supervisor–employee relationship by specifying the employee's role, mission, and goals, thereby assisting the employee in fulfilling his assignment properly. It establishes quantitative and qualitative standards that can be measured objectively and can provide an objective basis for affirmative remedial actions as necessary by the supervisor.

3. To provide an objective statement of job duties to enable anyone who considers himself qualified to review the details and qualifications before deciding (a) whether to seek a given job, and (b) whether to take the training identified as needed, to improve his chances of getting the job when vacancies become available.

4. To show the relationship of each job to others, thereby indicating possible career ladders and lattices for employees who possess the necessary traits. (Career ladders and lattices can be perceived in occupations, but not all incumbents in a given job in a career ladder have the aspiration, motivation, interests, temperaments, aptitudes, and GED to qualify for the higher level jobs.)

5. To provide an objective basis for job restructuring to resolve recruitment difficulties, to secure job enrichment, or to extend opportunities for employment to inexperienced minorities and women.

Methodology

The need to develop specific position descriptions at Wagner was evident from the outset. To make the best possible hiring decisions, it is critically important to have detailed knowledge about the tasks to be performed and the matching qualifications required. This information is necessary to maintain staff morale, to ensure the fulfillment of employer objectives, and perhaps most important of all, to "select" and to assign members of minority groups to jobs they can be trained to perform successfully. Understandably, some incumbent employees resent being skipped over in promotion or in transfer, and adjustment of newly hired staff whose appointment may be clouded by controversy is ordinarily hastened by solid performance on the job in accordance with accepted expectations of fellow workers and supervisors.

It was determined that Affirmative Action would be best served by preparing a position description for each of 116 nonfaculty positions at Wagner. There were 55 discrete occupations, employing 148 incumbents. How were the position descriptions to be prepared, and by whom? Several alternatives were available:

1. Request the supervisors to develop a position description for each job in their respective rosters.
2. Have the supervisors develop position descriptions based on the *DOT* definitions, or available generalized task inventories.[12]
3. Request each employee to prepare his own job description, subject to the approval of his supervisor.
4. Have the personnel office prepare all the descriptions, using their own criteria.
5. Train the personnel staff in job analysis techniques and have them do the work in accordance with the principles and techniques customary in the observation interview method of job analysis.
6. Have professional occupational analysts (OAs) prepare the descriptions.

Option 6 was chosen because in this prototype study it was necessary to determine the type of detail needed and to develop a suitable format experimentally. It was believed that best job would be done by experienced occupational analysts. The work was assigned to OAs on the staff of the New York State Employment Service, who normally provide technical employer services that assist employers in obtaining workers; they also recommend measures to reduce turnover and absenteeism. The procedure follows:

1. The personnel office provided information about the jobs utilized and quantitative data about the roster. The OAs prepared a staffing schedule listing the Wagner job titles by departments, relating ("converting") each to a *DOT* title and code and specifying totals employed, subdivided by male and female. Sample pages of the staffing schedule appear in Appendix I.
2. Jobs were studied by department. As the first step, the OA met with the department head to explain the objectives and the methods to be used, including reassurance that each draft would be sent to the department head for correction and approval.
3. Wherever possible, the OA spent a half-day (or less) observing the worker; in addition, an interview was conducted to obtain all the details required by the position description form. The OA took notes and discussed doubtful or unclear perceptions of duties with the supervisor.

4. The OA developed a draft from his notes, as well as his estimates of the Worker Function levels and Worker Trait factors.

5. The rough drafts were reviewed, corrected, and edited by the OA's supervisor.

6. The completed drafts were submitted to the personnel office for review and subsequent routing to the appropriate supervisor and department head. (Appendix J gives a sample position description of a Wagner College job.)

7. The personnel office reconciled the comments received, and after discussion with the OA, routed the position description for final typing.

The 116 position descriptions prepared represent 55 occupations. For example, 31 secretaries are employed, and "secretary" is one "job." The core job tasks are the same, but unique tasks associated with some secretarial assignments required different degrees of skills, knowledge, and experience, and different Worker Traits. For example, the secretary to the chairman of the biology department could function adequately with less interest in "business contact with people," ability to "exercise considerable judgment," or capacity to "communicate with people," than the secretary for the athletic department.

In a recent decision, a circuit court held that

> In developing criteria of job performance by which to ascertain the validity of its tests [the employer] . . . failed to engage in any job analysis. Instead, test results were compared with possibly subjective ratings of supervisors who were given a vague standard by which to judge job performance. Some form of job analysis resulting in specific and objective criteria for supervisory ratings is crucial to a proper concurrent validation study. To require less is to leave the job relatedness requirement largely to the good faith of the employer and its supervisors.[13]

By these standards, the Wagner position descriptions achieve a high level of validity and objectivity, because of the successive reviews described and perhaps more important because they were based on the USES job analysis methodology created by the Occupational Analysis Branch of the Department of Labor's Manpower Administration. The methodology is completely described in the *Handbook for Analyzing Jobs,* and in Chapter 3.

Interviewing and Counseling for Affirmative Action

Revised Order No. 4 names two areas that require discussions with employees: (*a*) communicating and explaining the plan to all employees, (*b*) providing counseling or activities related to counseling and placement. The relevant sections of Revised Order No. 4 are quoted below and compared with the steps taken at Wagner to implement each requirement. (See Chart 4)

CHART 4

Relevant Section of Revised Order No. 4	Implementation at Wagner
Section 2.22 (a5) "Discuss the policy thoroughly in both employee and management training programs."	Thorough interview of each nonfaculty employee, including all administrative levels below vice-president.
Section 2.21 (a11) "Communicate to employees the existence of the contractor's affirmative action program and make available such elements of his program as will enable such employees to know and avail themselves of its benefits."	Thorough interview with employees previously identified, with explanation of "bid procedure" and availability of complete position descriptions for review by each employee as wanted.
Section 2.22 (b5) "Review the qualification of all employees to insure that minorities and women are given full opportunities for transfers and promotions." Section 2.22 (b6) "Career counseling for all employees."	Setting up the Wagner "Opportunity File" to accommodate all bids and records of qualifications. Interviewing and counseling each employee and job seeker to help the individual appraise his relationship to his present job, and to discuss what more suitable jobs are available at Wagner or elsewhere.

The basic interview, given to all nonfaculty employees and job seekers, included as much counseling as needed. The employees ranged from key punch operators to the director of the student union, from bookstore manager to residence hall deans, from secretaries to the chief of electronic data processing. In addition, the highest administrative levels (registrar, controller, dean of faculties, and others) were "interviewed" to permit them to understand what their employees were experiencing. All the interviews began with a complete explanation of the Wagner Affirmative Action Plan.

The objectives of the interview were:

1. To explain Affirmative Action in sufficient detail to provide full understanding of the law and its orders and regulations.

2. To ask each employee how suitable he perceived his present assignment to be within his occupation; to identify with him his long-range career goals and to explain the possibilities for their fulfillment at Wagner; to help him to identify his vocational potentials in other occupations, if he appeared to be interested; to point out other possible jobs at Wagner for which he ap-

peared to be qualified or qualifiable, after training specified in the position description, and if so, to assist him in preparing a "bid" form to be placed in the appropriate in-house recruitment source file (the Opportunity File).

3. To prove to the worker that Wagner was interested in having him elect a course of action that could fulfill his aspiration levels and career expectations, consistent with the performance needs and requirements of the college and in conformity with the policy constraints of the Affirmative Action order and policies.

Standards for the Diagnostic Interview

Each employee was interviewed in the Personnel Office during his regular working hours. The elements of the procedure are outlined below.

1. The employee's education and training were elicited and reviewed, to ascertain relevance to the individual's current assignment. When a person's background appeared to be irrelevant, it was necessary to explore the reasons (employee no longer interested; employee liked the work even though his preparation for it was irrelevant; employee preferred another job or assignment that *would* utilize his prior training or education).

2. The employee's work experience for all jobs that were meaningfully related to his career plans was reviewed as a basis for identifying his interests and temperaments, the level of complexity characterizing (*a*) his actual abilities with respect to the Worker Function levels of his present job, and (*b*) his potentials for upward mobility with respect to jobs with higher Worker Function levels; his General Educational Development; and *his own* perceptions of his aptitudinal strengths. His education and training, insofar as these were relevant, were ascertained, and also his leisure time pursuits (if relevant—usually this subject was discussed only with people who had not had enough work experience to know what they wanted to do and how to implement their decisions through career choice and regular employment).

3. Whenever an employee expressed interest in a job other than his own, the interviewer showed him a copy of the position description for that job. This told the employee enough about the duties and requirements to enable him or her to relate current abilities, capacities, and potentials to the job, and perhaps to "bid" for it, as described earlier.

4. The interviewer advised the worker and job seeker as much as he appropriately and realistically could about the possibilities for fulfilling his or her vocational goals at Wagner and about steps that could be taken to improve one's qualifications, now or in the future.

5. The detail recorded on the diagnostic interview form enabled personnel technicians to construct a qualifications profile (see Chapter 3) within the context of the *DOT* Worker Traits system, which indicated the em-

ployee's aptitudes, interests, temperaments, educational attainment, and physical capacities. When no objective criteria were available, the interviewer estimated the extent to which the individual exceeded the qualifications profile levels on the Wagner Profile entered on the position description.[14] Included in this estimate were the statements made on the supervisory review form (described below). A sample of a completed diagnostic interview form appears in Appendix K.

Many versions of diagnostic interview forms had been used experimentally, in local offices of the New York State Employment Service. The present form is one of the standard instruments used to register job seekers, and complete instructions are an official part of the *Operations Manual*.[15] The instructions were made available to the personnel director at Wagner, along with the standards described earlier; thus the form could be used experimentally and changes for the college could be determined after experience had been gained. The modified form appears in Appendix L. The procedure for interviewing incumbents follows.

1. Each department head was requested to send all employees on his roster to the personnel office for a scheduled interview.

2. The interviewer studied each position description prior to the interviews, but the position description was available for reference during the sessions.

3. The interviewer reviewed with the employee the duties of his present job, to elicit (*a*) his attitudes toward each task (likes and dislikes; interests and temperaments); (*b*) his capability with respect to DATA, PEOPLE, THINGS levels, as well as his proficiency (qualitatively and quantitatively).

> (a) The interviewer reviewed the employee's prior jobs, using the same frame of reference, to establish the individual's qualification profile in narrative terms. In other words, the interviewer determined the incumbent's GED level, his interest and temperament preferences, and his physical capacities, by appraising the extent to which these matched the "requirements" of his prior jobs. Was his GED higher than the GED required by the job? Were his preferred interests and temperaments the same as those required by the job? How did they differ? Were the variances significant? When necessary, and for persons without prior work experience, the interviewer based subsequent estimations and documentations of the Worker Trait ratings on "leisure time pursuits."
>
> (b) Insofar as prior education and training appeared to be relevant, these areas were reviewed.
>
> (c) The individual's qualifications profile was estimated as well as possible.

(d)   The actual and *potential* profiles were examined against the same factors on the relevant position description.

(e)   The interviewer asked the individual about his perceptions of his present assignment, his aspirations, and his long-term career goals (where applicable, and if the interviewee was interested).

(f)   Where necessary, feasible, and desirable, the interviewee was told about other jobs at Wagner (and elsewhere) for which he or she might qualify if opportunities became available. Then the Interviewer reviewed relevant Worker Trait Groups to discover other options and to be able to specify the type of additional training considered to be necessary. He next attempted to pinpoint the occupations within the relevant groups that best accommodated the worker's qualifications profile.

(g)   Where indicated, the interviewer showed pertinent descriptions or described thoroughly jobs for which the interviewee appeared to be qualified or qualifiable and for which he expressed interest and aspiration.

(h)   The individual was taught how to prepare "bids" whenever he became interested in a job advertised in a Notification of Job Opening (described below).

(i)   Afterward the interviewer completed all postings, determined the Worker Trait Group page number (in Volume II, *DOT 3*) from the interviewee's *DOT* title and code, and filed it in the appropriate section of the Opportunity File (arranged by WTG page numbers).

(j)   The last step was to ensure that the objective of the interview had been accomplished—namely, that the interviewee had left with a feeling that Wagner was interested in his vocational progress, an awareness of his current career status and his possible opportunities for advancement or transfer, and good advice about the independent steps he should take, consistent with his aspiration levels, to grow and develop vocationally.

An interview conducted in this manner was considered to meet the requirements for counseling as specified in Revised Order No. 4, Section 2.22 (*b*5).

File Arrangement of Diagnostic Forms   During the interview, a diagnostic interview form was prepared for each incumbent and also for serious applicants for work at Wagner. Each person was identified by the appropriate nine-digit *DOT* code number [i.e., the first and second three-digit groups, plus a three-digit suffix code to designate the title) and Worker Trait Group *DOT* page number. Thus worker and job seeker files were arranged by WTGs, further subdivided by nine-digit *DOT* codes arranged serially. The arrangement is desirable because the diagnostic form file is the source of in-house recruitment. A second file, similarly arranged, contained the "bid" forms of all workers and job seekers.

Filing by Worker Trait Groups (WTG)   All the diagnostic and bid forms were filed by Worker Trait Groups, covered in Chapter 3. Recall that the WTG traits are translated into codes expressing levels of complexity at which a worker must perform with reference to DATA, PEOPLE, THINGS. For example, all occupations with the same (or closely related) pattern of Worker Traits related to Investigating, Protecting, and Related Work are assigned to the WTG bearing that title; this information appears on pages 416–417 of *DOT 3,* Volume II; page 416 describes the WTG, telling about all occupations in the group, the "Work Performed," the "Worker Requirements," Clues for Relating Applicants and Requirements," and "Training and Methods of Entry." The qualifications profile, however, designates the Worker Requirements (which were described in narrative terms) by the subcodes that describe the traits (i.e., GED, SVP, aptitudes, interests, and temperaments: see in Appendix B). In addition, each WTG lists the *related* WTGs. On following page(s) can be found all the occupations in the group having the same, or almost the same, traits. Because all do not have precisely the same traits, the first subcode given for a trait indicates that most of the constituent occupations require that trait (e.g., most occupations in that group are GED 5; a smaller number are GED 4). The SVP ranges from 5 to 8 for the constituent occupations. Similar commonalities are present for aptitudes, interests, temperaments, and physical demands. All occupations within the group are rated .168 or .268 for the DATA, PEOPLE, THINGS, levels. The reader may want to study Appendices A and B to fix these scales, levels, and hierarchies in his mind. Several factors are relevant and important.

1.   Each of the 14,000 codes is assigned to one WTG only. Some of the constituent occupations of a six-digit code group are split among two or more WTGs. For example, Water Boy and Child-Care Attendant carry the same six-digit code 359.*878* because both have the same relationship to DATA, PEOPLE, THINGS. However, Water Boy is in the WTG entitled "Miscellaneous Personal Service Work" (Food Serving, Portering, Valeting and Related Activities: *DOT 3,* Volume II, p. 507), whereas Child Care Attendant is in the WTG entitled Child and Adult Care (p. 479). Appendix M gives a sample WTG.

2.   Many of the groups were developed on the assumption that substitutions (e.g., for recruitment to meet shortages) are possible among occupations in the group.[16] Experience has indicated that such transfer may be possible (with or without moderate training) among the 40 WTGs

characterized by low levels of complexity with respect to DATA, PEOPLE, THINGS. Appendix G lists the 40 WTGs of lower complexity. (This research was directed by the writer for other purposes.) For the others with "higher competencies," additional training is sometimes necessary to qualify persons experienced in one occupation of a WTG to perform acceptably in another occupation in the *same* group. Additional comments on these possibilities appear in the final chapter.

Worker Trait Group filing allows intragroup transfers and also makes possible the development of manpower projections by WTGs (page number) subdivided by the first two digits of the *DOT,* code which represent "Work Fields" or materials, products, subject matter, or service (industries) or activities. This approach comprises the matrix described in the preceding chapter. A sample list of Wagner job titles within each Worker Trait Group appears in Appendix N.

The Supervisor's Review Form   To increase the objectivity of the interview, supervisors were asked to evaluate each employee's performance periodically, say, once every 6 months. In addition for a given employee under consideration for a new job vacancy, the supervisor's evaluation might have been solicited by the personnel office. If necessary, the personnel office requested specific comments on certain areas of the employee's work history or characteristics. For sample form see Appendix O.

The evaluation was to indicate only the employee's strengths; no mention was to be made of weakness unless specifically requested by the Personnel Office. The emphasis on the affirmative aspects of performance was intended to minimize nonobjective opinions concerning weakness. It was assumed that the instruction to specify employee strengths would influence the supervisor to be impersonal and not unduly subjective. The diagnostic interview was expected to reveal the tasks the employee liked least, giving the interviewer the opportunity to find out why. The aim was to disclose employee strengths in an affirmative climate, with the interviewer making every effort to reduce subjectivity. It was realistic to expect a high degree of objectivity because the interviewer worked within the guidelines of the *DOT* building blocks.

Because the supervisory review forms were to be used in considering incumbent workers for promotion, they were filed within the respective diagnostic interview forms.

The objective of Affirmative Action is placement, and we now turn to the aspects of the plan that are directly related to new hire and promotion.

Request for Consideration for Possible Job Opening ("Bid" Form)   A

CHART 5

Relevant Section of Revised Order No. 4	Implementation

Section 2.23 (a).
"An in-depth analysis of the following should be made . . . (3) The total selection process including position descriptions, position titles, worker specifications, application forms, interview procedures, test administration, test validity, referral procedures, final selection process and similar factors."

All the elements named were analyzed and are included in the Wagner Plan, excepting tests. The use of tests is not contemplated in any way.

Section 2.22 (b5)
"Review the qualifcations of all employees to ensure that minorities and women are given full opportunities for transfers and promotions."

When vacancies occured, the records of all employees and job seekers were reviewed in the Opportunity Files. This was consistently done.

Section 2.23 (a10)
". . . technical phases of compliance, such as a poster and notification to labor unions, retention of applications, notifications to subcontractors, etc."

All vacancies were posted. The Wagner Plan stimulated bids for any job for which any employee perceived himself to be qualified, regardless of whether vacancies existed.

"bid" form was filled out by any employee under the following circumstances:

1.   When he considered himself qualified for any job that existed at Wagner, regardless of whether there was an actual vacancy.

2.   When he saw on the bulletin board or was invited to file for, an opening advertised on the "Notification of Job Opening" form (described below).

By filing a "bid" form like the sample shown in Appendix P, an employee broadened the base for his upward mobility by declaring his interest in competing for promotion or transfer at any time. The practice also gave the college the opportunity to learn of all possible candidates for promotion and to notify an apparently (potentially) qualified individual of opportunities that had not come to the employee's attention. Similarly, the college could

CHART 5 (Continued)

Relevant Section of Revised Order No. 4	Implementation
Section 2.24 (d) "The contractor should evaluate the total selection process to insure freedom from bias and, thus, aid the attainment of goals and objectives.	The Opportunity File ensured that employees and outside applicants for a given vacancy were considered on the basis of qualifications (actual and potential) recorded on the individual records prepared for each incumbent and serious job seeker.
Section 2.24 (f) (2) "Make an inventory of current minority and female employees to determine academic, skill and experience level of individual employees."	The Opportunity File fully covered these requirements and was designed to ensure equal consideration of all candidates.
Section 2.30 "The purpose of a contractor's establishment and use of goals is to ensure that he meet his affirmative action obligation. It is not intended and should not be used to discriminate against any applicant or employee because of race, color, religion, sex, or national origin."	The Wagner Opportunity File ensured that all candidates were considered according to whether they had the requisite actual or potential skills; selection was to be based on the requirements of this section of the order and the needs for Affirmative Action.

stimulate bids by employees who did not consider themselves qualified, were timid, or did not think it "proper" to solicit consideration of themselves. Finally, this innovation proved to all employees that Affirmative Action is for the benefit of all groups in the community.

Employees interested in competing for a specific job opening could ask at the personnel office to see the appropriate position description.

All bid forms were filed by Worker Trait Group, then by nine-digit *DOT* code number. The bid file thus became a source file for locating candidates with skills, motivations, and aspirations that might qualify them for vacancies as they occurred.

Notification of Job Opening When the personnel office received advance notice of a termination, or a requisition for a new employee, it prepared a Notification of Job Opening, using as much detail from the matching position description as it considered necessary and relevant, and adding wage rates, fringe benefits (if not standard), hours, conditions of work, and so on. The completed notification (see sample, Appendix Q) was routed to all department heads for posting on bulletin boards and circulating to employees.

Where necessary and desirable, copies were sent to individual employees who had not filed "bids" for the job in question but appeared to be qualified. When "bids" were received in response to such an opening, the bid forms were interfiled with those previously received either in response to previous notifications or on the initiative of an individual (employee or job seeker). Whenever an opening occurred, the file was reviewed to determine whether to recruit in-house or outside through accredited agencies including the New York State Employment Service.

The bidding process enabled the personnel office to conduct its fact-finding operations objectively and to decide what recruitment actions were to be taken, consistent with the guidelines and requirements of the Affirmative Action policy.

File Arrangement   The announcements of job openings were filed alphabetically by job title, since the retrieval system was a "history file" to be used to recover the notifications for infrequent reference as needed.

Interview at the Gate   Section 2.21 (*b* 4) of Revised Order No. 4 requires the contractors to "Communicate to prospective employees the existence of the Contractor's Affirmative Action Program and make available such elements of his program as will enable such prospective employees to know of and avail themselves of its benefits."

The Wagner Plan was applicable to all nonfaculty employees and to outside job seekers. Each person applying at the gate was interviewed, using the same techniques and forms as for employees; bids were solicited; position descriptions were made available for review and discussion; and records were placed in the Opportunity File to await job vacancies. When vacancies occurred, all records for all candidates were reviewed, a selection was based on equal employment opportunity, consistent with the Affirmative Action goals and all other pertinent situational and administrative factors.

MECHANICS OF ENSURING AFFIRMATIVE ACTION

Chart 5 pairs the measures used to implement Affirmative Action at Wagner with the relevant Section of Revised Order No. 4. The three main factors were:

1.   Ensuring that all employees were made aware of vacancies and that all relevant tools and techniques were applied in "selection."

2. Establishing a means for considering all persons with requisite skills for vacancies as they arose.

3. Taking action to ensure equal employment opportunity.

SUMMARY

This chapter has presented the requirements of each component of Revised Order No. 4, together with the methodology designed to implement the program at Wagner College. All the components identified as quantitative and qualitative factors in achieving equal employment opportunity reflect the main features of the Wagner College Affirmative Action Plan.

Two observations made in Chapter 1 can now be addressed more precisely. The first is that the requirements of Revised Order No. 4 are meager and not definitive, particularly in the case of the specific qualitative data needed and the character of position descriptions, counseling interviews, and mechanics to be used in filling vacancies. The author's study reveals a need for an approach more innovative and detailed than that indicated by the language of the order. Second, and most important of all, each qualitative factor was applied to *all* employees and job seekers, without reference to race, color, religion, national origin, and sex. By thus making each person aware of his vocational potentials and of the opportunities at Wagner College or outside it, we ensured that the comprehensive needs of the individual were met, rather than the narrower requirements of Revised Order No. 4. In other words, the Wagner College Plan was intended to meet the objectives of Affirmative Action more fully and constructively than was required by Revised Order No. 4.

We now turn to the data collected as a result of using the methodology and perspectives defined, including an analysis of the costs, benefits, and implications of the Wagner Plan.

NOTES

1. Emphasis added.

2. Revised order No. 4 has been amended since the initial preparation of The Wagner Plan. The latest revision as of this writing is July 8, 1974, effective July 12, 1974.

3. *Federal Register,* Vol. 39, No. 135, July 12, 1974, states that "the term 'bona fide' occupational qualification" has been construed very narrowly under the Civil Rights Act of 1964. Under Executive Order 11246 as amended and this part, this term is to be construed in the same manner."

4. "Job classification," according to Revised Order No. 4, means "one or a group of jobs having similar content, wage rates, and opportunities" (Section 2.11). *Federal Register,* Vol. 39, No. 135 (July 12, 1974) states: "The phrase "job classification" was used in both sections [60-2.11(a) and (b)] but had different meanings in each. Additionally, the amend-

ment's purpose is to conform similar language in subsequent sections of Revised Order No. 4 (41 CFR 60-2), specifically 60-2.13(*d*) 60-2.23, 60-2.23(*b*) (1), 60-2.20(*a*) (1), and 60-2.24(*b*). The term "job title" will be substituted for the term "job classification" in 60-2.11(*a*). Job title means a particular, narrowly defined position in the traditional sense of the meaning of the word job . . . the term "job group" will be substituted for the term "job classification" in 60-2.11(*b*). Job group means one or a group of jobs having similar content, wage rates, and opportunities."

5. These are slight modifications of census categories. For definitions, see Standard Form 100, Joint Reporting Committee, 1800 G St. N.W., Washington, D.C., 20506.

6. Office of the Secretary, U.S. Department of Labor, issued January 23, 1973. This regulation sets forth guidelines for compliance officers.

7. The BLS and other governmental units apply the term Standard Metropolitan Statistical Areas (SMSA) to an area with social-economic ties to a city of at least 50,000 inhabitants. Additional criteria are used for special cases.

8. Cited as U.S. Equal Employment Opportunity Commission, Equal Employment Opportunity Report No. 1, Part 1, 1966, Volumes 1 and 2, 1967.

9. The conversion was not issued to local offices because they had no use for it. A conversion indicates for each code in one classification, the equivalent code in another classification.

10. Adapted from the basic matrix described in page 95 ff, representing supply-demand data obtained from the files of registered job seekers at the Staten Island office of the New York State Employment Service.

11. The term "position description" has a specialized meaning here. "Job descriptions" relate to basic jobs; "positions" in a job relate to specific job assignments. At Wagner College, position descriptions were prepared for each of some 30 secretaries. It is possible to characterize all such assignments in one establishment in one *job* description.

12. A set of inventories was developed by the California Occupational Analysis Field Center, one of 10 funded by the federal Manpower Administration. The inventories have been published as U.S. Department of Labor, Manpower Administration, "Task Analysis Inventories" (Washington, D.C.: Government Printing Office, 1973).

13. *Moody* vs. *Albemarle Paper Co.,* 41 U.S. Law Week 2474; CA 4, February 20, 1973.

14. The position description indicates the qualification profile for the job as it exists generally. The entry of the Wagner profile below it on the position description form indicates variances. See Chapter 5 for description of this area and its interpretation.

15. New York State Department of Labor, Manpower Services Division, *Procedures Manual,* II, *Forms* (ES66). These forms and the instructions had been developed by the writer several years earlier.

16. In forming other groups, the same kind of activity (Work Field) was the dominant criterion (see, e.g., Industrial Training, *DOT,* Volume II, p. 335).

17. Section 2.24 (*c* 1) of Revised Order No. 4 lists many agencies that are appropriate recruitment sources for minorities and women.

CHAPTER 5

FINDINGS

This chapter presents the findings of the operations of the Wagner College Affirmative Action Plan, to determine (1) whether the plan met the requirements of Revised Order No. 4, and (2) how much the USES Job Analysis Formulation and the *DOT* contributed to the effectiveness of the plan. The chapter is based largely on the analytical framework presented in Chart 1 of Chapter 4, and findings for each factor are presented in the following sequence:

Quantitative Factors
1.   Data relating to supply and demand requirements in the area surrounding the contractor's establishment.
2.   Goal setting by the contractor to correct identified deficiencies.
3.   Measurement of the extent to which the contractor demonstrated good faith in correcting deficiencies.
Qualitative Factors
1.   Preparing and updating position descriptions.
2.   Interviewing employees and job seekers and counseling them when needed.
3.   Expediting Affirmative Action processes by specific mechanics.

In each case, comments on costs, benefits, and implications for public policy are accompanied by an appraisal of the Plan's success in meeting the provisions of Revised Order No. 4.

QUANTITATIVE DATA

As explained in the previous chapter, several types of data are needed: (*a*) basic data on population and the work force, both employed and unemployed (see Chart 1), (*b*) data about persons with the requisite skills needed to meet employer needs (see Chart 2), (*c*) data for planning the contractor's expansion and replacement needs (retirements, resignations, deaths), including the determination of recruitment sources (see Charts 4 to 6). The sections that follow present the data collected for these purposes.

Basic Data on Population and Workforce

Revised Order No. 4 and Regulation 14, which sets forth guidelines for compliance officers, do not tell how data such as the compilation of Chart 1 are to be used. However, they might be used to establish participation rates in the labor force for minorities and women. The data should also make it possible to determine whether occupational training should be considered by the contractor when persons with the requisite skills are not available. For example, the federal compliance officer might determine whether a contractor who failed to hire minorities and women should have initiated training in his own facility or should have requested appropriate community officials (e.g. local occupational education and state employment service personnel) to do so.

Costs   No costs were incurred because government agencies and the New York State Department of Labor publish the data needed by the interested community. Contractors in states less advanced than New York would be obliged to prepare such data, and much of the material would have to be based on special tabulations obtained from the Census Bureau, usually for a charge. In large cities each contractor would be required to compile the same data unless all pooled their resources.

Benefits   Data on population and workforce are basic in planning manpower programs by government, and it is doubtful whether the costs could reasonably be borne by individual employers if each had to compile the same data. This points to a need for a standardized compilation by or under the auspices of the Equal Employment Opportunity Commission or the U.S. Department of Labor (which could ask all state Employment Security Agencies to comply).[1]

Supply-Demand Matrix

Chart 2 presents data for persons with *requisite skills* for those of the 114 Worker Trait Groups which accommodate all Wagner jobs; the detail compares demand (job openings) with supply (job seekers) as shown by an

CHART 1

POPULATION AND WORK FORCE: EMPLOYED AND UNEMPLOYED. STATEN ISLAND. 1970

Item	Total	Female	Male Minorities			Female Minorities		
			Negro	Spanish Speaking	Other	Negro	Spanish Speaking	Other
Population	295,400	151,100	7,800	2,400	1,000	8,000	2,500	1,000
Workforce	115,276	41,415	2,884	748	478	2,355	545	302
Percentage of workforce	100%	36.0%	2.5%	0.6%	0.4%	2.0%	0.5%	0.3%
Employed	112,075	40,090	2,718	741	473	2,327	525	286
Unemployed	3,201	1,325	166	7	5	28	20	16
Percentage Unemployed	2.8%	3.2%	5.8%	0.9%	1.0%	1.2%	3.7%	5.3%

Source: Bureau of the Census, "General Social and Economic Characteristics," 1970 census. Compiled from "Minority Manpower Statistics, with Special Reference to Their Application in Affirmative Action Compliance Programs," New York State Department of Labor, July 1971.

CHART 2
SUPPLY-DEMAND CHART

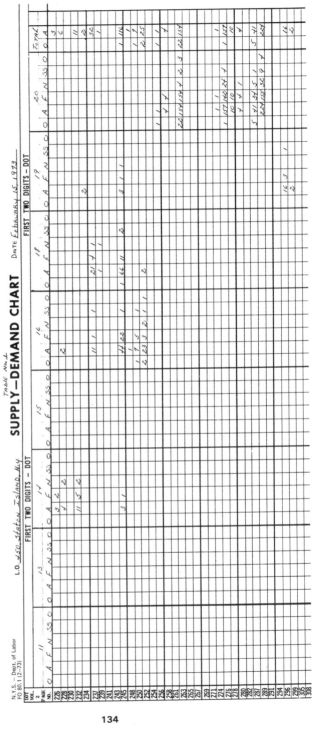

CHART 2 (Continued)

Table No. 1

SUPPLY—DEMAND CHART

N.Y.S. — Dept. of Labor
FO 80.1 (2-73)

L.O. _450 Staten Island N.y._   DATE _February 15, 1973_

FIRST TWO DIGITS – DOT

LEGEND
1st "O"=Openings
"A"=Applicants
"F"=Female
"NW"=Non-White
"SS"=Spanish Speak.
2nd "O"=Other

136

CHART 2 (Continued)

N.Y.S. — Dept. of Labor
FO 80.1 (2-73)

SUPPLY—DEMAND CHART

Table No. 1

L.O. _____ Staten Island N.Y.   Date February 15, 1973

FIRST TWO DIGITS – DOT

Column headers: 21, 22, 23, 24, 25, 26, 27, 28 (each with sub-columns O A F N 55)

Row numbers (DOT Vol. 2 Page No.): 225, 228, 230, 232, 234, 237, 239, 241, 243, 245, 248, 250, 252, 254, 256, 258, 261, 263, 265, 267, 269, 271, 274, 276, 278, 280, 282, 287, 289, 291, 294, 296, 299, 305, 308

CHART 2 (Continued)

Table No. 1

SUPPLY—DEMAND CHART Date February 15, 1973

L.O. 450 Staten Island, N.Y.

N.Y.S. — Dept. of Labor
FO 80.1 (2-73)

FIRST TWO DIGITS – DOT

FIRST TWO DIGITS – DOT

DOT VOL. 2 P AGE NO.	21				22				23				24				25				26				27				28				Total	
	O	A	F	N	SS	O	A	F	N	SS	O	A	F	N	SS	O	A	F	N	SS	O	A	F	N	SS	O	A	F	N	SS	O	A	F	N	SS	O	A
310																																
312																																
319																																
322																																
333																																
335																																
337																																
339																																
341																																
343																																
345																																
347																																
349																																
351																																
354																																
356																																
360																																
371																																
373																																
375																																
377																																
379																																
381																																
383																																
385																																
387																																
390																																
392																																
394																																
396																																
398																																
400																																
402																																
404																																
405																																
408																																
411																																
413																																
415																																
418																																

LEGEND
1st"O"=Openings
"A"=Applicants
"F"=Female
"N"=Non-White
"SS"=Spanish Speak.
2nd"O"=Other

422
425
427
330
433
435
444
447
461
464
466
468
471
473
475
477
479
482
484
486
488
491
493
496
499
501
503
505
507
509
511
514
516
519
522
524
525
528
TOT

CHART 2 (Continued)

Table No-1

SUPPLY–DEMAND CHART Date February 15, 1913

N.Y.S. – Dept. of Labor
FO 80.1 (2–73)

DOT Vol. 2

L.O. 440 Staten Island N.Y.

FIRST TWO DIGITS – DOT

FIRST TWO DIGITS – DOT

140

CHART 2 (Continued)

Table No. 1

SUPPLY–DEMAND CHART

N.Y.S. — Dept. of Labor
FO 80.1 (2-73)

L.O. 150 Staten Island N.Y. Date February 15, 1983

DOT VOL. 2 PAGE NO.	29 O	A	F	N	SS	O	30 O	A	F	N	SS	O	31 O	A	F	N	SS	O	32 O	A	F	N	SS	O	33 O	A	F	N	SS	O	34 O	A	F	N	SS	O	35 O	A	F	N	SS	O	36 O	A	F	N	SS	O	Total O	A
420																																																	
422																																																
425																																																
427																																																
430																																																
433																																							2	10	6	1	1		2	10
435																																																
444																																							1	2	2	1			1	2
447																			1																					2	1				4	
461														1																																	
464																																																
465																																																
468																																																
471																																																
473																																																
475																																																
477																																																
479		2	2					2	2																												2	84	67	43	2								2	88
482																																																
484																																																
486		9	2	1																																			9						9	
488																																																
491																																1																
493																																	1						1						1	
496																																																
499																									1	1	3												1								
501	1	76	33	2	1																																		1	7	8				1	7
503		6	3	1	1																									1							6	3							8	
505																																																
507								5						2	57	38	2	1												1									6					2	61
509																																																
511																																																
514																																																
516																																																
519																																																
522																																																
525																																																
528																																																
TDT	2	88	38	5	2	1		8	2	5			4	127	41	24	4		5	3	1				1	9	5				3	1	1				2	84	67	43	2		3	13	31	5	1	12	377

LEGEND
1st "O"=Openings
"A"=Applicants
"F"=Female
"NW"=Non-White
"SS"=Spanish Speak.
2nd "O"=Other

analysis of the files of the New York State Employment Service's local office in Staten Island, N.Y.

Part of the matrix is shown on pages 134–139. The entire matrix is 10 pages long. The rationale for the matrix is explained in Chapter 3, pp. 95–99 and is illustrated in Chart 9, Chapter 3. Column 1 of the matrix represents the 114 Worker Trait Groups comprising the *DOT*.[2] The column headings at the top of the form designate industries and activities (e.g., clerical). They comprise the first two digits of the first three *DOT* digits; the first two were used instead of the first three for ease of presentation and interpretation, since there are 84 *two*-digit groupings, which subdivide into 603 *three*-digit groupings.[3] For each two-digit grouping, the first column ("0") represents job openings on hand when the inventory was prepared in the state employment office on Staten Island; the remaining columns for each two-digit grouping are for registered job seekers: the columns are respectively for (A) Total Applicants (Job Seekers), (F) Females, (N) Negro, (SS) Spanish speaking, and other (Orientals and American Indians). Totals for openings and job seekers with requisite skills are supplied for each row and each column. In the *DOT* classification structure, each WTG falls into *specified* two-digit groupings only, and each WTG contains occupations having the same or almost the same trait configurations. Since only some occupations in the *first-two-digit code groups* meet this criterion, segments of first-two-digit *code groups* fall into specified *Worker Trait Groups*. Only a limited number of segments of first-two-digit code groups "fall" within any one WTG. Not all two-digit groups that comprise a WTG are indicated in Chart 2. Instead, data are shown for each two-digit division that contains occupations for which job seekers are actually registered in the state employment office on Staten Island.

In this matrix "substitutions" of job candidates for a given job vacancy ordinarily can be made horizontally among persons coded in the two-digit divisions that comprise that Worker Trait Group, with little or minimal additional training. For the 40 WTGs of lower levels of complexity, listed in Appendix G, such substitutions should be readily possible (see, e.g., *DOT 3*, Volume II, p. 360). A complete list of jobs that fit into this group appears on pages 361 through 369 of *DOT 3*, Volume II. For the remaining 74 groups, additional training will ordinarilly be essential to qualify persons skilled on one job in a (first) two-digit division for a job in another two-digit division within the *same* WTG. For example, a floor waxer should have no difficulty in qualifying to be a material handler, since both jobs are in the Material Handler WTG, which has a low level of complexity. The problem differs for a higher level group. Thus if a city manager is needed and none is available, the following types of persons within the same (higher level) WTG might well be considered: manpower research and planning director, export manager, budget officer, director of community organization. Such persons would require less training than persons whose traits "fit" into another WTG.

To fully understand the data, it must be realized that the detail on *supply* represents job seekers who requested placement service from the Staten Island NYSES office, including persons filing for unemployment insurance benefits. Since all unemployed persons seeking such benefits must register for employment at a state office, and since all employers of one or more except religious, charitable, and nonprofit agencies are covered by the New York State unemployment insurance law, most of the unemployed are included. However, the data do not account for the hard-core unemployed or others who do not look for work through the state agency. Similarly, *demand* represents only job vacancies placed by employers with this state Employment Service Office. Since estimates of job vacancies are not made routinely (by government agencies), no estimates are available for the entire job vacancy universe. For many years students of manpower have tried to estimate Employment Service placement *penetration rates* (i.e., the percentage of all hiring transactions made by the Employment Service). Such estimations range up to 25% of new hires made in the community. Since the employment offices fill about 65% of all job openings they receive, it is obvious that the number of job vacancies available to the Employment Service for referral of job seekers is below the total available in the geographic area served.[4]

Nevertheless, the employment service is surely the largest employment agency in the community that definitely has the greatest and most authentic data on people and their skills. This is not surprising because trained interviewers interview all job seekers, obtain their work history, and assign, with the concurrence of the job seeker, the job code and title representing his job preferences. Unemployment insurance claimants are additionally classified according to their best "work test" occupation, in accordance with the law, which requires each to accept a job for which he is "reasonably fitted by training and experience."

Costs   The matrix was generated manually by trained New York State Employment Service occupational analysts in 24 man-days. Such matrices are occasionally prepared by the state for upstate New York communities, but the time required for more frequent preparation exceeds present staff capacity. However, this limitation should not be permanent since preparation by computer is projected, perhaps in 1975. The data will be taken from regular reporting schedules, which means that the only additional costs will be for programming and computer operating time. It is possible, therefore, that publication of such data by the New York State Department of Labor is in sight. Preparation by computer is desirable for another reason. Since the data are located in the files of the local NYSES office, no contractors, even those with trained staff, have access to the source documents; thus contractors would not be able to prepare the matrix themselves. In the author's opinion, having such data available would assist the state in meeting its own planning needs and the needs of the employing community.

Benefits The benefits to be derived from the matrix are substantial for several reasons:

1. The matrix portrays in meaningful groupings, which are much more definitive than the major census categories, the supply and demand for persons with requisite skills in a given community. This knowledge would be useful to contractors in many aspects of manpower planning, in addition to planning for Affirmative Action. Chart 3 represents the Wagner matrix, which should be related to Chart 2 when planning recruitment. Contractors are required to present data by stated categories to determine underutilization[5] in any job classification (i.e., "one or a group of jobs having similar, content, wage rates, and opportunities," Section 2.11).[6] Reference to Appendix R indicates that as many as 65 Wagner job titles comprise one census category ("Office and Clerical.") It would be difficult to calculate the degree of underutilization for any one of the 65 titles. The benefit of using the Worker Trait Groups as the classification base is apparent from Chart 3, which reveals that Wagner job titles are accommodated by 25 WTGs. Only two (shown in the Position Description Column) have more than 10 job titles; one WTG has 10 titles, another has 9 titles, two have 6, two have 5, and the remaining 17 have 3 or fewer Wagner job titles.

2. The matrix might be used by compliance officers to determine whether contractors have recruited persons with requisite skills who might be available in local employment office files on job seekers.

3. The matrix provides local employment offices a basis for developing their annual plan of service, which includes a statement of their projected work programs for the next budget period, the positions needed, and the organizational and procedural changes required to fulfill the plans. The matrix indicates supply-demand imbalances, which *represent manpower problems* for which the Employment Service must provide such remedial services as developing suitable job openings for groups of job seekers and initiating vocational training courses where demand exceeds supply. Large establishments might find the matrix useful in their manpower planning.

4. As noted elsewhere, the New York State Department of Labor has begun to make manpower projections experimentally using the format outlined for the WTGs of lower levels of complexity[7] (entry and next higher levels). These projections (if continued) should also be valuable in manpower planning, including aspects of Affirmative Action planning, by the concerned community groups and employers.

First Two Digits, *DOT*

DOT Volume II page number	02 J	02 P	04 J	04 P	09 J	09 P	10 J	10 P	16 J	16 P	18 J	18 P	20 J	20 P	21 J	21 P	22 J	22 P	23 J	23 P	24 J	24 P	37 J	37 P	38 J	38 P	96 J	96 P	Number of Pos. Desc.	Total J	Total W
237					2	14	1	1	2	1	2	3																	19	7	19
239									1	2																			2	1	2
243													1	2	1	1	1	1	2	2									6	5	6
245					1	1	1	2	1	5	2	3																	9	5	11
250									2	8																			3	2	8
252									1	1																			1	1	1
258													1	2			1	2			1	11							5	3	15
261																											1	1	1	1	1
263													1	36															31	1	36
265																	1	1											1	1	1
267															1	2													1	1	2
269															1	1													1	1	1

271																	1	1											1	1	1
274															2	2				1	1								3	3	3
276							1	1					2	4															5	3	5
280															6	14													10	6	14
289													1	1						1	2								2	2	3
291																				1	1								1	1	1
296			1	9	1	1																							6	2	10
360																									1	1			1	1	1
416																							1	1					1	1	1
435													2	2															2	2	2
468	1	1																											1	1	1
482									2	2																			2	2	2
484									1	1																			1	1	1
Total	1	1	1	9	4	16	3	4	10	20	4	6	8	47	11	20	4	5	5	6	1	11	1	1	1	1	1	1	116	55	148

[a] Data as of February 15, 1973.

[b] J = jobs; P = Positions (perform same duties).
W = Workers.

5. The matrix is useful in counseling because an individual can be assisted to see himself in relation to the world of work when the counselor identifies relevant Worker Trait Groups. When projections based on the matrix are available, the information can be passed on to the counselee, who is then able to make a more informed career determination than might otherwise have been possible.

6. If further research indicates that the occupational matrix can be related to the input–output matrix (developed nationally), national manpower planning could be advanced significantly.

Wagner Job Titles

The supply-demand matrix should be used with Charts 3 and 4. Examination of Chart 4 confirms that Equal Employment Opportunity Commission (EEO) groups are closely related to major census groups. Sample pages of the complete tabulation of these data appears in Appendix R. Chart 4, however, gives an idea of the scope of the presentation: it lists the specific positions and the number of incumbents at Wagner classified by *DOT* and EEO (census) categories, and (2) shows the number of job seekers registered in Staten Island in matching job titles as of February 15, 1973.

The data of Chart 4 thus provide a basis for deciding about recruiting minority workers and women when deficiencies have been identified: reference to this tabulation indicates the possible availability of persons with requisite skills registered in the NYSES office on Staten Island. Note that the number of job seekers in Chart 4 is for the Worker Trait Groups as a whole rather than for the individual Wagner and *DOT* job titles. For example, the first three titles are in *group 237*; the total of 33 is available for *all* occupations in *that* group.

Again, the detail by Wagner job titles (column 5) converted to *DOT* job titles and codes (columns 2 and 3) grouped by census category (column 1) indicates the limitations of using census categories only. The Wagner College Plan, however, assumes that Charts 2 and 4 fully implement the requirements of Section 2.11 concerning the identification of *persons with requisite skills.* More specific determination will be possible by placing a job order for a vacancy in the Staten Island office of the NYSES; state personnel would review the files to determine whether any qualified person is available in the *precise* job title and code, and failing that, whether any individuals in related titles and codes within the *same* or related WTGs are available.

Costs   Since Chart 4 is a derivative of the matrix (Chart 2), about 2 hours were required to prepare it. There is one additional cost—namely, to relate Wagner titles to *DOT* codes, then to census groupings. Trained occupa-

CHART 4

WAGNER JOB TITLES CLASSIFIED BY *DOT* TITLES AND EEO MAJOR GROUPINGS

Census Category	*DOT* Title	*DOT* Code	WTG page	Wagner Title	Number of Positions	Job Seekers[a] Registered at NYSES Staten Island Office			
						Total	F	N	SS
Officials and managers	Academic Dean	090.118	237	Asst. Dean, Acad. Affairs	1	33	6	1	1
	"	090.118	237	Dean, Academic Affairs	1	33	6	1	1
	"	090.118	237	Dean of Faculty	1	33	6	1	1
	Administrative Assistant	169.168	245	Asst. to Dir. Grad. Studies	1	117	35	1	3
	"	169.168	245	Assistant to President	1	117	35	1	3
	"	169.168	245	Secretary II, Library	1	117	35	1	3
	Alumni Secretary	090.118	237	Dir. of Alumni Affairs	1	33	6	1	1
	Association Executive	189.118	237	Asst. Dir. Develop. Office	1	33	6	1	1
	"	189.118	237	Dir. of Development	1	33	6	1	1
	Dean of Students	090.118	237	Dean	2	33	6	1	1
	"	090.118	237	Dean of Students	1	33	6	1	1
	Department Head, College	090.168	245	Dir. of Graduate Studies	1	117	35	1	3
	Director of Admissions I	090.168	237	Assoc. Dir. of Admissions	1	33	6	1	1
		090.168	237	Dir. of Admissions	1	33	6	1	1
	No *DOT* coverage	T165.118	239	Dir. of Church Relations	1	1	0	1	0
	No *DOT* coverage	T165.118	239	Dir. of Foundation	1	1	0	1	0

CHART 4 (Continued)

Census Category	DOT Title	DOT Code	WTG page	Wagner Title	Number of Positions	Job Seekers[a] Registered at NYSES Staten Island Office			
						Total	F	N	SS
Director of Guidance		045.108	296	Asst. to Dir., Special Progs.	1	25	6	3	1
	" "	045.108	296	Dir. Special Programs	1	25	6	3	1
Dir. of Student Affairs		090.168	237	Dir., Wagner Union	1	33	6	1	1
Financial-Aids Officer		090.118	237	Asst. Dir., Financial Aid	1	33	6	1	1
	"	090.118	237	Dir. Financial Aid	1	33	6	1	1

[a] F = female; N = negro; SS = Spanish speaking.

150

tional analysts performed this task in 7 hours. Trained Wagner staff should be able to update such data in the future at slight cost. The chief task, locating the *DOT* title and code representing the Wagner title, should take but a few minutes for each identification, particularly since complete descriptions have already been prepared for each position. The *DOT* code identification has other uses, explained in subsequent sections of this chapter; thus this cost is minimal.

Benefits Many of the benefits of Chart 2 are applicable to Chart 4: the data presented are necessary and useful in pinpointing underutilization of minorities and women by WTG code. Since the data of Chart 4 allow one to do this more definitively than data presented only by census categories, Chart 4 seems to exceed the requirements of Revised Order No. 4. Moreover, this table should make it easier to plan recruitment and occupational training strategies, where the total number of job seekers with requisite skills registered at the Staten Island NYSES office is less than the projected Wagner need. Charts 5 and 6 were developed to meet such planning needs.

Personnel Status and Planning Sheet

Chart 5, a partial tabulation, expands Charts 2 and 4; it relates each Wagner job to its WTG and indicates from the matrix surpluses or shortages of persons registered in the local state employment office whose job titles are in the same and "related" groups as the Wagner title. Thus when a vacancy becomes available at Wagner, this table will tell whether the local state employment office has a possible shortage or surplus of job seekers with requisite skills. A phone call will establish whether persons with the necessary skills or potential skills are available. In cases of surplus recruitment through the local office may permit Wagner to fill the vacancies.

Chart 5 also expedites the type of "goal setting" for minorities and women required by Revised Order No. 4. Projected vacancies at Wagner can be entered in columns. The next-to-last column is for data concerning availability of trainees, to be obtained by special survey; also indicated is the standard Specific Vocational Preparation time needed to qualify inexperienced workers to perform acceptably. (The SVP time levels are explained in Appendix B.) Thus Chart 5 shows (*a*) vacancies projected, (*b*) possible availability of persons with requisite skills in the same or related WTGs, (*c*) whether trainable persons are available in the community, and (*d*) the training time period needed for the occupation in question.

Costs Since Chart 5 is a derivative table (from Charts 2 and 4) the additional time cost for preparing it is minimal, once projected vacancies have

CHART 5
PERSONNEL STATUS AND PLANNING SHEET

Wagner Job Title[a]	DOT Title	DOT Code
Academic Supervisor Spec. Progs.	Academic Dean	090.118.010
Accountant Business Office	Bookkeeper I	210.388.022
Administrative Asst. Alumni	Secretary	201.368.018
Affirmative Action Asst. Pers.	Employment Interviewer II	166.268.018
Alumni Records Clerk	File Clerk II	206.388.022
Assistant Cataloguer Library	Cataloguer	100.388.010
Assistant Dean of Acad. Affairs	Academic Dean	090.118.010
Assistant Dir. Financial Aid	Financial-Aids Officer	090.118.026
Assistant Director Admissions	Personnel Recruiter	166.268.030
Assistant Director Development	Association Executive	189.118.010
Assistant Director Wagner Union	Manager, Front Office	187.168.094
Assistant Supervisor Letter Shop	Chief Clerk, Print Shop	207.138.010
Assistant Supervisor Postal Cntr.	(Mailing Supervisor)	231.138.010
	(Mail Clerk)	231.588.014
Assistant to Dir. Special Progs.	Director of Guidance	045.108.018
Assistant to Dir. Graduate Studs.	Administrative Assistant	169.168.014
Assistant to President	Administrative Assistant	169.168.014
Assistant Treasurer Bus. Office	Treasurer	161.118.010
Faculty Secretary II	Secretary	201.368.018
Faculty Secretary II Education	Secretary	201.368.018
File Clerk Letter Shop	Clerk, General	209.588.018
General Services Manager Chem.	Receiving Clerk	222.387.018
General Services Sup. Purchasing	{ Receiving-and-Shipping Foreman	223.138.022
	{ Property Man	964.168.014
Graphotype Operator Letter Shop	{ Addressing-Machine Operator	234.582.010
	{ Embossing-Machine Operator II	208.782.014
Head Accountant Business	Accountant	160.188.010
Head Librarian Library	Library Director	100.118.010
HEOP Counselor Special Programs	Counselor II	045.108.010
Key Punch Operator Computer Cen.	Key-Punch Operator	213.582.010
Library Assistant, Catalog Dept.	File Clerk II	206.388.022
Library Assistant, Ordering	Expediter I	222.368.014
Library Assistant	Library Assistant	249.368.050
Mail CLERK Postal Center	Mail Clerk	231.588.014
Offset Printer Letter Shop	Offset Duplicating Machine Operator	207.782.026
Operator Switchboard	Telephone Operator	235.862.026
Payroll Clerk Business Office	Pay-Roll Clerk	215.488.010
Placement Officer Placement Off.	Placement Officer	166.268.034

[a] As indicated in job specs.
[b] These figures are not additive

been established. A special survey will be needed, however, to determine whether persons who can be trained to acquire skills are available. This can be partially determined by ascertaining the number available in related Worker Trait Groups.

WTG page	Number of Positions	Vacancies Expected	Job Seekers Registered at NYSES Staten Island Office: Data as of February 15, 1973								SVP	Trainable Job Seeker Available	
			Same WTG				Related WTGs						
			0	Shortage	5–9	10+	0	Shortage	5–9	10+		Yes	No
						Surplus				Surplus			
237	1					x				x	9		
280	1					x				x	7		
263	1					x				x	6		
250	2				x					x	5		
276	1					x				x	5		
276	2					x				x	7		
237	1					x				x	9		
237	1					x				x	7		
250	4				x			x			5		
237	1					x				x	8		
245	3					x			x		5		
243 }	1					x				x	6		
289 }						x				x	3		
296	1					x				x	2		
245	1					x				x	8		
245	1					x				x	8		
237	1					x				x	8		
263	1					x				x	6		
263	1					x				x	6		
289	1					x				x	2		
271	1					x				x	5		
243 }	1			x		x				x	6		
261 }										x	3		
274 }	1					x				x	3		
435 }						x				x	3		
252						x				x	8		
237	1					x				x	7		
296	1					x				x	7		
274	1					x				x	4		
276	1					x				x	5		
265	1					x				x	5		
258	1					x				x	4		
289	11					x				x	2		
435	1					x				x	3		
291	1					x				x	3		
280	2					x				x	7		
250	2					x				x	7		
	1												

Wagner Staffing Planning Sheet

Chart 6 is an occupational planning sheet for analysis of the composition of the current roster at Wagner. A separate sheet is used for each occupation, and the total vacancies projected are entered for each. Planning for one time frame (say, 6 months) is read horizontally, the date of each planning period being entered in the first column. The last three columns indicate the sources that can be used to recruit job seekers interested in such vacancies.

The benefits adduced in previous sections are applicable here. Most important of all, these approaches should lead to hiring minorities and women, within the letter and spirit of Revised Order No. 4. The requisite supporting detail can be recorded in the format of Chart 6.

Costs No additional costs accrue from the use of the *DOT* classification system, since some sort of record would be required if planning is practiced and planning data are recorded. Costs for posting are minimal.

Benefits Chart 6 indicates planning sequences and estimates over time. It will provide a cumulative record of plans to indicate to compliance officers the character of Wagner's "good faith efforts."

Additional Data Needed

Data are required for two other purposes: (*a*) setting goals, and (*b*) measuring the extent to which the goals have been achieved. Charts 5 and 6 have spaces for entering vacancies expected, and the extent to which they might be filled by recruitment, and by training. Since the intention for the foreseeable future is to fill *all* such vacancies at Wagner with minorities and women, specific quantitative goals are not needed yet.[8] Over time, successive entries on Chart 6 will reveal how satisfactorily the goals are being achieved.

Summary of Quantitative DATA

The *forms* and *methods* outlined in the preceding sections were derived from the methodology presented in Chapter 4. The richness of the data is shown by the character of the data elements that can be obtained by using the charts in accordance with the methodology. The material in Chart 7 is a summary.

From the data shown, the personnel office staff and a compliance officer can analyze the current situation at Wagner and assess the good faith efforts extended or planned to remedy underutilization through recruitment, promotion, or occupational training. Actual planning at Wagner (i.e., estimating vacancies by job title) is in process; thus the data are not presented here.

Without the need to ascertain the number of persons "generally available with requisite skills," the detail in Charts 4 and 6 (excluding the number of job seekers represented in the Staten Island NYSES file) would be sufficient to meet the requirements of Section 2.11. But in that case, the *DOT* would have made no quantitative contribution to Affirmative Action. The fact is, however, that having estimates of persons with requisite skills is critical in

WAGNER OCCUPATIONAL STAFFING PLANNING SHEET

Wagner Job Title:

DOT Title and Code:

Date	Current Employment						Projected Vacancies	Source in-house	Agencies	Training Course
	Total	Male	Female	N	SS	Other				

CHART 7[a]

	Wagner Data							Plan of Action			
					Goals			Recruitment and Training		Actions	
					Min.		Other				
Census Group	Job Title	Number of Positions	Estimated Vacancies		M	F	F	Persons with required skills	SVP	Number trainable	
(1)[a]	(2)[b]	(3)[c]	(4)[d]		(5)[e]	(6)[f]	(7)[g]	(8)[h]	(9)[i]	(10)[j]	(11)[k]

[a] Major census category.
[b] Wagner job title.
[c] Number of incumbents.
[d] Estimated vacancies.
[e] Minority males.
[f] Minority females.
[g] Nonminority females.
[h] Staten Island job seekers with required skills.
[i] SVP training time shown in DOT.
[j] Number of trainable minorities and women.
[k] Actions to be taken by Wagner.

achieving compliance with Affirmative Action requirements. Could these data be obtained by a method unrelated to the *DOT*? The only alternative available through current technology is to retrieve data from the 1970 census enumeration and update it (say) annually. This would require special surveys to meet the needs of all or most contractors. Detail would also be needed for many of the occupational titles used by the census.[9] Moreover, there is some question about the validity and reliability of such data, and the contractor's job titles do not always match those in the census, particularly if the former are not supported by position descriptions.

The use of local Employment Office files of job seekers should be a better data source, since the titles and codes are determined through personal interview by trained staff, and titles and codes are assigned on the basis of substantive facts related to *DOT* definitions.

Thus the utility of the *DOT* approach in data collection and decision making has been at least tentatively established. Our results permit us to conclude that contractors would be able to obtain information about persons with requisite skills registered in specific occupations,[10] and from these they could begin efforts to eliminate instances of underutilization. Contractors would save time in this process if they identified their positions by *DOT* title and code.

It also appears possible for state Employment Services to periodically issue data for all active job titles in the community. This would provide the necessary information for most of the job titles used by a contractor. The data would be presented by *DOT* title and code; each code could be identified by major census category, or by major *DOT* category, or both, thereby meeting the minimum standards of compliance officers as well as contractors.

The Wagner College Plan uses *DOT* not only to assemble and present occupational data, but to prepare position descriptions, provide counseling, and retrieve records of persons who expressed interest in being considered for other jobs at Wagner when vacancies occur. These elements are reviewed next, as succeeding sections reveal how effectively the *DOT* contributes to the fulfillment of Affirmative Action.

Revised Order No. 4 does not make detailed reference to the use of the *DOT* in preparing the reports (EEO-1) required by the Equal Employment Opportunity Commission pursuant to Section 709 (C) of Title VII of the Civil Rights Act of 1964. Nevertheless, all contractors are required to file an annual report, identified as Standard Form 100. The commission's report for 1966 does mention *DOT*:

(*d*) Item 1. Occupational Data. You are required to present your employment data by job category. In order to simplify and standardize the method of reporting, all jobs are considered as belonging in one of the nine broad occupations [shown in the table]. To assist you in determining how to place your jobs within the nine occupations, a description of job categories follows. . . . For further clarification, you may wish to consult the *Dictionary of Occupational Titles*, U.S. Department of Labor (U.S. Government Printing Office, Washington, D.C., 1965).[11]

EEO is aware of the potential benefits of reporting by *DOT* code; indeed, contractors are required to relate all their job titles at least to the major *DOT* categories (designated by the first digit of the full *DOT* code). The various tables prepared for Wagner make such reports by the college readily feasible.

QUALITATIVE FACTORS

Position Descriptions

The development of descriptions for the 116 positions at Wagner was critically important in implementing the qualitative aspects of the Wagner College Plan. (The descriptions also contributed peripherally to the accuracy of the quantitative data, since it became easier to classify accurately every job at Wagner College, thereby relating the job to the supply-demand matrix and other statistical arrays.)

The issues confronted in preparing the position descriptions were:

1. Is the degree of job detail excessive?
2. Are the position descriptions useful?
3. Can Wagner personnel technicians prepare the position descriptions?
4. What are the costs?
5. What are the benefits and related implications?

Degree of Job Detail Utilized and Its Value

The detail selected should conform to the objective. Appendix V shows different degrees of detail in various types of descriptions. At Wagner, the detail had to be sufficient to enable the analyst/technician to establish the worker trait qualifications profile (i.e., the specific traits and factors required to perform job duties acceptably).[12] Presumably, this strategy would allow us to achieve many applications contributing toward effective personnel management. These are: to establish criteria for initial hire, transfer, and promotion; to permit ready conversion of Wagner job titles to *DOT* titles, with effective recruitment through the state Employment Service (which would permit the preparation of an accurate matrix); to make possible the type of analysis necessary for job restructuring (redesign); to facilitate effective, accurate "bidding" for jobs (candidates could appraise their own chances on the basis of a complete statement of the work to be performed and the qualifications required); to provide a basis for accurately grouping related jobs together; to make possible the identification of "job descriptors" necessary for the application of computers to personnel management.

Although the use of computers in personnel management is in the developmental stage, some dramatic demonstrations reveal the significant potentials of this approach. The objective is to retrieve from among thousands of records for individuals, those which meet specified criteria for hire, for promotion, or for assignment to special projects. Two basic systems are involved: the use of a code number to represent the job title (*DOT* or employer job code), and the use of "descriptors," which ignore job codes and instead relate to specific characteristics (e.g., elements of the USES Job Analysis Formulation or other descriptors, such as "abilities" developed by other researchers). In addition, it is possible to use "key words" or other types of information about people or jobs to identify specific skills or knowledges.

Descriptors provide a broader base for retrieval than a job code because they cut across such codes. This is particularly desirable for two reasons: (1) job codes pigeonhole people in narrow ranges, and (2) job titles and codes reflect *job requirements,* and the latter may underrepresent specific individuals whose skills, knowledges, or abilities may be higher than those required by the job titles and codes that represent them in the file. The use of descriptors, therefore, enables the computer to tell the personnel department about the possessors of abilities and capacities that otherwise might not be discovered. This would be possible because a given individual's set of descriptors could be programmed to retrieve jobs that neither the individual nor the personnel department thought he could perform.

Position description forms were developed for use at Wagner; there is space for a description of the tasks performed; the skills, knowledges, and abilities required; and the worker traits and functions necessary for average successful performance (see sample, Appendix J). In addition, the "Worker Trait Profiles" established nationally can be compared with those determined to be needed at Wagner. A comparison of the variances between the 116 Wagner jobs and their national counterparts (Chart 8, lower left) indicates that the differences are not significant enough to warrant individual tailormade estimates by any contractor. In other words, the contractor need only identify all the tasks, relying on the applicability of the national "stereotypes" developed by the Manpower Administration.[13] (see Appendix S)

A more detailed analysis of this conclusion can be followed by observing the variances in Chart 8. The character of the variances can be ascertained

CHART 8

VARIANCES IN WORKER TRAIT RATINGS BETWEEN WAGNER COLLEGE AND
DOT 3 FOR THE 116 JOB TITLES

DOT Factor[a]	One-Step Difference	Two-Step Difference	Three-Step Difference	Total Congruent[b]
GED	10	—	—	106
SVP	21	6	1	88
Aptitudes	1	8	1	106

Number of *DOT* Factors in Common

	0	1	2
Interests	—	13	103
Temperaments	—	16	100
Physical demands	1	9	106
Working conditions	2	114	xxx

[a] See Appendix B for definitions of these factors and their levels.

[b] "Congruent" relates to the number of positions for which there was no variance. Sample pages from the table from which these data were summarized appear in Appendix S.

by reference to Appendix B, which lists and defines the Worker Trait Factors. Thus a one-step difference for GED (especially for levels 1, 2, and 3) is not by itself fully significant. For SVP, a one- or two-step differential, particularly in the lower range, is not significant: for example, SVP 1 represents a training period of "short demonstration only," SVP 2 requires training beyond short demonstration up to and as long as 30 days, SVP 3 represents training of longer than 30 days and as long as 3 months.

Aptitudes bring out a somewhat different set of considerations. There are five steps in rating aptitudes during a job analysis study. A one-step difference is not significant. A two-step variance might be critical, but not necessarily disqualifying for employment. Thus a worker who has moderate "spatial perception" in a job that requires greater strength in this area may perform acceptably because of motivation and will: he might be less efficient, having to work longer and harder on the task components requiring spatial perception; but he should be more effective on the other aspects of the job for which he has the necessary aptitudes. The variances in Chart 8 indicate that for 106 out of the 116 Wagner jobs, significant variations are not present.

Fewer variances were found for interests, temperaments, physical demands, and working conditions, as shown. The heading "Number of *DOT* Factors in Common" refers to the number of factors for which there was full congruence. All jobs in *DOT* are rated for the two dominant interests and temperaments. Temperaments in 100 of the 116 jobs had the same two temperaments shown in the national ratings; in 16 cases there was one temperament in common for the Wagner job and the national rating. Similarly, the Wagner and *DOT* ratings shared one interest for 13 jobs and 103 had both interests in common. The variances for physical demands and working conditions were not significant.

We cannot comment definitively on the necessity for the depth selected until greater experience has been gained, but some of the uses made indicate their potential. For example, certain Worker Traits were estimated during the counseling interviews, particularly interests and temperaments; these and the other traits were related to the qualifications profiles of other jobs at Wagner and outside it. Thus a residence hall dean requested assistance in picking out other jobs for which she might be qualified, and one suggestion emerging was "travel counselor." Workers generally expressed great interest in these explorations; many said the process helped them to become aware of possibilities they would not have perceived themselves.

As another spinoff of this technique, two possible bases for reorganization of some units were disclosed by a review of the position descriptions:

1. Possible centralizing of all counseling activities to replace counseling currently provided by deans of students and others in the residence halls, the placement office, and the HEOP unit,[14] and counseling in other units in the fields of finance, health, and mental health, and personal, religious, vocational planning, and academic problems.

2. Centralizing all secretaries in a pool rather than continuing to assign a secretary to each high-level staff member.

In both instances, the position descriptions provided a far more definitive base for such decision making than would otherwise have been possible.

Additional benefits were ascertained from responses to a questionnaire received by department heads along with drafts of the position descriptions covering the jobs under their supervision. (A facsimile of the questionnaire appears as Appendix T). The questionnaire solicited supervisors' views of the potential values of the position descriptions at Wagner. The results of the data entered on the questionnaires are tabulated in Chart 9.

Some of the respondents stated that the position descriptions could be also used as a basis for reassignment of responsibilities and for training new employees. One even alleged that some of the duties attributed to the employee were performed by the supervisor. Another said that "complexity

CHART 9
SUPERVISORS APPRAISAL OF POSITION DESCRIPTIONS

Question	Total	Initial Answer		After Correction	
		Yes	No[a]	Yes	No[b]
Detail					
1. Is the list of duties complete?	19	15	4	18	1
2. Are the requisite skills, knowledges, and abilities correctly identified?	19	19	—	—	—
3. Is the language readily understandable?	19	17	2	18	1
Uses					
1. Can the job specifications serve as a statement of the employee's duties and responsibilities?	19	17	2	19	—
2. Can it serve as a supervisory tool to evaluate the employee's performance?	19	16	3	18	1
3. Can it be used acceptably in setting qualifications for new employees?	19	17	2	18	1
4. Can it be used as a partial basis for determining which candidates should be selected for promotion?	19	17	2	18	1

[a] These respondents stated that their answer would be "yes" if the corrections they noted were made.
[b] These figures represent unequivocal disapproval after correction.

could discourage [the instrument's] effective use; insignificant duties were described; could be more concise." Negative opinions were in the minority, however, and both detail and depth seemed to be acceptable to the vast majority of respondents. A longitudinal study, say, 6 months hence, would yield more conclusive results.

Wagner personnel technicians prepared some of the position descriptions and feel confident that they can assume the entire task. The author's experience in training and supervising occupational analysts confirms that well trained personnel technicians can feasibly be trained to prepare such descriptions. Additional comments on training are presented in the summary.

Costs Trained occupational analysts not on Wagner's staff could complete a position description in 1 to 1.75 days. The time would be 0.25 day less if all elements of the qualifications profile were not estimated. Wagner personnel technicians estimate 1 to 1.25 days to be necessary for all but the simplest jobs (without estimating ratings for qualifications profiles), because they knew the incumbents and were familiar with the work performed. Therefore, the total time estimated to be required would range from 116 to 203 man days for preparing a position description for each nonfaculty position.

Benefits and Implications The benefits of preparing position descriptions can be summarized as follows: employer and employee have a basis for agreement over the requisite duties and qualifications; the descriptions constitute partial performance standards, which provide an improved basis for supervision; and the descriptions are essential for most personnel management areas, including selection, transfer, promotion, counseling, constructing job ladders, job restructuring, wage administration (including job price setting), and organizational analysis.

Job Ladders

An attempt was made to construct job ladders (see Chart 10). For example, the bookstore cashier might progress, with appropriate additional education and training, to cashier, business office and other successively higher level

CHART 10

JOB LADDER: CASHIER'S PROGRESS FROM BOOKSTORE TO HEAD ACCOUNTANT[a]

Wagner Title	*DOT* Title	*DOT* Code	WTG Page	GED	SVP
Head accountant	Accountant	160.188	252	5	8
Accountant	Bookkeeper I	210.388	250	4	7
Bookkeeper, students' accounts	Accounting clerk	219.488	280	4	5
Payroll clerk	Payroll clerk	215.488	280	4	5
Cashier, business office	Cashier I	211.368	267	4	5
Cashier, bookstore	Cashier II	211.468	269	3	2

[a] It is assumed that the bookstore cashier incumbent has the motivation and aspiration to take the necessary training to qualify for the next higher job.

titles, to head accountant. For each step in the ladder, Chart 10 indicates the Worker Trait Group page in *DOT 3,* Volume II, which describes the general duties, qualifications, and qualifications profile; the GED level, and the SVP level. Such levels generally represent upward progression. It is difficult to construct job ladders for a facility having only 116 positions; greater success in this direction would be possible for a much larger establishment. For example, one eastern university has 11,000 nonfaculty employees in 800 job titles. Job ladders and lattices could be constructed using Worker Function levels and Worker Trait factors as the criteria, as well as other factors described in this section.

Chart 10 represents a straight line sequence. A job lattice would indicate career routings for many jobs on an organization chart, in a lateral and diagonal progression as well as in a straight line sequence, thus cutting across occupational lines without reference to departments.

THE COUNSELING INTERVIEW

The objectives, standards, and the content of the interview, including counseling, have been described in earlier chapters. Briefly, all nonfaculty Wagner employees were interviewed, the salient data were elicited, and the interpretations and courses of action to be taken were recorded on a diagnostic form (see Appendix L).

The average interview required 1 hour, 7 minutes to (*a*) explain the scope and objectives of the Wagner Affirmative Action Plan (5–10 minutes), (*b*) complete a data sheet covering each interview (see Chart 11), and (*c*) prepare bids, when employees requested them. The author conducted 48 interviews, and two Wagner personnel technicians handled the remaining 100. The total time required was 165 hours.

The Personnel technicians were given intensive training in the *DOT* to qualify to conduct the interviews. At first there were lectures and discussions, with detailed explanations of job analysis, interviewing, and counseling concepts. To round out the training, the two personnel technicians audited about 15 interviews conducted by the author; an in-depth discussion of technique followed. At the outset, the technicians doubted their ability to conduct the interviews acceptably. After completing a dozen, they became more confident, however, and welcomed detailed, critical discussions of their recorded interviews. The personnel technicians conducted each interview alone, with only the interviewee present, and I believe that both women are now fully competent in this assignment.

At the conclusion of each interview, the interviewee was asked to appraise objectively the value of the interview, and a statement of the facts was recorded on the data sheet (see Chart 11). To obtain a more realistic ap-

CHART 11

DATA SHEET: REPORT OF AFFIRMATIVE ACTION INTERVIEW

| Dept. Faculty Secretary | Title Secretary | DOT Code 201.368 |
| Employee | | WTG p. # 263 |

| 1. Date of Interview April 24, 1973 | Time In 11:25 a.m. Time Out 1:00 p.m. | Net Time 1 hr. 35 min. |

2. Worker Traits: Comparison between employee's and those shown on job specification.
   Same. Plus Interest 3,9,0

3. Possible reasons for variance
   Prefers working with organized procedures and machines. Prefers activities resulting in tangible productive satisfaction. Likes to see finished product.

4. Jobs for which employee bid
   graph-0-type operator
   DOT Title: 9 digit code 213.582   WTG p. # 274
   Off-set printer

5. Employee reaction to the interview (favorable, unfavorable, etc.)
   Enjoyed interview. Was glad for explanation of program.

6. Comments:
   Seemed a little reluctant to express desire to bid on other job. At suggestion, was happy to put in 2 bids for lettershop.

FORM B · 11/1/72

praisal, a questionnaire (Appendix U) was sent to each employee interviewed, requesting his anonymous opinions. Chart 12 tabulates the views of the employees who returned the questionnaire.[15] To enhance the reader's appraisal of the data, Chart 13 summarizes the responses to each question.

Further refinement of the data appears in Chart 14, which indicates the combinations of questions checked by individual respondents. Note that some respondents checked no questions, and others checked one or more. Such data were tabulated for the first 57 questionnaires returned to indicate (a) no checks, and (b) the frequency of pairings of checks.

Questions 1, 2, and 3 (of Chart 13) relate specifically to the impact of the use of the *DOT* on the respondent. Question 4 is an end result of the interview as a whole, not *necessarily* related to *DOT*. In any event, although the totals indicate that the interviews were generally successful, the impact of *DOT* cannot be quantified. A longitudinal study would reveal the presence of any attitudinal lag (i.e., after a lapse of time, the respondents' more considered attitudes might emerge).

The following comments from three questionnaires are revealing:

I wish to commend the professional ability of Mrs. Ann Mochnick who conducted my interview. She put me at ease throughout the discussion and was very adept in her ability to explain Wagner's long-view personnel policies for its staff members. I went away with a renewed enthusiasm for my working career.

CHART 12

ATTITUDES TOWARD COUNSELING INTERVIEWS

Attitude Expressed	Total Responding	Favorable Responses		Unfavorable Responses	
		Number	Percentage	Number	Percentage
During interview	80	78	97.5	2	2.5
In the anonymous questionnaire	85	72	84.7	13	15.3

CHART 13
ANALYSIS OF EMPLOYEE ATTITUDES TOWARD THE INTERVIEWS

Found interview rewarding: 72 Not Rewarding: 13	
Question	Favorable Responses
1. Did it convince you that you were in the right field of work?	34
2. Did it help you clear up your own thinking about your career goals?	25
3. Did it make you aware of other suitable careers you had never considered before?	30
4. Did it indicate that Wagner was interested in your growth and development?	55

CHART 14
NUMBER OF ITEMS ON
QUESTIONNAIRE CHECKED BY
INDIVIDUAL RESPONDENTS

Responses to Question Number(s)	Number of Responses
(None)	10
1	3
1, 2	2
1, 2, 4	2
1, 3	1
1, 3, 4	3
1, 4	6
2	3
2, 3	2
2, 3, 4	1
2, 4	2
3	4
3, 4	3
4	7
1–4	8
	57

I feel the Affirmative Action Program should have a very positive, worthwhile affect on all Wagner employees.

It was extremely helpful to understand the purpose of the Affirmative Action Program and the reasons for Wagner expending the time and effort on this program.

The organization must show an *increased* amount of interest in the lives of its staff, in areas professional *and* personal, in order to keep the best of this group. When an individual feels that the organization doesn't care about him, he must question his loyalty and position in relation to the organization. Wagner has shown very little interest, I believe, in the professional or personal lives of its staff.

The observation that the majority of those interviewed apparently found the interview rewarding seems to support the hypothesis that the *DOT* and its building blocks make an important and valuable contribution to Affirmative Action. This is reenforced by two additional factors—namely, the number of "bids" received, and the comments made to the interviewer at the end of each session. Thus of the first 83 people interviewed, 21 (or 25.3%) filed bids for other jobs at Wagner. Perhaps most revealing of all were the oral comments recorded on the data sheets by the interviewers. Many employees found the interview useful and helpful. Others said the experience was enjoyable. A few believed that the interviews were either enjoyable or useful because they improved morale. Two of the 148 employees had a negative reaction. One was a supervisor who felt injured because he had not been sufficiently informed of the plan; his comments were summarized by the interviewer as follows: "Resented the idea of interview because he was not sufficiently aware of its objective. Considers he is fully aware of his goals. Therefore, this interview did not help him in any way." The other dissatisfied response was from an employee who was about to retire. Some representative comments follow:

Thought interview was most enlightening with respect to explanation of AA Program.

Enjoyed interview. Thought "bid" idea a good one.

Enjoyed interview. Good for growth on campus.

Interview was interesting and could be very valuable. "It is fun for people who are open to experience and to new ideas. Useful to explore self with another person. Felt lifted in spirit. Now know of options which may match my needs."

Found the interview fun. Plans to retire reasonably soon. Plans to continue her present job until then.

Enjoyed interview. Felt she already knew her best field of work.

Considers self too old to be choosing a new career, but found interview enjoyable.

Interview was very good. Helped to become aware of other job possibilities on campus. Stimulated ideas about future plans.

Interview was great stimulus toward thinking about his career. After his first interview (he had requested a second), helped him to develop best résumé he had ever prepared.

Thought interview was excellent. Helped him to document for himself certain earlier career decisions he had made.

Wanted assistance in clarifying his job aims. Believed he obtained this during intervies.

Found interview useful to the college and its employees.

Gave employee chance to express his job preferences.

Interview was excellent. Stimulated him to think about things he should have thought about before.

Interview enabled him to express himself and to bid on other jobs. Thought interview would be especially useful to young employees who are seeking self-clarification and some vocational direction.

Found interview useful. Now realizes she would like to return to former job as auditing clerk in a hospital.

Interview gave her the assurance she is in a field that is good for her.

Appreciated the interview very much. Stimulated her toward self-appraisal. Now she is sure she is in a suitable field for her.

Interview reenforced his feeling that he is currently working below skill; needs more responsibility.

Interview gave him confirmation of the validity of what he is doing. It shored him up. This was reassuring to him.

Thought interview was good and valuable, particularly since it identified job requirements and qualifications.

While she knows what she wants to be, feels great to discuss her ideas with personnel people.

Interview gave her chance to hear herself express job aims. Thought this reality testing was valuable.

Interview provided opportunity to exchange information with Personnel.

Helped personally. Feels college will not utilize the interview for good of employee of the college. No opportunity at college for promotion.

Helped to consolidate thinking about aims and goals. Thought interview opened "windows."

Was stimulated to think about self.

These interviews should lead to better campus relationships. Feels Personnel is geared toward every individual's well being.

Interview gave her hope. Suggests there is more need for in-house promotion to improve morale.

Interview was marvelous. Made her aware of the importance and scope of her job, and other jobs outside Wagner for which she now knows she is qualified. Thinks College should recognize contribution of nonfaculty employees.

Good opportunity to have a dialogue with Personnel, even though has no higher job aspirations.

Summary of Counseling Section

It appears that the interviews met the requirements of Revised Order No. 4, under which all employees are to be counseled. It is also clear that the majority of those interviewed found the interview rewarding. No one complained, either orally or by anonymous questionnaire, that the interview was too lengthy or included extraneous elements. If the oral comments can be regarded as a true expression of opinion, the interview was considered to be valuable in reenforcing career decisions previously made, in providing self-clarification concerning career aims, or in making employees aware of new potentials and career options in Wagner and/or outside it.

A number appreciated the opportunity for self-expression (reflecting in minor fashion what Mayo found at Hawthorne—that employees feel good when they become the center of attention).[16] Employees were made to realize the importance of the demonstration during the course of the interview, and their opinions of the value of the counseling were earnestly solicited. Although this might have enhanced the employee's opinions of the value of the Wagner College Plan and its technology, a more constructive benefit was probably present: the relevance of each employee's position to his potentials was discussed with him, and other options were described for his own appraisal. The attention might have flattered the employee beyond the value of the "counseling" he received, but the net impact on morale, if nothing else, seems to have made the counseling worthwhile.

Minimally, it appears that the interviewers contributed to gaining acceptance for Affirmative Action. For example, most of the employees stated that the Wagner Plan and the interviews would tend to build morale, provided the plan was followed—a few expressed skepticism that it would be. Some employees believed that the college administration ignored nonfaculty employees and their contribution to the institution. A few interviewees felt that they should receive the same attention as faculty (be asked to attend staff meetings, be kept informed of college issues and problems, and otherwise be made to feel that they were important participants in the college enterprise).

OTHER QUALITATIVE FACTORS

There are a few additional qualitative factors related to the mechanics used to secure Affirmative Action at Wagner: constructing job ladders, operating the "bid" procedure, posting notifications of job vacancies, locating and appraising all candidates for given vacancies, and planning and initiating recruitment actions on the basis of the available data and the circumstances.

The plan became fully operational in June 1973, but all components could not be implemented by that time. The supply-demand matrix was prepared, all position descriptions were completed, and all nonfaculty employees were interviewed and counseled. Files also were set up to accommodate all forms used. However, there were not many job openings. Budgetary problems became acute for many reasons, including a drop in student enrollment, and retrenchment, rather than expansion, was necessary. Thus no meaningful data of the values of these aspects of the Wagner College Plan are available. However, college officials and the director of personnel have expressed conviction that the plan as a whole has been eminently successful thus far; as soon as vacancies occur, the plan should ease the attainment of equal employment opportunity through the methods and procedures developed at Wagner. It is possible to assess the costs and to comment on the benefits, however.

Costs Vacancies were posted at slight cost. Additional costs were entailed in constructing job ladders, working out the bidding procedure, creating the Opportunity File. The costs of bidding were minimal because candidates prepared and submitted forms detailing their qualifications. Since all records would have to be filed somehow, no additional costs were attributable to the creation and maintenance of the Opportunity File, in which all the bids are placed. The cost of the career ladder samples constructed ranged from 1 to 3 hours for each cluster. The chief limiting technical factor is the lack of a complete technology for constructing career ladders. Worker Trait and Worker Function factors are critical, but another "ingredient" is needed, particularly to establish relationships among jobs including those with different Worker Trait patterns. The most promising ingredient is the "methods verbs" concept described in the *Handbook for Analyzing Jobs.*[17] Methods verbs are action words that describe work performed by employees in specific jobs (e.g., "types," "assembles," "grinds," "researches," "analyzes," "computes.") In practice, all jobs requiring "typing" would be identified and rated for Worker Functions and Worker Traits, particularly those which scale: GED, SVP, aptitudes, and physical factors (only partly since all physical factors do not scale). This would allow determinations of the progressively higher levels of complexity and trait patterns required to establish an upward sequence. Substantial research is needed to develop valid techniques for these purposes, but the current use of computers in "manpower matching" under the aegis of the Manpower Administration may provide a good experiential research base.

Benefits Since the Opportunity File and the bid procedure ensure that all persons will receive "automatic consideration" for each vacancy, the objectives of equal employment opportunity ought to be fulfilled through the Wagner College Plan. The Opportunity File is arranged by Worker Trait Groups, to broaden the base for "selecting" (considering) all qualified or qualifiable candidates for jobs. This method brings together under meaningful job classifications, all jobs that require the same configurations of traits. By filing the records of all job candidates according to this plan, we overcome technical coding and filing errors for given individuals; it is also possible to locate job seekers with the nearest qualifying traits when persons with the exact experience are not available.

Some offices of the New York State Employment Service have experimented with this method, but there are no definitive findings yet about its values. Some users are enthusiastic; others remain to be convinced. Differences of opinion are partly attributable to the difficulty of pinpointing the degree to which the method really "works." This is essentially a reporting problem. To keep score, the interviewer must report whether each placement resulted from the use of the method: for example, if a job seeker had a secondary skill in an occupation that is in the same Worker Trait Group as his last occupation, the method cannot be credited with the successful placement. Similarly, if a job seeker suggested interest in an occupation in a related WTG, and this attitude would not have been disclosed otherwise, the method's value would not be clearly documented. For valid assessments, many interviewers in representative locations, serving a representative sample of occupations, would have to be trained in the WTG concept and in the evaluation method to be used; close supervision would be necessary. This could not be done in the Employment Service when the Wagner College Plan was being developed and implemented. There is every reason to speculate, however, that the method has had useful and valuable results at least in those Worker Trait Groups, and for those occupations, in which substitutions are possible from one job to another in the same group, with minimal training.

CHAPTER SUMMARY

This chapter has presented the findings, costs, and benefits of all aspects of the Wagner College Affirmative Action Plan. The observation was made that the data support the proposition that the *DOT,* Third Edition, can contribute substantially to the achievement of the objectives of Affirmative Action. That is, the *DOT* approach can be applied to determinations of supply and demand, goal setting, corrections of deficiencies, preparation and updating of job descriptions, interviewing and counseling, constructing promotional ladders and lattices, and job restructuring.

A detailed statement of the conclusions reached, including replicability and policy connotations, appears in the next chapter, along with suggestions for future research. Finally, in a summary of recent developments, the seeming contradiction between the concepts of affirmative action and equal employment opportunity receives comment and clarification.

NOTES

1. The Manpower Administration issued guidelines (see their Reports and Analysis Letter No. 716, February 24, 1971) to be used by state Employment Security Agency labor market analysts "in developing estimates to meet requests by contractors . . . in connection with [Revised Order No. 4]." See also, note 5.

2. Fully explained in Chapter 3. These groups include occupations with the same configuration of occupationally related traits and factors. A complete list of the titles of the Worker Trait Groups appears in *DOT 3*, Volume II, beginning on page 217, identified by the same page number as in the matrix. This also appears in Appendix E.

3. A full list of the *DOT* two-digit groups appears in Appendix C; three digit groups are listed in *DOT 3*, Volume II, beginning on page 3.

4. More recently, government contractors began to list with the Employment Service all their vacancies under Executive Order 11598, now Public Law 92.540.

5. The initial phase of the Wagner College Affirmative Action Plan was completed in June 1973. In January 1974 the Equal Employment Opportunity Commission issued a guidebook for employers, suggesting that a survey be undertaken as a basis for setting Affirmative Action goals:

> This survey will help you to identify jobs, departments or units in which there may be significant *underutilization* or *concentration* of minorities and/or females and males. Underutilization has been defined as having fewer minorities or women in a particular job category than would reasonably be expected by their presence in the relevant labor market.

Appendix B, Volume 3 of that brochure (p. B-31) states

> However, excessive data collection is not necessary if your own employment survey reveals absence or serious underrepresentation of any group. Affirmative efforts to locate and/or train females and minorities for jobs where they are not represented will be more productive than intensive effort to locate data justifying their underutilization.

Following this paragraph are some three pages of data sources including those published by the Census Bureau, The U.S. Department of Labor's Women's Bureau, The Equal Employment Opportunity Commission, the Bureau of Labor Statistics, Educational Data Sources, and State and Local Data Sources. In addition, page B-5 describes a new "DATA PACKAGE FOR AFFIRMATIVE ACTION" as a

> . . . standardized packet of local work force statistics, including minimum data needed to analyze "underutilization" of minorities and women for Affirmative Action Plans. Data "packets" will be available at State Employment Security Offices for some areas in November, 1973, and are expected to be available for all areas by Spring 1973 (sic). The packets will include recent information by sex and minority status on: population and labor force, employment status, occupations of employed

persons, last occupations of experienced unemployed workers and occupational characteristics of job applicants at public employment offices.

Source: U.S. Equal Employment Opportunity Commission, *Affirmative Action and Equal Employment, A Guidebook for Employers* (Washington, D.C.: Government Printing Office, January 1974).

6. Note again that Section 2.11 has been amended effective July 12, 1974. The term "job title" (i.e., "a particularly narrowly defined position in the traditional sense of the meaning of the word job") replaces the term "job classification."

7. These groups accounted for 52% of all employment in New York State in 1968. The study projects that jobs in these lower level groups will represent 48.3% of all jobs to be filled 1968–1980. (From unpublished report, New York State Department of Labor, Bureau of Research and Statistics, 1972, p. 1b.) These groups, however, differ somewhat from those listed in Chart 2.

8. The Equal Employment Opportunity Commission's brochure, "Affirmative Action and Equal Employment," states: "Although Title VII bars preferential hiring simply to eliminate racial employment imbalances in relation to population ratios, Federal courts consistently have found numerical goals and timetables to be a justified and necessary remedy and means of eliminating the present effects of past discriminatory practices" (p. 11).

9. Census data are presented by a list of occupations comprising the categories. These differ substantially from *DOT* job titles. For many job titles in an establishment, therefore, census data would have to be estimated from broader groupings.

10. If many workers or occupations are involved, special funding might be required. If data are provided by computer (which is possible in some states), employers might have to be charged.

11. EEO Report, 1966, p. xxxi. The same statement appears in the commission's brochure "Affirmative Action and Equal Employment Opportunity," Volume 2, p. A-2 (*f*), January 1974.

12. Chart 1 of Chapter 1 displays the elements of the Job Analysis Formulation (including the qualifications profile). The Worker Traits and Worker Functions are defined in Appendices A and B.

13. It is expected that these will be published in the next *DOT* edition, scheduled for 1976. Further research, however, may show that the variances for "blue-collar" jobs are more substantial. See Appendix S for Wagner variances.

14. The New York State Higher Education Opportunity Program, which helps minority students adjust to campus life, grants up to $1,100 to educationally and economically disadvantaged New York State students.

15. Of the first 90 persons interviewed, 85 returned the questionnaire. The personnel office did not wish to pursue the matter further, since a pattern of attitudes had been obtained.

16. Research in job satisfaction and motivation as well as employee experience under the operations of so-called human relations technique have demonstrated that employees need a sense of belonging, recognition, and participation, in addition to the other values of their work experience, to reinforce their feelings of self-worth.

One great source of frustration for an employee is to be left out of his establishment's formal communication network, particularly if he thinks he should be included. Experience has shown that employees will submerge self to a larger goal if they believe the goal to be important and themselves to be part of it. (See my article, "Beyond Motivation," in *Harvard Business Review*, May-June 1960, p. 123.) For this reason the Wagner Plan provided that each employee should be made to feel that he was part of an important study; that his views were highly valued and needed in formulating policy for several aspects of the Plan.

17. See *Handbook for Analyzing Jobs*, pp. 87–148.

CHAPTER 6

DISCUSSION OF
THE ASSUMPTIONS

Before interpreting the findings of the study and making suggestions for
further research, let us restate and analyze the objectives of the legislation,
the issues affecting its implementation, the impact of the findings on future
social legislation, the considerations germane to the formulation of a national manpower policy, and the implications for public administration.

PRELIMINARY DISCUSSION: OBJECTIVES OF AFFIRMATIVE ACTION

The provisions of Revised Order No. 4 detail the steps to be taken by
"covered" contractors (employers) when specified types of quantitative
analysis indicate deficiencies in hiring and promoting minorities and
women. The objective is to eliminate discrimination through an enlightened
and sophisticated manpower technology. Although the coming of Revised
Order No. 4 was doubtless accelerated by the unrest in major cities in the
1960s, its content and scope are rooted in and stem from the Employment
Act of 1946, in which a national manpower policy was contemplated. The
equal employment opportunity derivation of the 1946 act was meant to
facilitate the optimum use and allocation of the nation's total human
resources without reference to race, color, religion, national origin, or sex as
a matter of social and economic policy.

Such policies indicate (a) that each of the constituent factors be
identified, (b) that a suitable technology be available for creative adaptation to emerging needs and imperatives, and (c) that the implementing
devices lead to the attainment of the social and economic objectives, either
initially or through a new synthesis of theory and implementation after feed-

back of operational results. In the author's opinion, such a sequence of events is based on certain assumptions; those relating to Revised Order No. 4 follow.

1.   Revised Order No. 4 assumes that techniques and methodologies are available for developing the requisite types of quantitative manpower analysis needed to establish whether minorities and women are equitably employed throughout the occupational spectrum.

2.   All or most employers are assumed to have developed a full functioning, scientific set of personnel management techniques, including use of position descriptions, identification of career ladders and lattices, and use of scientific selection and promotion criteria, as well as participatory supervisory methods; the will to obtain, train, and stimulate employees to work effectively toward full productivity is also assumed.

3.   The resolution of controversial aspects of vocational choice theory is assumed, and basic standardized techniques are to have been established to facilitate vocational decision making through counseling.

4.   It is assumed that minorities and women have internalized the desire to work and to produce, and potential employers and coworkers will accept the role of these individuals in the fulfillment of the stated objectives, provided the new workers can perform acceptably.

5.   It is assumed that the enactment of such social legislation can and will be readily implemented by the bureaucracies in government and in the private sector, within the guidelines set forth in the legislation.

6.   It is assumed that the "controls" leading to the fulfillment of the objectives of Revised Order No. 4 are logical and persuasive enough to be virtually self-enforcing, and recalcitrant or bigoted employers can be stimulated by legislation and a set of social and economic values and pressures to rethink their positions.

7.   It is assumed that Revised Order No. 4, along with all the other social and economic legislation stemming from the Employment Act of 1946, comprises a well-conceived, though not fully integrated national manpower policy that can be successfully operated and enforced through the provisions of the constituent statutes enacted since 1946.

Apparently it was believed that if these expectations were correct, the nation would enjoy equal employment opportunity and full employment, to be manipulated and adjusted in the event of disequilibrium through fiscal and monetary policy, and effective public administration.

The Wagner College study documents the lack of realism of the foregoing assumptions, both generally and specifically. The Civil Rights Act of 1964 and Revised Order No. 4 represent the type of legislation designed to be largely "self-implementing" (i.e., actions are to be initiated by the target group). The law presents broad guidelines and possibly specific instructions for initiating implementing action, with penalties for failure to comply. The areas of civil rights and income tax are examples. The government's role is restricted to providing forms and instructions and carrying out certain activities to ensure compliance. In contrast, the unemployment compensation law assigns responsibility for full implementation to a government agency, with the target group fulfilling its obligations as directed. The same preliminary steps are followed for both types of legislation: domestic pressures lead to consideration of the problem by the legislators; social planners, consultants, and interest groups assist in drafting the legislation, and hearings are held by congressional committees to test the "adequacy" of the proposed law.

Substantial differences occur, however, following enactment. A self-implementing law is published in the *Federal Register,* thus assuring initial publicity. Implementation by the target group is considered to be feasible because the statute is assumed to be completely self-explanatory and because appropriate technologies are available. The second type of legislation is characterized by an altogether different bureaucratic approach. Classically, the government agency concerned convenes a "work committee"[1] representing its legal department, the public information office, and staff and line units, to review the legislation exhaustively and to establish a "plan of operation" describing in general terms the policy, procedure, and systems needed to serve the target groups. Following clearance approval by the line and staff, each operating division develops the methods, techniques, and forms to be used by the target groups and by the operating local and central office (if any). The next step is to provide full publicity to the target groups, including oral presentations by line and staff as necessary. After operational experience has been gained, the agency develops remedial legislation or additional rules and regulations needed to correct deficiencies disclosed through analysis of operating statistics, complaints, or views of the staff. Line and staff may testify before the legislative committees engaged in drafting amendments.

The advantages of this type of administrative planning, and the problems resulting from the lack of it, are illustrated by the difficulties encountered in implementing Revised Order No. 4. Wagner College officials informed the author that they received from compliance officers little guidance in *substantive* areas. Instead, during an early meeting conducted by the Department of Health, Education, and Welfare (which was responsible for compliance by colleges and universities), contractors were informed that HEW assumed that contractors "would not want to be told how to implement the order." Contractors did not know how to proceed, however, and they anxiously sought assistance from consultants. A few contractors told the author that the consultants themselves could not supply sufficiently definitive suggestions for implementation.

The task of the Equal Employment Opportunity Commission represents an important variation from the examples of administrative management just described. In its role and scope it is quite unlike the Internal Revenue Service. The IRS administers tax legislation. Its employees are the substantive experts, issuing instructions and exercising compliance; and the feedback generates legislative and procedural changes to meet emerging conditions. Forms and instructions to taxpayers are improved over time, and a body of case law develops from experience. The successful performance of the Equal Employment Opportunity Commission's function, on the other hand, requires the synthesis of several disciplines, each of which should be reasonably standardized to ensure operational feasibility and compliance. These disciplines include personnel management (which itself represents a synthesis or at least an integration of several sociopsychological elements) and manpower planning (requiring practical methodologies and the availability of the basic data). Also needed is a manpower delivery system to facilitate the recruitment and training of the target groups. Each element of the synthesis is a substantive, controversial area over which neither the Equal Employment Opportunity Commission nor the Department of Labor or its designees can exercise control. At best, the commission and the agencies can stimulate contractors to use the techniques in the public domain that will best contribute to the attainment of equal employment opportunity. For example, can or should the agencies instruct contractors *how* to effect upward mobility? How to counsel? How to perform job analysis? At best, the agencies' role must be to motivate contractors to take measures to ensure these end products. At best, the agencies assume that contractors will equip themselves to do so. And hopefully, the agencies assume that the necessary innovations will emerge.

Another problem concerns the division of responsibility among the Equal Employment Opportunity Commission, the Department of Labor, and the Department of Health, Education, and Welfare. Title VII of the Civil Rights Act of 1964 established the Equal Employment Opportunity Commission to administer that title. However, according to Section 201 of Executive Order 11246, the Secretary of Labor is responsible for administering Parts II and III (covering nondiscrimination in employment by contractors and subcontractors, and the nondiscrimination provisions in federally assisted construction contracts, (respectively) of the order. Finally, Section 401 provides that:

The Secretary of Labor may delegate to any officer, agency, or employee in the Executive branch of the government, any function or duty of the Secretary under Parts II and III of this Order, except authority to promulgate rules and regulations of a general nature.

Thus the Equal Employment Opportunity Commission is named responsible for attaining equality in employment opportunity for covered nongovernment employers as defined. The Department of Labor or its designee has compliance authority for covered *government contractors*. As noted earlier, the Secretary of Labor has delegated compliance activities for colleges and universities (with the requisite government contracts) to the HEW.

The Department of Health, Education, and Welfare issued Higher Education Guidelines, Executive Order 11246, on October 1, 1972. The transmittal memorandum to college and university presidents included the following statement:

> The Department of Health, Education and Welfare stands by ready to assist in every way possible so that all institutions of higher education will be able to meet the requirements of the Executive Order and other Federal requirements, regarding non-discriminatory treatment. Once such measures have been installed and are operable, the commission would then determine if these implement Equal Employment Opportunity and hence are acceptable.[2]

The foregoing contingencies explain at least to the author's satisfaction why none of the agencies involved could or would issue adequate guidelines until some time *after* the various orders were effective. This view is reenforced by the difficulty, if not the impossibility, of preparing guidelines in advance of experience. This would have required the commission and the compliance agencies to provide "models" for fulfilling some of the requirements (after predicting the kinds of contingencies which might occur) and to distill and enunciate remedial *principles* in advance.

It is interesting to note the sequence of events in a prior, analogous situation. When unemployment insurance first became operational in New York, and long before benefits were payable, the author was assigned to prepare guidelines for the adjudication of cases resulting from the section of the law that required benefit seekers to accept "suitable employment" as vaguely defined in the statute. British experience with unemployment insurance was the basis for handling the assignment. These principles were rejected as a matter of policy by the New York agency's executive staff, however, after it was realized that British experience might lack relevance. More important, it was concluded that it would be better for referees and higher appellant bodies to distill principles out of the body of case law that would be developed through experience and would represent lower and higher level adjudications.

Apparently realization of the limitations of projecting guidelines in advance of experience comes to different agencies at different times: the Department of Health, Education, and Welfare issued its guidelines (for Executive Order 11246) in October *1972,* and the Equal Employment Opportunity Commission issued its guidelines for employers in January *1974.* Perhaps, too, this realization prompted the government official mentioned earlier to suggest that college personnel officers might not want to be told how to implement Revised Order No. 4.

Another significant complicating factor was stated previously—namely, that compliance activities are the responsibility of the Department of Labor or its designees. This organizational device (whatever its justification) separates the Equal Employment Opportunity Commission from some of its client groups. One wonders whether even under optimum conditions this strategy tends to retard the type of feedback needed as a basis for drafting and issuing interpretive statements and examples of effective plans and techniques used by some contractors in attaining Affirmative Action. In any event, the Office of Information of the Department of Labor stated in its release *Women & Work,* dated October 1974, "The U.S. Department of Labor and the Equal Employment Opportunity Commission sign[ed an] agreement to coordinate enforcement of federal equal employment opportunity regulations."

REALITY PROBLEMS FOR SOCIAL PLANNERS

A sharp difference exists between theoretical constructs and operating realities, and the rapid proliferation of manpower programs is a case in point. The federal Manpower Administration's United States Employment Service and its affiliated state agencies were confronted with a succession of laws touching many of the elements needed in a total manpower program, including vocational training under the Manpower Development and Training Act of 1962 (and its subsequent amendments), the Job Corps, the Neighborhood Youth Corps, Human Resources Development (HRD) policies, and the Work Incentive Program. These were doubtless designed by planners from relevant disciplines. There was heavy emphasis on helping minorities to become "job ready" and placing them in meaningful employment,[3] even though this caused many skilled and semiskilled job seekers to seek employment in whatever manner each thought best. This was the very contingency against which Bakke warned: he thought that all workers and all employers should be served by the employment and manpower services,[4] to the greatest extent possible. More complications occurred when New York State enacted a law requiring welfare recipients to pick up their checks at the local employment office, which was to offer them "any job in which they could engage." (Employers were not required to hire workers so referred.) In any case, the number of job opportunities available to the Employment Service diminished because many employers did not want to hire the "disadvantaged."

Problems also resulted because usual counseling techniques were difficult to apply to some members of the disadvantaged groups because of allegedly different social and cultural values, inability of some to crystallize their vocational needs and goals because of lack of prior work experience, individuals' lack of knowledge of their potentials and the types of jobs for which they could qualify, and because of applicant mistrust pending revalidation of "standard" testing procedures. Of course the sticky allegations had nothing to do with unfair practices based on race, sex, and so on, it was simply that the needed facilities and technology lagged behind program conceptualization. We now turn to reality issues in the bureaucracy.

Reality in the Bureaucracy

Ordinarily administrators in any type of organization want to accomplish program objectives with minimum effort (often because of insufficient funding) in a stabilized operating environment. Given adequate funding, the average bureaucrat wants to maintain the status quo, eschewing either substantive or mechanical innovation. Innovation comes only after substantial pressures have been experienced, either from the target group or as the result of insufficient funding.

Some bureaucrats have insufficient knowledge of operations. Some assume that once they establish basic policies, the development of techniques and systems by their technicians can be taken for granted. Additionally, when appearing before various groups and legislative committees, some bureaucrats are very outspoken and are likely to misrepresent the operational feasibility of proposed legislative changes. Poor leadership, inadequate communication, inability to set realistic priorities, pressures of interest groups, political considerations, and unrealistic civil service procedures in hire and promotion complicate the problem. The issues are further confused by changing social values within the community and among the target groups.

Attitudes of the Target Groups

In the 1960s the dynamics of the disadvantaged segments of the populace, new realizations of their needs, rapid changes in their values, and varied perceptions of their rights, obligations, and "power," began to exert new forces on public administration and the legislative process. This was and is particularly noticeable in the fields of education, employment, and politics. New needs emerged and continue to emerge with respect to the values and desirability of the rewards to be obtained through the Protestant ethic. Broad sections of youth and students experienced identity crises. Students became more articulate; some joined communes, questioning the meaning and value of traditional career patterns and benefits. University professors began to organize. High school teachers went on strike for higher wages. Government employees sought higher wages and were prepared to take "job actions," although this was proscribed by law. A new and substantial emphasis was placed on finding "meaningful" work that would help the individual toward "self-actualization," where job satisfaction rather than monetary profit was the main objective. For many, deeper values outweighed potential economic gain.

These, however, are not the only realities. For example, some years ago, certain supporters of equal opportunity were disturbed because minorities were not represented in middle and higher echelons of management. One heard the complaint that too few members of minority groups occupied policy-making positions. Some government officials attributed this situation to the failure of large numbers of minority groups to "file for" the required merit system examinations, and pass high enough to be appointed. They were informed that the examinations were inadequate and served to screen out minorities who did not possess the established "credentials," which were said to be subjective and inappropriate.

Others expressed a contrary view. They charged that "reverse discrimination" was no remedy, alleging that government agencies and private establishments set out to demonstrate their interest in equal employment opportunity by favoring minorities when granting promotions, even though this adversely affected some nonminorities who were "better qualified." Some employees carried their opposition to the courts.

These realities cannot be minimized. Some situations can be ameliorated by technologies such as the *DOT*. Others can be resolved by court decisions that address the legal aspects without necessarily touching on the human questions involved when nonminorities rightly or wrongly perceive that equal employment opportunity policies have robbed them of promotions.

Perhaps the most important remedy is education, to promote the sober understanding that the nation cannot endure unless equal employment opportunity is a reality. Unfortunately, short-term compulsory methods seem to be needed to begin the process of eventually securing equal employment opportunity for all. The plight of other ethnic and religious minorities some 50 years ago is clearly remembered. Discrimination against these groups is now rare. It was overcome gradually, often because of supply-demand imbalances that forced employers to hire minorities; and once this occurred, it was found that minority employees were well-qualified, able workers.

One might well ask whether a democracy can afford to permit any minority to continue to be subjected to the hazards of slow-acting evolutionary processes. One might well ask whether any country can survive on less than the optimum utilization of its total workforce. One might also ask whether there is any basis or any reason for denying equal employment opportunity to any person. Finally, one can reasonably assume that once minorities have caught up (i.e., have taken the necessary training and have obtained the knowledge and experience needed to perform acceptably), equal employment opportunity will be self-generating, and prodding by government will no longer be required.

These realities pose serious short-term dilemmas, however, and undoubtedly agonizing decisions will have to be made by administrators and personnel directors who want to do the right thing. How can one provide equal employment opportunity when it means injuring valued employees who merit promotions? Technology may resolve certain specific problems. For example, jobs might be restructured to make possible a promotion for a well-qualified nonminority employee, while providing a port of entry for a member of a minority group. Such solutions are not always possible. The handling of difficult cases must be based on a consideration of all the facts. And in some instances hard decisions must be justified by the broader, long-term results anticipated.

We next assess the extent to which the findings of the Wagner College Affirmative Action Plan relate to the considerations of this section and contribute to the resolution of some of the technical issues raised. In other words, what were the benefits of the plan and its spinoffs in the present climate and state of national, social, and economic values? What is the potential payoff?

LESSONS LEARNED FROM THE WAGNER PLAN

The Wagner College Affirmative Action Plan may be regarded as a case study in social and legislative planning and public administration. However, it is clear that the legislation and the ensuing orders produced less than the intended implementation thruout the economy.

Because the substance and objectives of the program are complicated by extremely sensitive moral, social, and technical issues, the drafters of Revised Order No. 4 should have taken extraordinary care to ensure that the order was clear and feasible enough to be expeditiously implemented. Such planning was necessary to fulfill interest group expectations and the needs of contractors, most of whom are among the 500 leading corporations in the country.

The Department of Labor's Manpower Administration made several efforts to assist employers in meeting the quantitative requirements of Revised Order No. 4. Early in 1971 the Manpower Administration established guidelines for use by the affiliated state Employment Service agencies in developing the statistical information required by Revised Order No. 4:

> At present, current statistical data on the minority work force are not available for most labor areas. The 1970 Census of Population, when available, will provide reasonably comprehensive and recent data on the minority population, employment status, and major occupational group of employed and unemployed minority workers in each SMSA (Standard Metropolitan Statistical Area) and individual county in the country.... In the meantime, existing data may provide some useful indicators relating to materials needed by Federal contractors for this program. The following guidelines ... are transmitted for the use of State agency labor market analyst staff in developing estimates to meet requests by contractors and other Government agencies in connection with this order.[5]

A subsequent federal letter updated the guidelines because the 1970 census had become available.[6]

Similarly, another release from the Manpower Administration stated that

> ... although compliance and enforcement activities are not within the province of State Employment Security Agencies, State agencies should provide factual information and technical assistance to employers covered by these orders.[7]

These approaches dealt with the quantitative aspects of implementation (i.e., the preparation of the basic data needed in goal setting). The more complicated legal problems were not covered until January 1974, when the Equal Employment Opportunity Commission issued its two-volume guidebook for employers entitled "Affirmative Action and Equal Employment." By this time many cases had been decided in court, and Revised Order No. 4 was 3 years old. However, the most controversial area, and the one presenting the most technical difficulties comprises personnel management and human issues, and this subject still is not adequately covered by official guidelines.

One can well understand the dilemma confronting the administrators responsible for securing compliance. The overriding objective was and had to be equal employment opportunity. The legal aspects, at least initially, seemed to be tenuous. Personnel management issues were in controversy, and in many establishments the techniques used for hire and promotion were primitive. Under such conditions, and in analogous subject areas, good administrators tend to be flexible and probing: they initiate strong compliance actions when there is a disinclination to follow the mandate at all, and they are constructive and flexible when the efforts are sincere and bona fide. Most of all, the good administrator would seriously consider publishing a description of an employer's exemplary efforts to attain the objectives, especially if at least one employer was able to "find a way" on his own initiative and through his own creativity.

The Wagner experience demonstrated what many administrators learned long ago. Government must, at the very least, provide a point of view and a realistic direction for any proposed program. This should be followed by a partnership of the legislators, academicians, bureaucrats, and interest groups, with the ideas of bureaucratic line and staff units heavily weighted, to harmonize theory and feasibility in operable programs. It has become increasingly clear that no one of the groups involved in social legislation and its implementation can work effectively without interacting with all the others.

The Wagner study has documented the need for a sharper perception of roles and accountabilities of the four groups enumerated. There has been too great a lag in intercommunication and feedback in all directions. Too much time has been lost from conceptualization to implementation to feedback to redirection. The one essential is that all the concerned groups work as a unit from the beginning, and throughout the life of a legislative enactment, with particular attention to the viability of the programs. Theory must be tempered by and adjusted to operating and technological realities if objectives are to be fulfilled.

How much change will occur because of the legislation and its effective implementation? The Wagner experience has indicated that change did occur, within the college bureaucracy, within the employee group, and generally throughout the campus. As stated in the previous chapter, employees sensed a new direction and expressed new hope. It appeared that the college was interested in all employees—that because of Affirmative Action, personnel management measures would be taken to assist interested employees toward self-actualization. Wagner officials were, therefore, prepared to implement a program that they realized was operable and acceptable to their employees. But was this attitude attributable to the requirements of the law, or was it adopted because the objectives of the program were just, and the plan developed to implement these desirable social goals was sensible and beneficial? Or perhaps this program was adopted because the college would lose federal money if noncompliance were proved, and they were already in a financial bind? One wonders whether acceptance and viability are due to the small staff and the compact campus. A longitudinal study is needed to sort out and evaluate the relative importance of each of these issues, as well as to estimate whether these affirmative values will continue.

A more specific issue is the net value of the technology used (i.e., the USES Job Analysis Formulation and the *DOT*). How much did these contribute to Affirmative Action at Wagner, and how great a contribution can they be expected to make to general economic well-being if they become more widely used? In making such as assessment it is obviously necessary once again to keep in mind that many factors are needed to secure the intended objectives and that the USES job analysis technology is only one. Moreover, such an evaluation must be composed of the following steps:

1. Determine the extent of the reduction of frictional and structural unemployment in a given establishment or community through improving hiring and promotion criteria (assuming that other jobs are available for the structurally displaced). The assumption is that the job analysis technology makes possible the assignment and reassignment of qualified workers to jobs they can and want to perform; thus job vacancies will be filled more quickly, and turnover and absenteeism will be minimized.

2. Appraise the benefits of the uses of this technology in job restructuring, job enrichment, and morale improvement.

3. Ascertain how much the improvements can help in reducing the number of unemployed immediately and in the future, in minimizing the costs of unemployment compensation, and in pointing the direction for a more productive capital-labor mix.

4. Examine whether the technology can make workers more content through the provision of meaningful work which might contribute to their growth, development, and effectiveness. Did productivity increase?

5. Ascertain how much this definitional technology can contribute to the formulation of a national manpower policy, recognizing that it can be used in many aspects of personnel management, individual career planning, and the measurement and forecasting of manpower imbalances.

Replication of the Wagner model to establishments of varying sizes in different industries, and a series of longitudinal studies, can provide answers to these questions. For the present, the findings of the Wagner study form a preliminary basis for future evaluations and will indicate the type of research needed for these purposes.

NOTES

1. For an explanation of the functioning of a work committee, see Clement J. Berwitz, "The Work Committee, an Administrative Technique," *Harvard Business Review,* Vol. 30, no. 1 (January–February 1952), pp. 110–124.

2. U.S. Department of Health, Education and Welfare, *Higher Education Guidelines,* Executive Order 11246 (Washington D.C.: Office of the Secretary, Office and Rights, October 1, 1972.)

3. The most recent statement appears in the Comprehensive Employment and Training Act of 1973 (PL 93-203, S. 1559, December 28, 1973): "It is the purpose of this title to establish a program to provide comprehensive manpower services throughout the Nation.

Such program shall include the development and creation of job opportunities and the training, education, and other services needed to enable individuals to secure and retain employment at their maximum capacity" (Section 101). This actually restates similar intentions which appeared in the Manpower Development and Training Act of 1962, and in statements made by high level government officials including President Lyndon B. Johnson.

4. See E. Wight Bakke, *A Positive Labor Market Policy* (Columbus, Ohio: Charles E. Merrill, 1963), Chapter 6.

5. U. S. Department of Labor, Manpower Administration, Reports and Analysis Letter No. 716, February 24, 1971, p. 2 (mineograph copy).

6. U. S. Department of Labor, Manpower Administration, Reports and Analysis Letter No. 816, August 28, 1973 (Xerox copy).

7. U. S. Department of Labor, Manpower Administration, TESPL. 2764; December 7, 1972.

CHAPTER 7

SUMMARY OF
THE STUDY RESULTS

This report has included a methodology for Affirmative Action and a statement of the preliminary findings on its initial use at Wagner College. The presentation began with the premise that the design and its implementation apparently exceeds congressional and administrative intentions. Revised Order No. 4 emphasized the need to achieve equal employment opportunity by fostering a more equitable employment penetration of minorities and women across the occupational spectrum. We postulated that the best way to meet this goal would be to provide Affirmative Action to *all* segments of the population, whether employed or unemployed, and without reference to race, color, religion, national origin, or sex; and selected the USES Job Analysis Formulation and its derivative *Dictionary of Occupational Titles* (*DOT*) as the technology to achieve these aims. The objective was to determine how well these instruments would function.

The problem was presented within the context of a nation groping toward the development of a manpower policy of which Affirmative Action is but one component. Other factors mentioned in earlier chapters include the need to determine and predict supply-demand imbalances in manpower. We stressed the need to link the issues and problems created by such imbalances to the following areas:

1.   Input-output analysis, to determine the sectors of enterprise to be expanded and manipulated through policies such as those pertaining to fiscal and monetary matters (including tax incentives for giving employment to persons on welfare) and vocational training;

2.   Improving selection and promotion criteria through the preparation

of complete and realistic position descriptions leading to accurate selection and promotion criteria;

3. Determinations of occupational training needs, quantitatively and qualitatively (course content), to ensure that qualified workers are available where and when needed;

4. Creating an adequate and responsive (public) manpower delivery system that can provide placement and vocational counseling services taking advantage of computer technology;

5. Identifying equitable opportunities for rewarding employment for the disadvantaged and minorities to overcome prior neglect;

6. Mounting an affirmative program to restore welfare recipients to full participation in the nation's economy.

Chapter 4 presented the Wagner College Plan and the legal requirements of Revised Order No. 4, which the plan implements. Chapter 5 outlined the quantitative and qualitative support for the hypothesis that *DOT 3* can contribute to the achievement of the aims of equal employment opportunity to be attained through affirmative action. The quantitative facts are related to the presentation of the necessary data, with particular reference to the determination of the availability of minorities and women with requisite skills in a contractor's immediate or surrounding locale, or in the area in which he can recruit. Many of the basic data on population and work force must be presented by census and (Equal Employment Opportunity Commission) major categories, but the EEO-1 Report does suggest consulting the *DOT* for "further clarification" although the precise reason is not clear.

The most critical item of information is the availability of persons with requisite skills. It was pointed out that this can be obtained only by special surveys of current job seekers. The best source for such data is generally conceded to be the files of job seekers registered at state Employment Services, which are affiliated with the Manpower Administration. The Employment Services use the *DOT* as the sole vehicle for presenting occupational data. Although *placements* are reported by the Standard Industrial Classification Code, that code is not used to identify job seekers. The conversion of *DOT* codes to census codes is possible, but it is feasible only if performed centrally, since state Employment Services report their transactions for computer processing under the national Employment Security Automated Reporting System program. Conceivably therefore, the state Employment Services could supply such data for the "active" occupations in an area and this is now under consideration at least for some states.

Reporting by *DOT* code makes possible the preparation of (*a*) a supply-demand matrix for local Employment Service "jurisdictions," and (*b*) projections by *DOT* Worker Trait Groups, at least for jobs of lower levels of complexity. Such projections might be possible for all 114 Worker Trait Groups. Moreover, the *DOT* matrix might be related to the national input-output matrix. If this worked out, the benefits of input-output analysis would be applicable to national *occupational* manpower planning, which, for example, might provide national incentives designed among other things, to equalize supply and demand. Thus from the quantitative point of order, the value of *DOT is* supported. A review of the qualitative factors provided equally significant observations.

The USES Job Analysis Formulation comprises a series of building blocks as a structured frame of reference, ensuring that all significant details are obtained and classified. This technique was used in developing position descriptions for the 116 nonfaculty positions at Wagner; the "qualifications profile" for each was recorded and compared with the nationally developed "stereotyped" profiles. Little significant difference was disclosed, and a contractor who must fill the types of jobs found at Wagner College is probably safe in assuming that his staff will not have to make qualifications profiles, since those for his jobs closely parallel national patterns. Further studies are required to establish whether this is true for other occupations, particularly in the blue-collar area; this postulate may not hold where local job variables or job combinations are significant. Supervisors and department heads at Wagner found that the depth and detail employed in the position descriptions was necessary and would be useful to achieve many of the objectives of personnel management, including interviewing and counseling employees and job seekers applying at the gate.

Each employee at Wagner (and each outside job applicant) participated in an interview structured on the building blocks of *DOT*. We wanted to (*a*) assist each employee toward self-clarification of his job aims at Wagner or outside it, and (*b*) stimulate him to "bid" at any time for any job for which he thought we was qualified or qualifiable. A third objective of the interview was to explain the Affirmative Action Plan. Each employee's opinion of the value of the interview was solicited (and recorded) at the conclusion of each interview; several weeks later, employees were requested to fill out, anonymously, a questionnaire inquiring about their views of the value of the interview. The vast majority agreed that the interview was rewarding. Many stated that the interviews also fully explained Affirmative Action.

Attention was directed to the other elements and mechanics for Affirmative Action: posting job vacancies, soliciting bids, filing all records in an Opportunity File (arranged by Worker Trait Groups). The file is to be used as an inventory of skills of all employees, and as a means of retrieving names of employees and job seekers, including minorities and women, to fill any vacancy, thereby ensuring objective consideration of all interested persons with requisite skills in selection.

Throughout Chapter 4, as well as in the preceding chapter, attention was focused on the specific requirements of Revised Order No. 4, and the devices designed to implement each. It appears that the Wagner Plan meets these requirements. Moreover, from the qualitative point of view it is clear that the *DOT* (and the USES Job Analysis Formulation) did contribute to fulfilling the aims of Affirmative Action.

COSTS AND FEASIBILITY OF REPLICATION

The Wagner experience demonstrated that the plan can work at Wagner, will little or no additional cost for the first year of operation. Additional costs will be necessary to update the position descriptions from time to time, and to interview-counsel each employee as necessary. Thus the following additional future costs would be necessary: (*a*) for updating position descriptions (1.25–1.75 days for each, including preparation of the initial draft and correcting for 25%[1] determined to be necessary by supervisors, and (*b*) for counseling interviews (1 hour each).

The costs of file maintenance were negligible. Therefore, the Wagner Affirmative Action Plan appears to be desirable and feasible for that institution, and only minimal, tolerable costs are foreseen. To replicate the plan in other establishments, four areas require consideration: (*a*) initial training in the *DOT* and the USES Job Analysis Formulation; (*b*) preparing position descriptions; (*c*) counseling employees; (*d*) developing a retrieval file, which also becomes an inventory of skills, knowledge, abilities, and job preferences of all employees.

INITIAL TRAINING OF STAFF

The first Wagner staffers to be trained were the personnel director and two women recently promoted from responsible secretarial jobs to be personnel technicians. Both technicians were high school graduates with a background of one or two college courses. The initial training was 15 hours (not continuous) followed by demonstrations and dialogues over a period of 9 months.[2] After the explanatory sessions, the technicians observed trained New York State occupational analysts interview incumbents and their supervisors in connection with preparing position descriptions; they also listened in on counseling interviews conducted by the author. The personnel director and the two technicians now believe that they are able to prepare good position descriptions and to conduct successful counseling interviews. I fully concur.

This amount of intensive training is not feasible with any one contractor under government auspices. Such services can be contracted with private consulting firms at substantial cost (i.e., for staff training, for preparing position descriptions, for conducting counseling interviews). Interested individuals can become self-taught, but experience has indicated that interaction with an expert, through lectures or in conversation, is desirable. Alternatively, representatives from state Employment Services and the 10 Occupational Analysis Field Centers can be asked to conduct brief seminars with employer representatives. Special additional government funding might be needed if this activity is to be extensive.

One long-term solution to the training problem involves colleges and universities. Many institutions offer courses in job analysis and in the *DOT*, but few provide these in sufficient depth. (Recently, however, the University of Missouri and the New School for Social Research, in New York, have begun to offer integrated courses of study in "Manpower Science.") The need is for courses in the *DOT*, job analysis, counseling, and related subjects, designed to qualify students to become practitioners in this area of the "human resources discipline." Such training should also qualify students in such elements as job restructuring, constructing career ladders and lattices, and designing manpower matching systems for computer operations. These elements were not attempted by Wagner personnel technicians. Under such a broad training program, qualified staff could be available in personnel departments to perform all aspects of personnel management, including those comprising the Wagner Plan. It is evident that such training is feasible, but most of it must be provided outside government. In the long run, this would best be accomplished through established college and university courses like the one offered by the School of Industrial and Labor Relations of Cornell University.[3]

Assuming the competency of personnel technicians to prepare position descriptions, how practical is it to require each facility to prepare this material at a cost of 1.5 man days each for the initial work, plus typing drafts, reviews by supervisors, correction, and final typing? For example, a large eastern university has a roster of 800 jobs. Processing time would be 9,600 hours for initial preparation of position descriptions and an additional 2,400 hours for correcting drafts after review. Six technicians could perform the job in a minimum of one year. As stated in earlier chapters, other options are available. Perhaps the most useful would be to request the Manpower Administration to develop a new type of job description, more detailed than the *DOT* definition but less detailed than the job analysis schedules prepared in individual establishments. The material would be developed from job analysis schedules, when prepared. A list of abbreviated schedules could be made available for purchase by interested employers at a nominal fee.

For the time being, personnel technicians can use the *DOT* definitions, locating for each establishment job title, the equivalent *DOT* title and description. This would serve as a base for reviewing the job duties associated with a given position, and updating the detail in the *DOT* definition as necessary. Personnel technicians would then adapt the definitions to meet local needs at perhaps a third the cost that would be incurred by individual establishments starting from scratch.

Many employers prepare job and position descriptions, but often include insufficient detail for the type of personnel management contemplated by the Wagner College Plan. Each facility would have to determine the additional depth needed to update its position descriptions. A desirable spinoff would occur if each such description were identified by *DOT* title and code, thus measurably increasing the ability of local offices of the state Employment Service to meet employer needs when referrals are requested. Most authorities on personnel management agree that written position descriptions are indispensable, and the need for developing such material in the detail used at Wagner has been established. The costs of preparation must be borne by contractors.

COUNSELING INTERVIEWS

Since the Wagner experience indicated that 84.7% of those interviewed considered the session to be rewarding, it seems reasonable to make every attempt to conduct a full counseling interview with each employee at the time of hire, and say, annually thereafter. This would not only serve the needs of Affirmative Action but also should make all employees more productive (assuming that individuals will produce more if they believe themselves to have their best possible assignment, and provided vacancies are available and transfers are made). The average time cost for the interview is one hour for the personnel technician, plus one hour's absence of the employee from production.

The character and extent of counseling will vary among organizations. Degree of counseling is a function of the organizational climate, personnel policies in the organization and in the home community, and the temper of the times. If the time cost for such interviews exceeds the facility's budget, the type of counseling conducted at Wagner could be scheduled on a request basis only; that is, all employees would be notified that career counseling is available but will be provided only on request.

CAMPUS ATTITUDES

From the beginning, the interviews conducted by the author generated positive attitudes toward the program. Campus feedback is evolving as more of the employees are interviewed. Some of the employees told the personnel office they "couldn't wait" until they had *their* interview. The personnel technicians reported that most of the interviewees found the experience very rewarding. For some, the interview provided a forum for attitudes toward supervisors and higher administrative levels. Some employees were grateful for the chance to "bid" for other jobs because they were afraid to tell their supervisors they wanted another assignment. The personnel director has stated that *few* of the many employers with whom Wagner deals have shown the kind of interest in their employees required by the Wagner Plan. She believes that the operation of the plan has been most salutary on the campus, having improved employee morale beyond her expectations. And the president of the college has expressed his appreciation in a letter, which appears in Appendix W. In conclusion, the Wagner Plan documented the need for the type of counseling used in the Hawthorne experiment and also demonstrated the values of occupational counseling for upward mobility at Wagner and outside it.

DEVELOPING A RETRIEVAL FILE

The Wagner College personnel file of all employees is arranged by Worker Trait Group, then by six-digit *DOT* code and title. For each six digit code and title, Supplement 1 of the *DOT* indicates the Worker Trait Group that accommodates it. File dividers for each WTG were printed with a list of "related Worker Trait Groups" (i.e., WTGs with occupations that are related to the WTG in question). When a vacancy occurred, the six-digit title and code for the job was identified by Worker Trait Group. Reference was to the specific six-digit code and title in that group, to locate candidates with the requisite traits, skills, knowledge, ability, and experience. If the first search was unsuccessful, job candidate records in other codes in the same six-digit code group were reviewed. (Recall that a code group comprises one or more titles, each coded with the same six digits. Thus the 14,000 defined titles in the *DOT* are identified by 3,000 six-digit codes.) If the second search was unavailing, reference was made to other six-digit codes in that WTG, then to related Worker Trait Groups (as printed on the file divider), and the process was repeated. Any facility that uses *DOT* codes and titles should have little difficulty in creating such a file.

Computerized files may be more rewarding for large installations than the foregoing method, and the Employment Services in 12 states are experimenting with system designs and computer programs. New York State uses the *DOT* code and title and some 35 other descriptors. In practice, the record of each employee and job seeker would be coded for all 36 factors, and the computer would select the five most qualified individuals on the basis of preestablished "weights" for given descriptors. To operate such a system, personnel technicians must know the concepts thoroughly and be fully versed in the structure of the *DOT*.

Another variant of computer manpower matching substitutes some of the *DOT* and job analysis building blocks for a specific code. This approach would overcome coding limitations and coding errors: six-digit codes pigeonhole people. What is needed is a means to cut across code lines on the basis of commonalities such as Worker Trait factors, thus broadening a job seeker's chances of being selected for suitable job openings. It is the author's opinion that this will be common practice in the future. The extremely high costs of developing and maintaining computerized manpower matching systems would be reduced if the government made its best designs and programs available at minimum cost to any employer who wanted them. Since the identification and location of job candidates for promotion or initial hire must occur after job vacancies are disclosed, a suitable file is necessary for storing and retrieving candidate records. Most employers maintain at least rudimentary files, arranged by job title or alphabetically by candidate name. The Wagner College Plan employs the Worker Trait Group method of filing, and any employer who uses the *DOT* coding structure can adopt or adapt it. In the long run, and for large installations, the best method may prove to be computer retrieval, including programs that eliminate overrefined job classifications; this would require the use of "descriptors" that cut across and in fact ignore job titles, for many are nondescriptive.

SUMMARY

A substantial investment in staff time was necessary to install and to operate the Wagner College Affirmative Action plan, but the benefits outweighed the costs. However, the Wagner College Plan cannot be replicated in other establishments without an expenditure of considerable time and money. This has serious policy implications for employers, the government agencies concerned with compliance, and the sectors of the national government responsible for the formulation of long-term manpower programs and policies. The factors involved are concepts, techniques, and costs. Many of the ingredients needed to formulate such programs and policies are known, available, or in use. It remains to assemble those which are viable within a total system context, and to target for further research and development elements whose contributions are inadequate or limited. Before discussing the types of research needed, it would be well to consider the policy implications of the use of the *DOT* and the data gathered in the Wagner study.

NOTES

1. New York State supervisory occupational analysts report this percentage to be reasonably constant.

2. Four months on-the-job training by a skilled expert supervisor would be adequate, but the longer period was necessary at Wagner because neither the author nor the technicians were always available to one another.

3. In the fall of 1973, at the request of the Industrial and Labor Relations School of Cornell University, the author trained and monitored graduate students in the preparation of position descriptions for some nonfaculty jobs at Cornell. This pilot program may be expanded.

CHAPTER 8

POLICY IMPLICATIONS
OF THE STUDY

In this presentation, the variables were restricted to optimum conditions in a tight labor market situation (i.e., demand exceeds supply). Under such conditions, employers ordinarily cannot find workers with the precise experience, skills, and knowledges to permit maximal production immediately after hire. Instead, employers are forced to seek minimally qualified or *qualifiable* candidates who have related experience or potentials to produce acceptably after training on the job. These are the circumstances under which *DOT 3* makes it strongest contribution to personnel management.[1] The Worker Traits formulation and structure should allow trained placement practitioners skilled in the *DOT* technology to help the employer make the best possible accommodation to labor market restrictions.

Similarly, skilled counselors, fully informed about the *DOT* technology, should be able to assist the counselee to identify his occupational assets and liabilities in keeping with his self-concept and aspiration levels. Having done this through an evolving counseling process, the skilled counselor should be able to help the counselee relate his identified assets to the world of work *and* the matching job opportunities available at given times. Where supply in the occupation of his choice exceeds demand, the task is to help the counselee make the best adjustment possible in a "directed" fashion (i.e., to accept only jobs that are within the "career direction" the counselee has decided to follow).

It is evident that the *DOT* offers a rational system in a relatively unstable occupational world in which unforeseen contingencies operate directly or indirectly, often adversely, on rational decisions made on the assumption that a stable, controllable condition would prevail, at least in the short run. This is the area in which government can play an effective role. Suppose that data can be gathered and presented in a timely fashion, and that fiscal and monetary policy have been sufficiently tested and accepted to enable the administration to adopt courses of action designed to bring supply and demand into equilibrium. Under these conditions, much of the type of planning envisioned in this presentation by employers, job seekers, and counselees will be more realistic and more readily accomplished.

To bring such a state into being requires new perspectives by government, employers and workers. Since the Employment Act of 1946, the federal government has mounted a series of programs designed to rationalize the economy. Those which concern manpower were intended to assist the individual to determine the kind of work most suitable to him and to make it possible for people to receive the necessary training and experience under government funding. One of the most explicit government pronouncement was Revised Order No. 4, which requires that qualified or qualifiable minorities and women be given the opportunity to prove *their merits* in gainful employment. Since the Wagner College study, another dimension was added by government in the Comprehensive Employment and Training Act (December 28, 1973). Note the following section, for example.

TITLE V—NATIONAL COMMISSION FOR MANPOWER POLICY

FINDINGS AND DECLARATION OF PURPOSE

SEC. 501. (*a*)   The Congress finds and declares that the responsibility for the development, administration, and coordination of programs of training and manpower development generally is so diffused and fragmented at all levels of government that it has been impossible to develop rational priorities in these fields, with the result that even good programs have proved to be far less effective than could reasonably be expected. The Congress further finds that the lack of a coherent, flexible, national manpower policy reduces our prospects of solving economic and social problems which threaten fundamental national interests and objectives.

(b)   Accordingly, the purpose of this title is to establish a National Commission for Manpower Policy which will have the responsibility for examining these issues, for suggesting ways and means of dealing with them, and for advising the Secretary [of Labor] on national manpower issues.

Employers however, are just beginning to understand these intentions; thus such measures as Executive Order 11598 (now P.L. 92-540) require government contractors to list their vacancies with state Employment Services, thereby making opportunities available to veterans, particularly Vietnam era veterans. Similarly, Affirmative Action measures were formulated to require contractors to hire and promote without reference to race, color, religion, national origin, or sex. Perhaps more important, as Chapter 1 indicated, many employers understand neither the requirements of the jobs in their establishments nor the qualifications needed for successful average performance. We have seen that the *DOT* can contribute significantly to resolving such problems, provided the employer *accepts* its underlying premises and tests them by utilizing the *DOT* approach. It is equally important for employers to change their perspective about employees (i.e., to accept the fact that workers perceive themselves to be entitled to meaningful work, consistent with production requirements). Recent trends in motivational research and job recruitment indicate that many employers have concluded that such measures will be in their own self-interest as well as their employees'. However, many employers are unaware of the potential contribution of the *DOT* approach and the benefits it can bring in this area.

Workers, too, require new perspectives. Too many workers believe that a job need not or should not be fulfilling. Instead of attempting to secure assistance in clarifying their job aims, needs, and potentials, they accept the first available job, regardless of whether it suits them. Many drop out of school to follow the same pattern. It is clear that more work is needed in the schools and churches, and through community efforts, to change the current worker and employer orientation—to teach people that work should be rewarding psychologically as well as monetarily and that individuals should chart out their own career direction, after counseling that begins in the elementary schools and continues throughout the individual's occupational lifetime. If this were done, people would make conscious compromises in accepting available temporary work until they find a more suitable job that fits their career planning.

The Department of Labor and other federal agencies continue to finance projects by nongovernment investigators on aspects of manpower and to engage consulting firms to develop or evaluate manpower systems. Each such project is "monitored" by the funding government agency in the sense that steps are taken to ensure that schedules are met and the research follows the initial guidelines developed. However, there is little evidence that any one agency or interdepartmental committee representing the agencies is coordinating the research and evaluating it to ensure that the results are synthesized and made available to the agencies of jurisdiction for consideration and use in their developmental work.[2] This indicates the desirability of setting up a federal instrumentality to review the state of the art, to solicit the assistance of the universities and other experts, to explore the "gaps," and to coordinate all the contributing efforts. Chapter 1 underscored the importance of such a total systems approach.

It appears that it is essential for government, employers, the individual, and the manpower delivery system to reappraise their perspectives on their respective roles, obligations, and rewards. The passage of the Comprehensive Employment and Training Act suggests that government is at last pointed in the right direction—some 27 years after the Employment Act of 1946. This seems to confirm that the manpower delivery system (the state Employment Services being the largest unit) will implement this philosophy within the framework stated. Hopefully, individuals will begin to accept as fact the government's findings that individuals are entitled to meaningful jobs that contribute to the fulfillment of their potentials. And with such measures as the requirement to initiate Affirmative Action for all employees, employers too will see the light; then, ideally, they will learn that this stimulus is in the direction of their self-interest.

The chief residual issue, however, is the availability of the technology for securing individual, employer, and national supply-demand equilibrium. As stated in earlier chapters, this subject is controversial. Little unanimity exists, for example, on vocational choice and occupational counseling theory. A substantial amount of research is in process, but each investigator appears to follow his own predilections. Research projects under government funding are subject to loose monitoring, with little if any effort exerted toward a directed, coordinated approach to fill in the gaps and to resolve controversies. Some workers are centering their research on changing or adapting some of the *DOT* building blocks to resolve what they consider to be the *DOT* shortcomings.

Most of the enactments dealing with manpower provide funding for research and development. Note, for example, the implications of the following section of the Comprehensive Employment and Training Act of 1973.

Part B—Research, Training, and Evaluation

RESEARCH

Sec. 311. (*a*) To assist the Nation in expanding work opportunities and assuring access to those opportunities for all who desire it, the Secretary shall establish a comprehensive program of manpower research utilizing the methods, techniques, and knowledge of the behavioral and social sciences and such other methods, techniques, and knowledge as will aid in the solution of the Nation's manpower problems. This program will include, but not be limited to, studies, the findings of which may contribute to the formulation of manpower policy; development or improvement of manpower programs; increased knowledge about labor market processes; reduction of unemployment and its relationships to price stability; promotion of more effective manpower development, training, and utilization; improved national, regional, and local means of measuring future labor demand and supply; enhancement of job opportunities; skill training to qualify employees for positions of greater skill, responsibility, and remuneration; meeting of manpower shortages; easing of the transition from school to work, from one job to another, and from work to retirement; opportunities and services for older persons who desire to enter or reenter the labor force, and for improvements of opportunities for employment and advancement through the reduction of discrimination and disadvantage arising from poverty, ignorance, or prejudice.

Hopefully, some of these funds will be used to develop further the *DOT* technology, which, the Wagner College Plan indicates, offers the most powerful means now available to meet the multifaceted requirements of securing Affirmative Action. It is the author's opinion that only government can supply the funding, the total objectivity and commitment, and the means for testing needed to establish the technology. Although many of the views and findings of "competing" independent researchers are interesting, the magnitude and scale of the research needed is beyond the means ordinarily available to an individual investigator. And many workers in this field are devoting their current efforts to making slight changes or adaptations of the *DOT* and USES Job Analysis Formulation. (Appendix H relates some *DOT* traits to Super's Work Values Inventory.) The nation could use a human resources Manhattan District project to discover and to test a new technology.

RESEARCH NEEDED IN JOB ANALYSIS

The developers of the current USES Job Analysis Formulation have stated on many occasions, particularly during installations and training sessions, that the framework now used is not "final," that it is but a step in the right direction. The experience of the 10 Occupational Analysis Field Centers has confirmed that the system is viable and seems to be adequate for studying jobs. Its usefulness in other applications remains to be validated. For this reason, the USES is conducting field research[3] into the adequacy of some aspects of the *DOT*. Additional research and demonstration projects looking into the possible substitution of "vocabularies" for *DOT* codes in computer-assisted placement should disclose the values and deficiencies of the system, particularly since these vocabularies include the building blocks of the Job Analysis Formulation as well as other factors that reflect competencies including "knowledges."[4] Further areas for suggested research follow.

The Job Analysis Formulation

It is not certain whether the components of the Job Analysis Formulation are complete: do Worker Functions; Work Fields; Machines, Tools, Equipment, and Work Aids; Materials, Products, Subject Matter, and Service; and the Worker Traits (GED, SVP, aptitudes, interests, temperaments, physical factors, and working conditions) embrace *all* the parameters needed to describe jobs and job relationships? Further research may be needed to answer some of the following questions. For example, is each ingredient of each component valid? What is the relative contribution of each to the total system? Under what conditions can each be subordinated to the other components, and to other elements comprising the Job Analysis Formulation? What is the best method for studying jobs: the observation–interview method wherein a trained occupational analyst studies the worker at his job, watching his observable moves and discussing them with the worker, his supervisor, and the personnel office? Is there a better, less costly way?

It is now essential to look at the two areas for research involving the worker side of the question: those which concern vocational guidance, and those which relate to self-concept, aspiration levels, and motivation. The *DOT* addresses only the former. It rests on the premise that the factors that describe jobs can also be used to diagnose people. Thus it assumes that the individual's traits can be identified and related to jobs defined in the same "trait terms."

The Wagner College study indicated that the building blocks of the *DOT* can be used as a structured frame of reference to identify employee traits and needs, which can then be related to other jobs, either in the establishment or outside it. Much more research is needed, however, to validate this approach in the following respects: (*a*) to determine whether the *DOT* building blocks are sufficiently complete for the purpose, (*b*) to ascertain how specific traits and factors can be estimated for specific workers and job seekers, and (*c*) to learn how much the individual's trait levels (e.g., for GED) can be improved and how.

Although additional research is needed with respect to the adequacy of the *DOT* structure in studying *job requirements,* it seems that the greatest priority should be given to the foregoing considerations, which relate to *worker* characteristics. This is particularly necessary because the structure used for studying jobs has served successfully for many years in relation to jobs needed in constructing the *DOT*. However, few directions have been issued[5] and used for *worker* diagnosis, and much of what has been formulated has not been subjected to controlled research.

The relation of the research described, and its potential impact on the structure of the *Dictionary of Occupational Titles* as such and its use as an information system, and instrumentation system, and a retrieval system,[6] are explored in the next section.

THE DICTIONARY OF OCCUPATIONAL TITLES

As an Information System

Several areas require further research and development before the *DOT* becomes a fully adequate information system.

The Definitions   The current definitions are intended as abbreviated statements of the data appearing on job analysis schedules, and the content should reflect all elements of the job analysis building blocks; however, many definitions do not fulfill these goals. The deficiency seems to stem from uneven editing of job definitions, and possibly different standards of supervision for the occupational analysts in the field centers that prepared the job analysis schedules.

Consideration should be given to expanding the definitions almost to the point necessary to serve as generalized job specifications, to be particularized for given positions by employer personnel technicians trained in job analysis. The Wagner experience tentatively indicated (*a*) that too much time was required to develop such specifications, and (*b*) that the variations in the Worker Traits for a given job assignment, as compared with those assigned by the *DOT,* are not substantial and are not unduly significant. Time and energy would be saved, and employer acceptance might come more swiftly, if the additional detail were provided to expedite the preparation of position descriptions. Some attention should be given to combining job titles and job definitions, particularly for low level jobs. Present practice requires the preparation of a job analysis schedule for every set of tasks comprising a job in a given establishment. This allows us to identify all constituent jobs within an industry,[7] but it compounds the problem of locating definitions in the *DOT* and complicates the present classification structure. One solution lies in listing all the titles found during the research, and defining them, but using a lesser number of codes. This would reduce coding problems drastically.

DOT as an Instrumentation System

"Tool" uses of the *DOT* include the classification structure, the use of the Worker Trait Groups in counseling and in recruitment, the use of the *DOT* building blocks in job restructuring, the construction of career ladders and lattices, and the use of the *DOT* building blocks as a frame of reference to determine applicant and employer needs.

The DOT Classification Structure   In the placement function, the primary uses of the *DOT* structure are to hasten the finding of related jobs for job seekers when jobs in their precise occupational code are not available, and to assist employers to recruit qualified workers when they cannot locate persons coded in the relevant occupational codes. In addition, data can be presented concerning employment and unemployment now and at future intervals, and *DOT* can help to relate counselee facts to the world of work to facilitate career exploration and career decision making. Thus the needs can be characterized in two dimensions: placement versus manpower projections. The chief problem in presenting manpower projections is to develop the projections: as a first step, the data are most readily obtained by *industries*, using such instruments as the Standard Industrial Classification Code to accommodate estimates made by economists and by employers for the goods they produce or the services they provide. To meet the needs identified in previous sections, projections must also be developed for *job seekers*, many of whose jobs cut across industrial lines. The solution appears to be to use an occupational matrix, in which the employment of specific occupational segments as a percentage of the totals for given industries are established by special surveys. This is the type of approach used in the BLS matrix.[8] Another refinement would be the development of such estimates by a methodology more closely related to the *DOT* (i.e., determining the percentage relation of *DOT* occupations to census occupations and relating this to Worker Trait Groups). This approach, which was selected by the New York State Department of Labor's Division of Research and Statistics,[9] leads to a review of the criteria used in the middle three digits of the nine-digit *DOT* code, reflecting levels of complexity for DATA, PEOPLE, THINGS. These levels, however, do not reflect Worker *Traits,* which are specified only in the Worker Trait Groups. However, in developing the matrix used by the author to represent the supply-demand situation for the area in which Wagner College is located (see Chart 2, Chapter 5), *Worker Trait Groups,* rather than Worker Function levels (i.e., the middle three digits) were used. Hence the issue is to determine which elements of the Job Analysis Formulation should be represented in the middle three digits: (*a*) the current levels of complexity for DATA, PEOPLE, THINGS; (*b*) Worker Trait Groups as presently constituted; or (*c*) other factors.

This area requires considerable research. The chief constraints are the needs (*a*) to develop that alternative that will be most useful for placement and for counseling (to relate counselee facts to matching career areas), (*b*) to create a solution that can be linked to the need for making manpower projections, and (*c*) to establish a further linkage to input-output analysis, since all these factors must be considered in developing a national manpower policy. Another important objective is a structure that will streamline employer manpower planning efforts; it should include the potentials for establishing promotion ladders and lattices while simultaneously using the building blocks of the Job Analysis Formulation as criteria for promotion and possibly job evaluation. It is the author's opinion that all the needed ingredients are available. Only further research and testing can identify the factors (such as GED or aptitudes) that best accommodate all the needs and goals named earlier.

The Worker Trait Groups designate the types of workers, rather than the types of jobs. The BLS matrix uses job titles, which designate *job* rather than *worker* requirements. The Worker Trait matrix is advantageous because for a given supply-demand imbalance, it reflects the kinds of workers available for jobs that are either in existence or should be developed for a community (by attracting the kind of enterprise that would hire such job seekers).

The Worker Trait Groups

As stated in earlier sections, the 114 WTGs cluster jobs by Worker Trait configurations; the groups are then identified by Worker Function levels, by group title, and by the number of the page in Volume II of *DOT 3* on which they are defined. An example appears below and on continuing pages.

The concept appears to be feasible, and demonstrations conducted by the author appear to document its validity, but the design of the groups is not consistent. Some embrace job titles with a range of SVP from 3 to 7. Some comprise a few titles, and others comprise several thousand. Additionally, although the clusters present common elements, in some instances substitutions are possible only after some incumbents have had substantial training, which means that substitution is not altogether realistic for practical placement purposes except for those individuals who had the training and experience in prior jobs. In some 40 Worker Trait Groups characterized by low levels of complexity substitutions seem to be feasible (see Appendix G). Much more research is needed to resolve these issues.

MANAGERIAL WORK

.168

Work Performed

Work activities in this group primarily involve organizing and coordinating the functions of a unit, department, or branch of an organization or establishment. Certain activities are concerned with the managing of one organization that is part of a larger chain or of an establishment of limited size and diversification. Also included is the planning and coordination of a singular program, project, or other organized endeavor, either public or private, originated for a specific purpose.

Worker Requirements

An occupationally significant combination of: ability to plan, initiate, and execute programs; ability to understand, interpret, and apply procedures and directives; numerical facility to analyze and use statistics and maintain production and inventory controls and records; leadership qualities; verbal facility; and the ability to relate to people in order to motivate and direct employees and to maintain good employer-employee and customer relationships.

Clues for Relating Applicants and Requirements

Successful experience in applicable work field at lower levels.
Academic preparation in pertinent coursework, such as business management.
Leadership qualities as indicated by elective offices held in academic or community environment.
Expressed interest in assuming management responsibilities.

Training and Methods of Entry

Promotion from within is the most common method employed for filling positions in this group. In some cases, however, employers desire new ideas, new techniques, new procedures, and new personalities, and recruit from outside the organization.

Most of the larger employers consider only those individuals who are recent college graduates. They look for an educational background consisting of appropriate personnel, vocational, business, merchandising, or similar coursework, and then provide their new employees with management-trainee programs which usually entail a combination of special training seminars and actual on-the-job training.

RELATED CLASSIFICATIONS

Administration (.118; .168) p. 237 [in *DOT 3*, Volume II]
Consultative and Business Services (.168; .268) p. 248
Supervisory Work (Clerical, Sales, and Related Activities) (.138) p. 243
Engineering, Scientific, and Technical Coordination (.168) p. 375

QUALIFICATIONS PROFILE

GED: 4 5
SVP: 6 7 8

Apt.	G	V	N		S	P	Q		K	F	M		E	C
	2	2	3		4	4	2		4	4	4		5	5
	1	1	2											

Int: 5 2   3
Temp: 1 4 5 9 0
Phys. Dem: S   L

07	**MEDICINE AND HEALTH**
077.	**Dietetic Work**
077.168	DIETETIC INTERN (profess. & kin.)
	DIETITIAN (profess. & kin.)
	DIETITIAN, ADMINISTRATIVE (profess. & kin.)
079.	**Medicine and Health, n.e.c.**
079.168	SUPERVISOR, CENTRAL SUPPLY (medical ser.)
09	**EDUCATION**
090.	**College and University Education**
090.168	DEPARTMENT HEAD, COLLEGE OR UNIVERSITY (education)

DIRECTOR OF INSTITUTIONAL RESEARCH (education)
SCHOLARSHIP COUNSELOR (education)

091.	**Secondary School Education**
091.168	MUSIC SUPERVISOR (education)
096.	**Home Economics, Agriculture, and Related Education**
096.168	DISTRICT EXTENSION SERVICE AGENT (gov. ser.)
	HOME-SERVICE DIRECTOR (profess. & kin.)
	SPECIALIST-IN-CHARGE, EXTENSION SERVICE (gov. ser.)

WEED-CONTROL SUPERVISOR (gov. ser.)

099. **Education, n.e.c.**
099.168 DIRECTOR, EXPERIMENTAL SCHOOLS IMPROVEMENT PROJECTS (education)
10 **MUSEUM, LIBRARY, AND ARCHIVAL SCIENCES**
100. **Library Work**
100.168 CHIEF LIBRARIAN, BRANCH OR DEPARTMENT (library)
FILM LIBRARIAN (library)
LIBRARIAN (library)
BOOKMOBILE LIBRARIAN (library)
CHILDREN'S LIBRARIAN (library)
PATIENTS' LIBRARIAN (library)
YOUNG-ADULT LIBRARIAN (library)
LIBRARIAN, REFERENCE LIBRARY (library)
LIBRARIAN, SPECIAL COLLECTIONS (library)
101. **Archival Science Work**
101.168 ARCHIVIST (profess. & kin.)
11 **LAW AND JURISPRUDENCE**
119. **Law and Jurisprudence, n.e.c.**
119.168 TITLE SUPERVISOR (profess. & kin.)
14 **ART WORK**
141. **Commercial Art**
141.168 PRODUCTION MANAGER, ADVERTISING (profess. & kin.)
143. **Photography**
143.168 TELEVISION-FILM FIELD COORDINATOR (motion pic.; radio & tv broad.)
15 **ENTERTAINMENT AND RECREATION**
*†. **Music**
152.168 MUSICAL PROGRAM DIRECTOR (radio & tv broad.)
153. **Athletics and Sports**
153.168 RACING SECRETARY AND HANDICAPPER (amuse. & rec.)
159. **Entertainment and Recreation, n.e.c.**
159.168 ANNOUNCER SUPERVISOR (radio & tv broad.)
ARTIST AND REPERTOIRE MAN (amuse. & rec.)
DIRECTOR (motion pic.; radio & tv broad.)
DIRECTOR, PROGRAM (radio & tv broad.) II
PRODUCTION MAN, INTERNATIONAL BROADCASTING (radio & tv broad.)
16 **ADMINISTRATIVE SPECIALTIES**
160. **Accounting and Auditing**
160.168 AUDITOR, COUNTY OR CITY (gov. ser.)
162. **Purchasing Management**
162.168 BUYER, GRAIN (grain & feed mill.; whole. tr.) I
BUYER, TOBACCO, HEAD (whole. tr.)
CLEAN-RICE MAN (grain & feed mill.)

SUPERVISOR, PROCUREMENT SERVICES (any ind.)
163. **Sales and Distribution Management**
163.168 HOME-LIGHTING-DEMONSTRATOR SUPERVISOR (light, heat, & power)
MANAGER, ADVERTISING (print & pub.)
164. Advertising Management
164.168 ACCOUNT EXECUTIVE (profess. & kin.)
DIRECTOR, MERCHANDISING DISPLAYS AND SPECIALTIES DEPARTMENT (paper goods)
165. **Public Relations Management**
165.168 DIRECTOR, TOURIST (gov. ser.)
166. **Personnel and Training Administrator**
166.168 BENEFITS-AND-SERVICE-RECORDS SUPERVISOR (any ind.)
DIRECTOR, CAST (motion pic.)
DIRECTOR OF PLACEMENT (education)
MANAGER, EMPLOYMENT (profess. & kin.)
PORT PURSER (water trans.)
SPECIAL AGENT (insurance)
168. **Inspecting and Investigating, Managerial and Public Service**
168.168 MANAGER, CREDIT AND COLLECTION (any ind.)
REGULATORY ADMINISTRATOR (tel. & tel.)
169. **Administrative Specialities, n.e.c.**
169.168 ADMINISTRATIVE ASSISTANT (any ind.)
ADMINISTRATIVE SECRETARY (any ind.)
CHEIF CLERK (any ind.)
ORDER DEPARTMENT SUPERVISOR (any ind.)
MANAGER, COPYRIGHT (radio & tv broad.)
MANAGER, ELECTRONIC DATA PROCESSING (profess. & kin.)
MANAGER, OFFICE (any ind.)
PROPERTY-DISPOSAL OFFICER (gov. ser.)
REGISTRAR, VITAL STATISTICS (gov. ser.)
18 **MANAGERIAL WORK, N.E.C.**
180. **Agricultural, Forestry, and Fishing Management**
180.168 AIRPLANE PILOT-CONSERVATION OFFICER (gov. ser.)
ARTIFICIAL-BREEDING DISTRIBUTOR (agric.)
FIELD SUPERVISOR, SEED PRODUCTION (agric.)
GENERAL MANAGER, FARM (agric.; whole tr.)
GROUP LEADER (agric.)
MANAGER, PRODUCTION, SEED CORN (agric.)
MIGRANT LEADER (agric.)

SUPERINTENDENT (agric.; can. & preserv.)

SUPERINTENDENT, PRODUCTION (agric.)

181. **Mining Management**
181.168 MANAGER, FIELD PARTY, GEOPHYSICAL PROSPECTING (petrol. production)
MINE FOREMAN (mining & quarrying)
SUPERINTENDENT, DRILLING AND PRODUCTION (petrol. production)

182. **Construction Management**
182.168 CONTRACTOR (const.)
ROADMASTER (r.r. trans)
SUPERINTENDENT, CONCRETE-MIXING PLANT (const.)
SUPERINTENDENT, CONSTRUCTION (const.)
SUPERINTENDENT, MAINTENANCE OF WAY (r.r. trans.)
SUPERVISOR, BRIDGES AND BUILDINGS (r.r. trans.)

183. **Manufacturiing Industry Management**
183.168 BREWMASTER (malt liquors)
CAR BUILDER, MASTER (loco. car bldg. & rep.)
GENERAL FOREMAN (any ind.) II
GENERAL FOREMAN (malt liquors)
GENERAL SUPERINTENDENT, MILLING (grain & feed mill.)
LOGGING CONTRACTOR (logging)
MANAGER, FOOD PROCESSING PLANT (can. & preserv.)
SERVICE SUPERVISOR, LEASED MACHINERY (mach. mfg.)
WINE MAKER (vinous liquors)

184. **Transportation, Communication, and Utilities Management**
184.168 CABLE FOREMAN, SUPERVISING (tel. & tel.)
DIRECTOR, OPERATIONS (radio & tv broad.)
DIRECTOR, OPERATIONS, BROADCAST (radio & tv broad.)
DIRECTOR, PROGRAM (radio & tv broad.) I
DIRECTOR, BROADCAST (radio & tv broad.) I
DIRECTOR, INTERNATIONAL PROGRAMS (radio & tv broad.)
PRODUCTION CHIEF (radio & tv broad.)
PRODUCTION CHEIF, INTERNATIONAL BROADCAST (radio & tv broad.)
DIRECTOR, SPORTS (radio & tv broad.)
DISPATCHER, CHIEF (petrol. production; petrol. refin.; pipe lines) I
FLIGHT SUPERVISOR, PHOTOGRAMMETRY (bus. ser.)
GENERAL AGENT, OPERATIONS (r.r. trans.)

INCINERATOR-PLANT-GENERAL FOREMAN (sanitary ser.)
MAINTENANCE SUPERVISOR (light, heat, & power)
184.186 MANAGER, BUS TRANSPORTATION (motor trans.)
MANAGER, LOCKER PLANT (motor trans.; whole. tr.)
MANAGER, STATION (air trans.)
MANAGER, TELEGRAPH OFFICE (tel. & tel.)
MANAGER, TERMINAL (motor trans.)
MANAGER, TRAFFIC (air trans.; motor trans.; water trans.)
MANAGER, TRAFFIC (any ind.)
MANAGER, TRAFFIC (motor trans.) I
MANAGER, TRAFFIC (radio & tv broad.)
MANAGER, TRAFFIC (tel. & tel.) I
MANAGER, TRAFFIC (tel. & tel.) II
MANAGER, WAREHOUSE (any ind.)
MANAGER, CHIEF, MATERIAL (petrol. production)
PORT-TRAFFIC MANAGER (water trans.)
SERVICE SUPERVISOR (light, heat & power)
STATION MASTER (r.r. trans.)
STATIONS-RELATIONS-CONTACT REPRESENTATIVE (radio & tv broad.)
SUPERINTENDENT, COLD STORAGE (any ind.)
SUPERINTENDENT, COMPRESSOR STATIONS (pipe lines)
SUPERINTENDENT, DISTRIBUTION (light, heat, & power) I
SUPERINTENDENT, DISTRIBUTION (light, heat, & power) II
SUPERINTENDENT, DIVISION (air trans.)
SUPERINTENDENT, DIVISION (motor trans.; r.r. trans.)
SUPERINTENDENT, ELECTRIC POWER (light, heat, & power)
OPERATION SUPERVISOR (light, heat, & power)
SUPERINTENDENT, GENERATION (light, heat, & power)
SUPERINTENDENT, SYSTEM OPERATION (light, heat, & power)
SUPERINTENDENT, TRANSMISSION (light, heat, & power)
SUPERINTENDENT, GAS PLANT (light, heat & power)
SUPERINTENDENT, MAINTENANCE OF EQUIPMENT (motor trans.; r.r. trans.)
SUPERINTENDENT, MARINE (water trans.)
SUPERINTENDENT, MEASUREMENT (petrol. production; pipe lines)

SUPERINTENDENT, METERS (light, heat, & power)

SUPERINTENDENT, PIPE LINES (pipe lines)

SUPERINTENDENT, POWER (r.r. trans.)

SUPERINTENDENT, STATION (tel. & tel.)

SUPERINTENDENT, STATIONS (air trans.)

SUPERINTENDENT, STATIONS (motor trans.; r.r. trans.)

SUPERINTENDENT, TERMINAL (water trans.)

WHARFINGER, HEAD (petrol. refin.; pipe lines)

SUPERINTENDENT, TESTS (light, heat, & power)

ELECTRICAL-TESTS SUPERVISOR (light, heat, & power)

SUPERINTENDENT, TRANSPORTATION (any ind.)

SUPERINTENDENT, WATERWORKS (waterworks)

SUPERVISOR OF TRANSMISSION (waterworks)

SUPERVISOR OF WAY (r.r. trans.)

SUPERVISOR, TERMINAL (motor trans.)

TERMINAL-SERVICES AGENT (motor trans.)

TESTING-AND-REGULATING CHIEF (tel. & tel.)

TRAFFIC CHIEF, RADIO COMMUNICATIONS (tel. & tel.)

TRANSPORTATION-MAINTENANCE FOREMAN (any ind.)

TRANSPORTATION SUPERVISOR (gov. ser.)

WATER-AND-SEWER-SYSTEMS SUPERVISOR (waterworks)

WATERMASTER (gov. ser.)

WHARFINGER, CHIEF (water trans.)

185. **Wholesale and Retail Trade Management**

185.168 COMMISSARY MAN (any ind.)

CONCESSION SUPERVISOR (ret. tr.)

MANAGER, DENTAL-SUPPLY HOUSE (bus. ser.)

MANAGER, DISTRIBUTION WAREHOUSE (whole. tr.)

MANAGER, DOUGHNUT SHOP (whole. tr.)

MANAGER, FOOD CONCESSION (hotel & rest.)

MANAGER, FRANCHISE PROMOTION (bus. ser.)

185.168 MANAGER, MERCHANDISE (ret. tr.; whole. tr.)

Con. MANAGER, PARTS (ret. tr.; whole tr.)

MANAGER, STORE (ret. tr.) I

MANAGER, STORE (ret. tr.) II

MANAGER, TOBACCO WAREHOUSE (whole. tr.)

SERVICE MANAGER (auto. ser.)

VENDING-STAND SUPERVISOR (gov. ser.)

WHOLESALER (whole. tr.)

CONVERTER (whole. tr.)

IMPORTER-EXPORTER (ret. tr.; whole. tr.)

186. **Finance, Insurance, and Real Estate Management**

186.168 BUILDING-SUPPLIES-AND-MOTOR-VEHICLE SUPERVISOR (tel. & tel.)

FOREIGN-EXCHANGE TRADER (banking)

MANAGER, APARTMENT HOUSE (hotel & rest.) I

MANAGER, HOUSING PROJECT (profess. & kin.)

MANAGER, INSURANCE OFFICE (insurance)

MANAGER, PROPERTY (real estate)

MANAGER, RENTAL DEPARTMENT (petrol. production)

MARKET MASTER (ret. tr.; whole tr.)

OPERATIONS OFFICER (banking)

RESERVE OFFICER (banking)

SECURITIES TRADER (banking)

SUPERVISOR, CREDIT UNION (finan. inst.)

187. **Service Industry Management**

187.168 APPLIANCE-SERVICE SUPERVISOR (light, heat, & power)

CATERER (per. ser.)

DIRECTOR, AGRICULTURAL LABOR CAMP (profess. & kin.)

DIRECTOR, FOOD AND BEVERAGE (hotel & rest.)

DIRECTOR, FUNERAL (per. ser.)

DIRECTOR, HOBBY SHOP (amuse. & rec.)

DIRECTOR, NURSES' REGISTRY (medical ser.)

DIRECTOR, SCHOOL LUNCH PROGRAM (hotel & rest.)

DIRECTOR, VOLUNTEER SERVICES (medical ser.)

EXECUTIVE HOUSEKEEPER (hotel & rest.; medical ser.)

HUNTSMAN (amuse. & rec.)

MANAGER, BARBER SHOP (per. ser.)

MANAGER, BEAUTY SHOP (per. ser.)

MANAGER, CAFETERIA OR LUNCHROOM (hotel & rest.)

MANAGER, CAMP (const.)

MANAGER, CATERING (hotel & rest.)

MANAGER, CEMETERY (per. ser.)

MANAGER, CONVENTION (hotel & rest.)

MANAGER, DANCE STUDIO (education)

MANAGER, DENTAL LABORATORY (medical ser.)

MANAGER, FRONT OFFICE (hotel & rest.)

MANAGER, GOLF CLUB (amuse. & rec.)

MANAGER, LIQUOR ESTABLISHMENT (hotel & rest.)

MANAGER, MARINE SERVICE (ship & boat bldg. & rep.; water trans.)

MANAGER, MUTUEL DEPARTMENT (amuse. & rec.)

MANAGER, RECREATION ESTABLISHMENT (amuse. & rec.)

MANAGER, FISH AND GAME CLUB (amuse. & rec.)

MANAGER, GUN CLUB (amuse. & rec.)

MANAGER, RESIDENT (hotel & rest.) I

MANAGER, RESTAURANT OR COFFEE SHOP (hotel & rest.)

MANAGER, SALES (clean., dye., & press.)

MANAGER, SERVICE DEPARTMENT (whole. tr.)

MANAGER, SKATING RINK (amuse. & rec.)

MANAGER, STORAGE GARAGE (auto. ser.)

MANAGER, THEATER (amuse. & rec.)

MANAGER, TRAVELING (hotel & rest.)

MANAGER, VEHICLE LEASING AND RENTAL (auto. ser.)

MANAGER, WINTER SPORTS (amuse. & rec.)

ORGANIZER (profess. & kin.) I

PRODUCER (amuse. & rec.)

PRODUCER (motion pic.)

PRODUCER ASSISTANT (motion pic.)

PROGRAM DIRECTOR, GROUP WORK (profess. & kin.)

PROGRAM DIRECTOR, SCOUTING (nonprofit organ.)

SUPERINTENDENT, BUILDING (any ind.) II

SUPERINTENDENT, LAUNDRY (laund.)

SUPERINTENDENT, MAINTENANCE (air trans.)

SUPERINTENDENT, MAINTENANCE (motor trans.)

188. **Public Administration Management**

188.168 ASSESSOR-COLLECTOR, IRRIGATION TAX (gov. ser.)

BUSINESS ENTERPRISE SPECIALIST (gov. ser.)

CHIEF PROCTOR (gov. ser.)

CHIEF WARDEN (gov. ser.)

CUSTOMS AGENT (gov. ser.)

CUSTOMS COLLECTOR, ASSISTANT (gov. ser.)

CUSTOMS OFFICER (gov. ser.)

DIRECTOR, CLASSIFICATION AND TREATMENT (gov. ser.)

DIRECTOR, FINANCIAL RESPONSIBILITY DIVISION (gov. ser.)

DIRECTOR, SECURITIES AND REAL ESTATE (gov. ser.)

DIRECTOR STATE-ASSESSED PROPERTIES (gov. ser.)

ELECTION PROCEDURES ADVISOR (gov. ser.)

FEDERAL AID COORDINATOR (gov. ser.)

MANAGER, HOUSING AUTHORITY (gov. ser.)

MANAGER, RENT-CONTROL OFFICE (gov. ser.)

PARK SUPERINTENDENT (gov. ser.)

CHIEF, BOATING DIVISION (gov. ser.)

POSTMASTER (gov. ser.)

PROPERTY-UTILIZATION OFFICER (gov. ser.)

REVENUE AGENT (gov. ser.)

SUPERINTENDENT, MAILS (gov. ser.)

SUPERINTENDENT, SANITATION (gov. ser.)

UNCLAIMED PROPERTY TRUST OFFICER (gov. ser.)

189. **Miscellaneous Managerial Work, n.e.c.**

189.168 DIRECTOR, SERVICE (ret. tr.)

JUNIOR EXECUTIVE (any ind.)

MANAGER TRAINEE (any ind.)

SECURITY OFFICER (any ind.)

SUPERINTENDENT, MAGAZINE AREA (ammunition)

SUPERINTENDENT, MAINTENANCE (any ind.)

SUPERINTENDENT, PLANT PROTECTION (any ind.)

19 **MISCELLANEOUS PROFESSIONAL, TECHNICAL, AND MANAGERIAL WORK**

193. **Radio Operating**

193.168 CHIEF CONTROLLER (gov. ser.)

FIELD SUPERVISOR, BROADCAST (radio & tv broad.)

RADIO CHIEF (air trans.)

SUPERINTENDENT, RADIO COMMUNICATIONS (gov. ser.)

195. **Social and Welfare Work**

195.168 CASEWORK SUPERVISOR (profess. & kin.)

COMMUNITY ORGANIZATION WORKER (profess. & kin.)

DIRECTOR, CAMP (profess. & kin.)

DIRECTOR, FIELD (nonprofit organ.)

DIRECTOR, RECREATION CENTER (profess. & kin.)

SUPERINTENDENT, RELIEF CAMP (gov. ser.)

196. **Airplane Piloting and Navigating**

196.168 CHIEF PILOT (air trans.)

197. **Managerial and Technical Work, Water Transportation**

197.168 DREDGE CAPTAIN (water trans.)

FERRYBOAT CAPTAIN (water trans.)

MASTER, PASSENGER BARGE (water trans.)

MASTER, RIVERBOAT (water trans.)

	MASTER, SHIP (water trans.)		COMMANDING OFFICER, MOTOR
	PURSER (water trans.)		EQUIPMENT (gov. ser.)
198.	Managerial Work, Railroad Transpor-		DETECTIVE CHIEF (gov. ser.)
	tation		POLICE CAPTAIN, PRECINCT (gov.
198.168	CONDUCTOR, MIXED TRAIN (r.r.		ser.)
	trans.)	40	PLANT FARMING
	CONDUCTOR, PASSENGER CAR (r.r.	406.	Horticultural Specialty Work.
	trans.)	406.168	NURSERYMAN (agric.)
	CONDUCTOR, PULLMAN (r.r. trans.)	409.	Plant Farming, n.e.c.
	CONDUCTOR, ROAD FREIGHT (r.r.	409.168	MANAGER, FARM (agric.)
	trans.)	41	ANIMAL FARMING
29	MISCELLANEOUS MERCHANDIS-	412.	Poultry Farming
	ING WORK	412.168	MANAGER, HATCHERY (agric.)
292.	Route Work	44	FORESTRY
292.168	ROUTEMAN (print. & pub.)	442.	Forestry Products Production, Except
31	FOOD AND BEVERAGE PREPARA-		Logging
	TION AND SERVICE	442.168	MANAGER, DISTRICT (forestry)
313.	Cooking, Large Hotels and Restaur-		SUPERVISOR, COAST DISTRICT (for-
	ants		estry)
313.168	EXECUTIVE CHEF (hotel & rest.)	449.	Forestry, n.e.c.
35	MISCELLANEOUS PERSONAL	449.168	CHIEF CRUISER (forestry; logging)
	SERVICES	46	AGRICULTURAL SERVICES
352.	Hostess and Steward Service, n.e.c.	469.	Agricultural Services, n.e.c.
352.168	DIRECTOR, RECREATION (hotel &	469.168	CONTRACTOR, FIELD HAULING
	rest.; water trans.)		(agric.)
37	PROTECTIVE SERVICES	91	TRANSPORTATION WORK, N.E.C.
375.	Police and Related Work, Public Ser-	910.	Railroad Transportation
	vice	910.168	PASSENGER REPRESENTATIVE (r.r.
375.168	COMMANDING OFFICER, HARBOR-PO-		trans.)
	LICE (gov. ser.)	96	AMUSEMENT, RECREATION, AND
	COMMANDING OFFICER, HOMICIDE		MOTION PICTURE WORK,
	SQUAD (gov. ser.)		N.E.C.
	COMMANDING OFFICER, INVESTIGA-	964.	Theatrical and Related Entertainment
	TION DIVISION (gov. ser.)		Production, n.e.c.
	COMMANDING OFFICER, MOTORCY-	964.168	MANAGER, STAGE (amuse. & rec.)
	CLE SQUAD (gov. ser.)		

Construction of Career Ladders and Lattices

The occupational group arrangement in Volume II lists jobs for a given three-digit group, by Worker Function levels,[10] indicating a possible career ladder from jobs with lower to higher Worker Function levels within a given three digit group. This is possible for some individuals however, only if the Worker Trait configurations follow each rung of the Worker Function ladder. No method has been advanced for constructing job ladders and lattices *among* and *across* three-digit code groups. Such ladders are now being developed empirically, but additional research is needed to establish a methodology.

In constructing career ladders, the following factors might be critical. The succession of higher level jobs in the ladder may require the following:

Item	*JA Elements Involved*
Broader or deeper knowledge of the subject matter	Work Fields, MPSMS, GED, SVP, Aptitudes, Interests, Temperaments
Greater degree of skill, responsibility, judgment	Work fields, Worker Functions, GED, SVP, Aptitudes, Interests, Temperaments, Physical Factors
Different or additional skills	Work fields, MPSMS, Worker Functions, GED, SVP, Aptitudes, Interests, Temperaments, Physical Factors
Different types of environments	MPSMS (as from industry to government) Physical Factors, Working Conditions

The foregoing indicates that a skill progression, vertical, or diagonal, might involve different traits as well as higher capacities. The former represents conditions to which the worker must adjust such as interests, temperaments, physical factors, environmental, and working conditions. The latter indicates higher levels of ability as in Worker Functions (DATA, PEOPLE, THINGS), GED, SVP, and Aptitudes. Both may of course involve different and more difficult methodologies and technologies (work fields) as well as different MPSMS that the promotee must be willing and able to learn.

Any one of the job analysis factors may be vital in determining possible career ladders. In many instances, work fields—and their constituent "methods verbs"—may be most critical in discovering relationships, such as *typing*. For example, the ladder to *linotype operator* might well involve *typing*. Such a relationship may be disclosed by sorting all jobs by the *action verbs,* thus leading to preliminary clusters of jobs. The next step might entail further analysis by other factors of the Job Analysis Formulation using trait homogeneities and the scaled factors (Worker Functions, GED, SVP, and Aptitudes) as the criteria. The end product would be career ladders or lattices.

DOT As A Retrieval System

Retrieval is based on a filing system (manual or in computer storage) with suitable indexing. The items to be retrieved include (*a*) names of qualified job seekers to match job vacancies, (*b*) job vacancies to match available job seekers, (*c*) career areas to match counselee's qualifications profile for evaluation by counselor and counselee, (*d*) occupational information, including job descriptions or specifications for counselees or for workers bidding for job vacancies as needed.

The *DOT* classification code of nine digits and the Worker Trait Group clusters meet the needs listed at least minimally. Additional research is needed as shown below.

Items *a* and *b* involve the same parameters. The problem is that a specific match by a nine-digit code can be limiting and self-defeating, since a slight difference in code and the other descriptors (job location, salary, industry preference, etc.) are "eliminators"[11] if sole reliance is placed on them. A corollary problem is that most retrievers expect and require the retrieval system to locate suitable job seekers or vacancies, as the case may be, with virtually 100% efficiency, thereby reducing the interviewer-retriever to a clerical level of competency. For fully competent interviewers, the optimal degree of the "initial" (by the code) match might well be 60 to 70%. Hence it would be most desirable to create a retrieval system that overcomes the limitations of a nine-digit code and has sufficient built-in flexibility to enable the interviewer to manipulate the data professionally to obtain best results.[12] This will require research and field testing, scheduled for 1975. The goal is theoretically being approached by the computer-assisted placement system used by the New York State Employment Service, in which various descriptors are weighted in an established manner. Again, substantial amounts of additional research and tryout are vitally needed.

Retrieval in connection with career exploration (counseling) and in locating matching potential vacancies in a "bid" procedure, or to meet the needs of economically displaced persons (e.g., aerospace technicians), requires the same types of computerized descriptors. Descriptors that cut across industrial and occupational lines cannot be found without heavy efforts in research and development. For example, a computer can identify occupations or vacancies (whichever is in the data bank), if the *job seeker's characteristics* are identified and included in the "search" request. With this refinement many otherwise unidentifiable career areas or jobs could be disclosed for *specific* displaced aerospace technicians.

Many governmental and commercial bodies prepare occupational briefs or monographs describing the work performed, the qualifications, the monetary factors, and so on. One problem is the nature of the content needed.[13] Deriving methods of filing, retrieving, and updating the information is another, and more research is clearly needed. It is the writer's opinion that occupational information should be stored on tape and retrieved by computer. Some testing has been done along these lines.[14] What is needed is a definitive test to establish the value of the computer in career exploration for a given counselee, with capacity to identify possible careers and to retrieve instantly a printout of the matching occupational monograph (for the occupations "selected") for career exploration.

RESEARCH NEEDED TO IMPROVE AFFIRMATIVE ACTION METHODOLOGY

The Wagner College Affirmative Action Plan was initially constructed for nonfaculty occupations, which represent a relatively small segment of the occupational spectrum. The *DOT* building blocks were assumed to be useful in developing descriptions; in conducting worker and job-seeker diagnostics; in retrieving suitable jobs to match worker potentials; in locating suitable workers, including minorities and women, to fill job vacancies either at the entry or promotional level; in performing job restructuring; and in determining current and projected supply-demand relationships at Wagner and elsewhere on Staten Island. Since not all the results were sufficiently definitive, additional research leading to the following end products is needed:

• Position descriptions covering all jobs, with the qualifications profiles indicated. Additional research, for example, will reveal the extent to which jobs at each installation studied vary in content and qualifications profile from the sample on which the *DOT* definitions are based. The findings will indicate the extent to which the Manpower Administration should prepare this type of job description to meet the needs of most users, including employers, thereby reducing duplication of effort by establishments interested in preparing job or position descriptions. The Manpower Administration will also have to choose a way to make the descriptions available (e.g., from printouts from computers located regionally, on "requisition" and at minimal cost).

• The development of suitable *descriptors* to locate for each employee other jobs in the *establishment* which he can perform with minimal retraining, particularly when technological or economic factors cause reductions in force. In large installations, this undoubtedly is best performed by computer, within the constraints noted. The research needed here is much the same as for some of the already listed factors.[15]

• Determinations, through research, of variations in techniques needed to attain Affirmative Action in establishments of varying sizes, across industries, with different types of working populations, and in different geographical sections of the United States. It may be found that many of these variables are functions of the climate of the times, the management and personnel policy of a plant, the level of sophistication and reality testing of employees, promotional policies, the availability of promotional opportunities, willingness to restructure jobs to cope with specific contingencies, availability of opportunities to match workers' perceived needs for growth and development, economic conditions, and relevant national policies leading to economic, cultural, and political equilibrium.

CONCLUDING OBSERVATIONS

Regarded as a manpower technology, the USES Job Analysis Formulation and the *DOT* have substantial potential impact on many of the problems discussed in this presentation, although it has little relevance to some. On balance, however, these techniques, under government auspices (as researcher, developer, or coordinator of research) should contribute to the development of a national manpower policy directed toward the optimum utilization and allocation of the nation's human resources. Almost by definition, much of the governing criteria for such a policy must incorporate the requirements of Affirmative Action.

It seems evident that equal employment opportunity under Affirmative Action is on the horizon as a fact rather than as a theory. It appears, too, that the Wagner College Affirmative Action Plan represents a step in that direction.

Recent Developments in Affirmative Action

In the introductory sections we took note of the contradictions within Revised Order No. 4. The point was made that the order seems to require *preference* to minorities and women, even though other provisions state that all personnel actions must be based on equal employment opportunity without reference to race, color, religion, national origin, or sex. Three very recent releases explore this area and are worthy of review.

In an article in *Fortune,* Seligman[16] characterizes four different attitudes displayed by contractors: "passive nondiscrimination" (no reference to minorities or sex in personnel transactions); "pure affirmative action" (hiring the most qualified, with no reference to sex or race); "affirmative action with preferential hiring" ("in this posture the company not only ensures that it has a larger labor pool to draw from but systematically favors women and minorities in the actual decisions about hiring"); and "hard quotas" (setting numerical quantities for hiring minorities and women according to the percentage of each group with respect to some base figures). Seligman believes that "the real issue is preferential hiring, which many government agencies are promoting."

Seligman looks at the operating aspects of Affirmative Action and states that guidelines were not developed by the Office of Federal Contract Compliance; rather, "it was left for the Nixon administration to make [Affirmative Action] operational." He discusses the setting of goals and timetables where minorities and women comprise a lower proportion of incumbents in a given establishment than one would expect "by their availability"; he looks at and questions options for the determination of appropriate "utilization rates." Seligman also explores employment standards, including test scores, and reviews briefly the *Griggs* vs. *Duke Power* case in which Chief Justice Burger "upheld the EEOC contention that Title VII has placed on the employer the burden of showing that any given requirement must have a manifest relationship to the employment in question." He discusses the question of preferences and whether the law requires hiring the "less qualified." He comments on reverse discrimination and its implications for morale and litigation. He observes "that the government's actions have . . . undermined some of the old-fashioned notions about hiring on the basis of merit." He remarks

> one would have to be skeptical of the long-term future of any program with so many anomalies built into it. For a democratic society to systematically discriminate against the majority seems quite without precedent. To do so in the name of nondiscrimination seems mind-boggling. For humane and liberal-minded members of the society to espouse racial discrimination at all seems most remarkable.

Having reached this conclusion, Seligman continues:

> It seems safe to say that at some point, even if government does not abandon its pressures for preference, more businessmen will begin resisting them. It should go without saying that the resistance will be easier, and will come with better grace, if those businessmen have otherwise made clear their opposition to any form of discrimination.

In another perspective, however, Seligman quotes a Labor Department official (William J. Kilberg) as follows: "in situations where there has been a finding of discrimination, and where no other remedy is available, temporary preferential hiring is legal and appropriate."

These problems were tackled head-on by a joint memorandum prepared by the Department of Labor, the Justice Department, the Civil Service Commission, and the Equal Employment Opportunity Commission, to reconcile "the demands for merit selection and equal employment opportunity in State and local employment."[17] The memorandum states that the Nixon administration specifically rejected the concept of quotas and preferential hiring, and that "under the Intergovernmental Personnel Act, the Civil Service Commission has an obligation to attempt to move state and local governments toward personnel practices which operate on a merit basis."

The memorandum says that no problem exists where hiring is based on ability and merit, that the cases of individuals who have been adversely affected by discrimination should receive priority when the next vacancy occurs, and that goals are permissible because they recognize that persons are to be judged on individual ability—thus having goals is consistent with the principles of merit hiring.

These views were clarified by the following enunciation of principle:

In some job classifications, in which the newly hired person learns on the job the skills required, and where there is no extensive education, experience or training required, as a prerequisite to successful job performance, many applicants will possess the necessary basic qualifications to perform the job. While determinations of relative ability should be made to accord with required merit principles, where there has been a history of unlawful discrimination, if goals are set on the basis of expected vacancies, and anticipated availability of skills in the marketplace, an employer should be expected to meet the goals if there is an adequate pool of qualified applicants from the discriminated-against group from which to make selections; and if the employer does not meet the goal, he has the obligation to justify his failure.[18]

It seems reasonable to conclude that where true equal employment opportunity exists, no special actions are required by the employer; that where deficiencies have been noted, the employer should establish goals for Affirmative Action; that in no case should merit and availability be subordinated to ability except where actual discrimination has been practiced, and in such instances the employer should meet the goals preferentially, to fill his vacancies if an "adequate pool of qualified applicants from the discriminated-against group exists from which to make selections. . . ."

In January 1974, the Equal Employment Opportunity Commission issued a two-volume brochure to guide employers.[19] Volume 1 furnishes a synthesis (with documentation) of the legal basis for Affirmative Action.

The message conveyed by these legal rulings is clear: *if a statistical survey shows that minorities and females are not participating in your workforce at all levels in reasonable relation to their presence in the population and the labor force, the burden of proof is on you to show that this is not the result of discrimination,* however inadvertent. There is a strong probability that some part of your system is discriminating, and that unless you make changes you may be subject to legal action.

The changes required were summarized by the Supreme Court:

"What is required . . . *is the removal of artificial, arbitrary and unnecessary barriers to employment* when the barriers operate invidiously to discriminate on the basis of racial or other impermissible classification."

The "artificial, arbitrary and unnecessary barriers" identified by the Supreme Court and by many other federal courts, include practices and policies of *recruitment, selection, placement, testing, systems of transfer, promotion, seniority, lines of progression,* and many other basic *terms* and *conditions* of employment. . . .

Removing these barriers requires positive, affirmative action to develop new policies and practices that provide all persons opportunity for employment on an equal basis.[20]

The remedies called for derive from the legal rulings, and the guidebook continues:

Numerical Goals and Timetables

It is clear from these legal developments that where violations of the law are found, broad remedial action to "remove vestiges of past discrimination . . . eliminate present and assure the non-existence of future barriers to full enjoyment of equal job opportunities" will be required, and that remedial action often requires some kind of special treatment for a period of time.

Courts increasingly are requiring companies and unions to provide pre-apprentice and apprentice training, to hire, promote and train minorities and females who have suffered from discrimination in specified numerical ratios, in specified job categories, until specified remedial goals are reached. . . .

Although Title VII [of the Civil Rights Act of 1964] bars preferential hiring simply to eliminate racial employment imbalances in relation to population ratios, Federal courts consistently have found numerical goals and timetables to be a justified and necessary remedy and means of eliminating the present effects of past discriminatory practices. . . .[21]

The EEOC guidebook gives additional guidance on the collection and interpretation of the data specified in Revised Order No. 4 and discussed in Chapter 4 of this book. Forms are also provided to accommodate the data. Instructions for setting of goals and timetables involve the following:

1. Setting Long-Range Goals

Long range goals and timetables will be needed to eliminate employment discrimination and effects of past discrimination. Your survey of present employment and analysis of underutilization and concentration by job category will provide the basic data for formulating such goals and timetables.

The ultimate long-range goals of your affirmative action program should be representation of each group identified as "underutilized" in each major job classification in reasonable relation to the overall labor force participation of such group. This goal may be modified to the extent that you can prove that valid *job-related* selection standards reduce the percentage of a particular group qualified for a particular job classification. . . .

Long-range goals should not be rigid and unchangeable. They cannot be based upon exact predictable statistics. For example, studies indicate that many qualified women not in the present labor force could become "available" if job opportunities were open to them. Similarly, many members of minority groups now in the workforce could become "qualified" if better jobs and opportunities for training and promotion become open to them.

2. Setting Annual Intermediate Targets

Once long-range goals have been set for each underutilized group in each job category, specific, numerical annual targets should be developed for hiring, training, transferring and promoting, to reach these goals within the indicated time frame.[22]

The guidebook then covers other aspects of Affirmative Action, including the use of tests (in substantial detail), selection standards and procedures, counseling, and job restructuring (in far less detail). For example, the guidebook states that only validated standards can be used in selection. Statements of job qualifications "must be significantly related to job performance"; employee selection procedures subject to these guidelines include all tests, "and other requirements such as personal histories, biographical information, background requirements, specific educational or work experience requirements, interviews (scored or unscored), application forms (scored or unscored)."[23] Moreover, job analysis should be used "to identify actual tasks performed, their frequency, and importance of specific employee traits or skills needed for the job."

Surely these guidelines will be helpful to employers in meeting Affirmative Action requirements. However, instructions on how to interview, how to counsel, and how to conduct job analysis are omitted in the guidebook. It was these very details that the author had to develop for Wagner College in order to secure equal employment opportunity through Affirmative Action.

Thus we can conclude: (*a*) that the determination of valid job requirements and actual matching *employee* qualifications is critical if true equal employment opportunity is to become a reality, and (*b*) that Affirmative Action in accordance with Revised Order No. 4 will not be needed as a stimulus once such objectivity has been achieved and employers have internalized the goal of hiring and promoting on the basis of merit and ability.

In some sections of the country job discrimination based on national origin and religion has given way to hiring and promotion based on merit and ability. It is reasonable to assume that over time the same condition will obtain for women and minorities (despite the so-called visibility factor). Can this process be expedited? Is there a technology that will enable employers and government to learn what they need to know to establish suitable courses of action?

This book began with the assumption that many of the problems and much of the controversy concerning manpower theory and personnel management practice resulted from a paucity of technique. It tested the proposition that many of the problems and issues could be resolved by the *DOT* and the Job Analysis Formulation on which it is based.

The Wagner College Project indicated that the tested technology did in fact contribute substantially to the achievement of Affirmative Action. It demonstrated that if this approach is used creatively and flexibly, many needs of workers, job seekers, and employers can be fulfilled. More than that, the Wagner College test documented that this objective approach (to be further extended through research) provides Affirmative Action to *all* concerned on the basis of merit and ability, which should eventually minimize the need for laws designed to stimulate employers to hire and promote without reference to race, color, religion, national origin, or sex.

The value of the *DOT* (and the Job Analysis Formulation) derives from its nature: it is essentially a fact-finding technique and tool based on scientific principles. It was developed through research without preconception and without prejudgment. It seems clear that full utilization of such principles will lead to individual fulfillment as well as the fulfillment of employer and national needs in a dynamic society.

NOTES

1. *DOT* makes a strong contribution to career exploration and occupational counseling under any labor market conditions. Determinations concerning which job to take, hopefully within a "career direction", would of course depend on the availability of job opportunities.

2. *Personnel and Guidance Journal,* Vol. 49, No. 3 (November 1970) states "The impact and consequences of technology upon (vocational) guidance are so potentially powerful, that it would be sheer folly to neglect the need for national planning and monitoring of guidance technology" (p. 181). Attention was also directed to the introduction of a bill in Congress to create an Office of Technology Assessment under the Comptroller General of the United States, to assess technology and predict the probable consequences, and to protect against adverse results.

3. A study to determine the feasibility of the USES job analysis technique in restructuring jobs in the human services field is now underway.

4. These projects are under the sponsorship of the Manpower Administration; research is now underway in eight states. Four other states have ongoing systems called "manpower-matching systems."

5. *The Counselor's Handbook,* issued by the U.S. Department of Labor's Manpower Administration in 1965 and recalled shortly after release because it was felt it did not sufficiently relate to the disadvantaged, addressed some of the issues just enumerated.

6. The writer used this analytical framework in an article entitled "*DOT,* An Information Instrumentation and Retrieval System," *Newsletter of the New York Personnel and Guidance Association, Inc.* [New York State Branch of the American Personnel and Guidance Association], Vol. 6, (April 1971), p. 11.

7. This is necessary for the *classification* structure, particularly for presenting data on employment and unemployment, and for supply-demand projection.

8. For a description of the matrix, see U.S. Department of Labor, Bureau of Labor Statistics, "Occupational Employment Patterns for 1960 and 1975" (BLS Bulletin 1599); and "Tomorrow's Manpower Needs" (BLS Bulletin 1737) (Washington, D.C.: Government Printing Office, revised 1971).

9. New York State Department of Labor, Division of Research and Statistics, "Manpower

Requirements of Lower-Level Jobs in New York State," Appendix C—Technical Note, December 22, 1971 (unpublished).

10. The (first)-three-digit groups represent an industry or activity, as stated in previous chapters. These groups are listed in the occupational group arrangement, *DOT 3*, Volume 11, pages 33–213.

11. If a job seeker wishes to work in a specific locality in which no jobs are available, the computer will not print out jobs elsewhere even though they meet the job seeker's requirements in all other respects.

12. Thus the interviewer might use a nine-digit code as the first search strategy. If this is unsuccessful, the interviewer could use any of the other descriptors singly or in combination (GED and aptitudes, adding interests or temperaments, or work fields, etc.) until the "best" match is obtained.

13. See Glen N. Pierson, Edwin Whitfield, and George Claeser, *Career Information: The VIEW System* (San Diego, Calif.: San Diego County Department of Education).

14. See, for example, the study by D. B. Youst entitled "The Rochester Career Guidance Project," *Educational Technology,* Vol. 9 (1969), pp. 34–41. *Personnel and Guidance Journal,* [Vol. 49, no. 3, (November 1970), p. 193], devoted its full space to these issues.

15. During a plant visit, the author noticed that a newly installed "numerical control" machine caused the termination of 100 solderers. However, the firm did not intend to consider the individuals for other jobs for which it was actually recruiting, perhaps because of ignorance of the procedures described in this book.

16. Daniel Seligman, "How Equal Opportunity Turned Into Employment Quotas," *Fortune* (March 1973), pp. 160–168.

17. General Administration Letter NO. 1488, "Federal Policy on Equal Employment Opportunity in State and Local Government Personnel Systems," June 8, 1973. The memorandom was transmitted to state employment security agencies by the Manpower Administration.

18. Ibid.

19. U.S. Equal Employment Opportunity Commission, "Affirmative Action and Equal Employment Opportunity." (Washington, D.C.: The Commission, January 1974).

20. Ibid., Vol. 1, p. 7.

21. Ibid., p. 11.

22. Ibid., p. 27, Vol. 1.

23. Ibid., p. 35, Vol. 1.

APPENDIX A

EXPLANATION OF RELATIONSHIPS WITHIN DATA, PEOPLE, THINGS HIERARCHIES

Much of the information in this edition of the Dictionary is based on the premise that every job requires a worker to function in relation to Data, People, and Things, in varying degrees. These relationships are identified and explained below. They appear in the form of three hierarchies arranged in each instance from the relatively simple to the complex in such a manner that each successive relationship includes those that are simpler and excludes the more complex.[1] The identifications attached to these relationships are referred to as worker functions, and provide standard terminology for use in summarizing exactly what a worker does on the job by means of one or more meaningful verbs.

A job's relationship to Data, People, and Things can be expressed in terms of the highest appropriate function in each hierarchy to which the worker has an occupationally significant relationship, and these functions taken together indicate the total level of complexity at which he must perform. The last three digits of the occupational code numbers in the Dictionary reflect significant relationships to Data, People, and Things, respectively.[2] These last three digits express a job's relationship to Data, People, and Things by identifying the highest appropriate function in each hierarchy to which the job requires the worker to have a significant relationship, as reflected by the following table:

DATA (4th digit)		PEOPLE (5th digit)		THINGS (6th digit)	
0	Synthesizing	0	Mentoring	0	Setting Up
1	Coordinating	1	Negotiating	1	Precision Working

DATA (4th digit)	PEOPLE (5th digit)	THINGS (6th digit)
2 Analyzing	2 Instructing	2 Operating-Controlling
3 Compiling	3 Supervising	3 Driving-Operating
4 Computing	4 Diverting	4 Manipulating
5 Copying	5 Persuading	5 Tending
6 Comparing	6 Speaking-Signaling	6 Feeding-Offbearing
7 } No significant	7 Serving	7 Handling
8 } relationship	8 No significant relationship	8 No significant relationship

DATA

Information, knowledge, and conceptions, related to data, people, or things, obtained by observation, investigation, interpretation, visualization, mental creation; incapable of being touched; written data take the form of numbers, words, symbols; other data are ideas, concepts, oral verbalization.

0 *Synthesizing:* Integrating analyses of data to discover facts and/or develop knowledge concepts or interpretations.
1 *Coordinating:* Determining time, place, and sequence of operations or action to be taken on the basis of analysis of data; executing determinations and/or reporting on events.
2 *Analyzing:* Examining and evaluating data. Presenting alternative actions in relation to the evaluation is frequently involved.
3 *Compiling:* Gathering, collating, or classifying information about data, people, or things. Reporting and/or carrying out a prescribed action in relation to the information is frequently involved.
4 *Computing:* Performing arithmetic operations and reporting on and/or carrying out a prescribed action in relation to them. Does not include counting.
5 *Copying:* Transcribing, entering, or posting data.
6 *Comparing:* Judging the readily observable functional, structural, or compositional characteristics (whether similar to or divergent from obvious standards) of data, people, or things.

PEOPLE

Human beings; also animals dealt with on an individual basis as if they were human.

0 *Mentoring:* Dealing with individuals in terms of their total personality in order to advise, counsel, and/or guide them with regard to problems that may be resolved by legal, scientific, clinical, spiritual, and/or other professional principles.

1 *Negotiating:* Exchanging ideas, information, and opinions with others to formulate policies and programs and/or arrive jointly at decisions, conclusions, or solutions.

2 *Instructing:* Teaching subject matter to others, or training others (including animals) through explanation, demonstration, and supervised practice; or making recommendations on the basis of technical disciplines.

3 *Supervising:* Determining or interpreting work procedures for a group of workers, assigning specific duties to them, maintaining harmonious relations among them, and promoting efficiency.

4 *Diverting:* Amusing others.

5 *Persuading:* Influencing others in favor of a product, service, or point of view.

6 *Speaking-Signaling:* Talking with and/or signaling people to convey or exchange information. Includes giving assignments and/or directions to helpers or assistants.

7 *Serving:* Attending to the needs or requests of people or animals or the expressed or implicit wishes of people. Immediate response is involved.

THINGS

Inanimate objects as distinguished from human beings; substances or materials; machines, tools, equipment; products. A thing is tangible and has shape, form, and other physical characteristics.

0 *Setting Up:* Adjusting machines or equipment by replacing or altering tools, jigs, fixtures, and attachments to prepare them to perform their functions, change their performance, or restore their proper functioning if they break down. Workers who set up one or a number of machines for other workers or who set up and personally operate a variety of machines are included here.

1 *Precision Working:* Using body members and/or tools or work aids to work, move, guide, or place objects or materials in situations where ultimate responsibility for the attainment of standards occurs and selection of appropriate tools, objects, or materials, and the adjustment of the tool to the task require exercise of considerable judgment.

2 *Operating-Controlling:* Starting, stopping, controlling, and adjusting the progress of machines or equipment designed to fabricate and/or process objects or materials. Operating machines involves setting up the machine and adjusting the machine or material as the work progresses. Controlling equipment involves observing gages, dials, etc., and turning valves and other devices to control such factors as temperature, pressure, flow of liquids, speed of pumps, and reactions of materials.

Setup involves several variables and adjustment is more frequent than in tending.

3 *Driving-Operating:* Starting, stopping, and controlling the actions of machines or equipment for which a course must be steered, or which must be guided, in order to fabricate, process, and/or move things or people. Involves such activities as observing gages and dials; estimating distances and determining speed and direction of other objects; turning cranks and wheels; pushing clutches or brakes; and pushing or pulling gear lifts or levers. Includes such machines as cranes, conveyor systems, tractors, furnace charging machines, paving machines and hoisting machines. Excludes manually powered machines, such as handtrucks and dollies, and power assisted machines, such as electric wheelbarrows and handtrucks.

4 *Manipulating:* Using body members, tools, or special devices to work, move, guide, or place objects or materials. Involves some latitude for judgment with regard to precision attained and selecting appropriate tool, object, or material, although this is readily manifest.

5 *Tending:* Starting, stopping, and observing the functioning of machines and equipment. Involves adjusting materials or controls of the machine, such as changing guides, adjusting timers and temperature gages, turning valves to allow flow of materials, and flipping switches in response to light. Little judgment is involved in making these adjustments.

6 *Feeding-Offbearing:* Inserting, throwing dumping, or placing materials in or removing them from machines or equipment which are automatic or tended or operated by other workers.

7 *Handling:* Using body members, handtools, and/or special devices to work, move, or carry objects or materials. Involves little or no latitude for judgment with regard to attainment of standards or in selecting appropriate tool, object, or material.

Note: Included in the concept of Feeding-Offbearing, Tending, Operating-Controlling, and Setting Up, is the situation in which the worker is actually part of the setup of the machine, either as the holder and guider of the material or holder and guider of the tool.

NOTES

1. As each of the relationships to People represents a wide range of complexity, resulting in considerable overlap among occupations, their arrangement is somewhat arbitrary and can be considered a hierarchy only in the most general sense.

2. Only those relationships which are occupationally significant in terms of the requirements of the job are reflected in the code numbers. The incidental relationships which every worker has to Data, People, and Things, but which do not seriously affect successful performance of the essential duties of the job, are not reflected.

APPENDIX B

EXPLANATION OF WORKER TRAIT COMPONENTS

Those abilities, personal traits, and individual characteristics required of a worker in order to achieve average successful job performance are referred to as worker traits. Occupational information presented in Volumes I and II [of the *DOT*] is based in part on analysis of required worker traits in terms of the six distinct worker trait components described in this appendix. These six components have been selected for this purpose because they provide the broadest and yet most comprehensive framework for the effective presentation of worker trait information. Within this framework the user will find data concerning the requirements of jobs for: (1) the amount of general educational development and specific vocational preparation a worker must have, (2) the specific capacities and abilities required of him in order to learn or perform certain tasks or duties, (3) preferences for certain types of work activities or experiences considered necessary for job success, (4) types of occupational situations to which an individual must adjust, (5) physical activities required in work situations, and (6) physical surroundings prevalent in jobs.

Information reflecting significant worker trait requirements is contained explicitly or by implication, in the job definitions in Volume I. In the Worker Traits Arrangement in Volume II, the qualifications profile for each worker trait group shows the range of required traits and/or levels of traits for the first five of these components. Numbers or letters are used to identify each specific trait and level. In this appendix, these identifying numbers and letters appear in italics.

The worker trait components are:

    I.   Training time (general educational development, specific vocational preparation)
    II. Aptitudes
    III. Interests
    IV. Temperaments
    V. Physical demands
    VI. Working conditions[1]

TRAINING TIME

The amount of general educational development and specific vocational preparation required for a worker to acquire the knowledge and abilities necessary for average performance in a particular job.

General Educational Development

This embraces those aspects of education (formal and informal) which contribute to the worker's (a) reasoning development and ability to follow instructions, and (b) acquisition of "tool" knowledges, such as language and mathematical skills. It is education of a general nature which does not have a recognized, fairly specific, occupational objective. Ordinarily such education is obtained in elementary school, high school, or college. It also derives from experience and individual study.

The following is a table explaining the various levels of general educational development.

GENERAL EDUCATIONAL DEVELOPMENT

Level	Reasoning Development	Mathematical Development	Language Development
6	Apply principles of logical or scientific thinking to a wide range of intellectual and practical problems. Deal with nonverbal symbolism (formulas, scientific equations, graphs, musical notes, etc.) in its most difficult phases. Deal with a variety of abstract and concrete variables. Apprehend the most abstruse classes of concepts.	Apply knowledge of advanced mathematical and statistical techniques such as differential and integral calculus, factor analysis, and probability determination, or work with a wide variety of theoretical mathematical concepts and make original applications of mathematical procedures, as in empirical and differential equations.	Comprehension and expression of a level to —Report, write, or edit articles for such publications as newspapers, magazines, and technical or scientific journals. Prepare and draw up deeds, leases, wills, mortgages, and contracts. —Prepare and deliver lectures on politics, economics, education, or science.
5	Apply principles of logical or scientific thinking to define problems, collect data, establish facts, and draw valid conclusions. Interpret an extensive variety of technical instructions, in books, manuals, and mathematical or diagrammatic form. Deal with several abstract and concrete variables.		—Interview, counsel, or advise such people as students, clients, or patients, in such matters as welfare eligibility, vocational rehabilitation, mental hygeine, or marital relations. —Evaluate engineering technical data to design buildings and bridges.
4	Apply principles of rational systems[a] to solve practical problems and deal with a variety of concrete variables in situations where only limited standardization exists. Interpret a variety of instructions	Perform ordinary arithmetic, algebraic, and geometric procedures in standard, practical applications.	Comprehension and expression of a level to —Transcribe dictation, make appointments for executive and handle his personal mail, interview and screen people wishing to speak to him, and

Level	Reasoning Development	Mathematical Development	Language Development
6	furnished in written, oral, diagrammatic, or schedule form.		write routine correspondence on own initiative. —Interview job applicants to determine work best suited for their abilities and experience, and contact employers to interest them in services of agency. —Interpret technical manuals as well as drawings and specifications, such as layouts, blueprints, and schematics.
3	Apply common sense understanding to carry out instructions furnished in written, oral, or diagrammatic form. Deal with problems involving several concrete variables in or from standardized situations.	Make arithmetic calculations involving fractions, decimals and percentages.	Comprehension and expression of a level to —File, post, and mail such materials as forms, checks, receipts, and bills. —Copy data from one record to another, fill in report forms, and type all work from rough draft or corrected copy.
2	Apply common sense understanding to carry out detailed but uninvolved written or oral instructions. Deal with problems involving a few concrete variables in or from standardized situations.	Use arithmetic to add, subtract, multiply, and divide whole numbers.	—Interview members of household to obtain such information as age, occupation, and number of children, to be used as data for surveys, or economic studies.

| 1 | Apply common sense understanding to carry out simple one- or two-step instructions. Deal with standardized situations with occasional or no variables in or from these situations encountered on the job. | Perform simple addition and subtraction, reading and copying of figures, or counting and recording. | —Guide people on tours through historical or public buildings, describing such features as size, value, and points of interest. Comprehension and expression of a level to —Learn job duties from oral instructions or demonstration. —Write identifying information, such as name and address of customer, weight, number, or type of product, on tags, or slips. —Request orally, or in writing, such supplies as linen, soap, or work materials. |

Specific Vocational Preparation

The amount of time required to learn the techniques, acquire information, and develop the facility needed for average performance in a specific job-worker situation. This training may be acquired in a school, work, military, institutional, or avocational environment. It does not include orientation training required of even every fully qualified worker to become accustomed to the special conditions of any new job. Specific vocational training includes training given in any of the following circumstances:

1. Vocational education (such as high school commercial or shop training, technical school, art school, and that part of college training which is organized around a specific vocational objective);

2. Apprentice training (for apprenticeable jobs only);

3. In-plant training (given by an employer in the form of organized classroom study);

4. On-the-job training (serving as learner or trainee on the job under the instruction of a qualified worker);

5. Essential experience in other jobs (serving in less responsible jobs which lead to the higher grade job or serving in other jobs which qualify).

The following is an explanation of the various levels of specific vocational preparation.

Level	Time	Level	Time
1	Short demonstration only.	5	Over 6 months up to and including 1 year.
2	Anything beyond short demonstration up and including 30 days.	6	Over 1 year up to and including 2 years.
3	Over 30 days up to and including 3 months.	7	Over 2 years up to and including 4 years.
4	Over 3 months up to and including 6 months.	8	Over 4 years up to and including 10 years.
		9	Over 10 years.

APTITUDES

Specific capacities and abilities required of an individual in order to learn or perform adequately a task or job duty.

G INTELLIGENCE: General learning ability. The ability to "catch on" or understand instructions and underlying principles. Ability to reason and make judgments. Closely related to doing well in school.

V   VERBAL: Ability to understand meanings of words and ideas associated with them, and to use them effectively. To comprehend language, to understand relationships between words, and to understand meanings of whole sentences and paragraphs. To present information or ideas clearly.

N   NUMERICAL: Ability to perform arithmetic operations quickly and accurately.

S   SPATIAL: Ability to comprehend forms in space and understand relationships of plane and solid objects. May be used in such tasks as blueprint reading and in solving geometry problems. Frequently described as the ability to "visualize" objects of two or three dimensions, or to think visually of geometric forms.

P   FORM PERCEPTION: Ability to perceive pertinent detail in objects or in pictorial or graphic material; To make visual comparisons and discriminations and see slight differences in shapes and shadings of figures and widths and lengths of lines.

Q   CLERICAL PERCEPTION: Ability to perceive pertinent detail in verbal or tabular material. To observe differences in copy, to proofread words and numbers, and to avoid perceptual errors in arithmetic computation.

K   MOTOR COORDINATION: Ability to coordinate eyes and hands or fingers rapidly and accurately in making precise movements with speed. Ability to make a movement response accurately and quickly.

F   FINGER DEXTERITY: Ability to move the fingers and manipulate small objects with the fingers rapidly or accurately.

M   MANUAL DEXTERITY: Ability to move the hands easily and skillfully. To work with the hands in placing and turning motions.

E   EYE-HAND-FOOT COORDINATION: Ability to move the hand and foot coordinately with each other in accordance with visual stimuli.

C   COLOR DISCRIMINATION: Ability to perceive or recognize similarities or differences in colors, or in shades or other values of the same color; to identify a particular color, or to recognize harmonious or contrasting color combinations, or to match colors accurately.

Explanation of Levels

The digits indicate how much of each aptitude the job requires for satisfactory (average) performance. The average requirements, rather than maximum or minimum, are cited. The amount required is expressed in terms of equivalent amounts possessed by segments of the general working population.

The following scale is used:

1 The top 10% of the population. This segment of the population possesses an extremely high degree of the aptitude.

2 The highest third exclusive of the top 10% of the population. This segment of the population possesses an above average or high degree of the aptitude.

3 The middle third of the population. This segment of the population possesses a medium degree of the aptitude, ranging from slightly below to slightly above average.

4 The lowest third exclusive of the bottom 10% of the population. This segment of the population possesses a below average or low degree of the aptitude.

5 The lowest 10% of the population. This segment of the population possesses a negligible degree of the aptitude.

Significant Apptitudes

Certain aptitudes appear in boldface type on the qualifications profiles for the worker trait groups. These aptitudes are considered to be occupationally significant for the specific group (i.e., essential for average successful job performance). All boldface aptitudes are not necessarily required of a worker for each individual job within a worker trait group, but some combination of them is essential in every case.

INTERESTS

Preferences for certain types of work activities or experiences, with accompanying rejection of contrary types of activities or experiences. Five pairs of interest factors are provided so that a positive preference for one factor of a pair also implies rejection of the other factor of that pair.

1 Situations involving a preference for activities dealing with things and objects.

vs. *6* Situations involving a preference for activities concerned with people and the communication of ideas.

2 Situations involving a preference for activities involving business contact with people.

vs. *7* Situations involving a preference for activities of a scientific and technical nature.

3 Situations involving a preference for activities of a routine, concrete, organized nature.

vs. *8* Situations involving a preference for activities of an abstract and creative nature.

4 Situations involving a preference for working for people for their presumed good, as in the social welfare sense, or for dealing with people and language in social situations.

vs.

9 Situations involving a preference for activities that are nonsocial in nature, and are carried on in relation to processes, machines, and techniques.

5 Situations involving a preference for activities resulting in prestige or the esteem of others.

vs.

0 Situations involving a preference for activities resulting in tangiblo, productive satisfaction.

TEMPERAMENTS

Different types of occupational situations to which workers must adjust.

1 Situations involving a variety of duties often characterized by frequent change.

2 Situations involving repetitive or short cycle operations carried out according to set procedures or sequences.

3 Situations involving doing things only under specific instruction, allowing little or no room for independent action or judgment in working out job problems.

4 Situations involving the direction, control, and planning of an entire activity or the activities of others.

5 Situations involving the necessity of dealing with people in actual job duties beyond giving and receiving instructions.

6 Situations involving working alone and apart in physical isolation from others, although the activity may be integrated with that of others.

7 Situations involving influencing people in their opinions, attitudes, or judgments about ideas or things.

8 Situations involving performing adequately under stress when confronted with the critical or unexpected or when taking risks.

9 Situations involving the evaluation (arriving at generalizations, judgments, or decisions) of information against sensory or judgmental criteria.

0 Situations involving the evaluation (arriving at generalizations, judgments, or decisions) of information against measurable or verifiable criteria.

X Situations involving the interpretation of feelings, ideas, or facts in terms of personal viewpoint.

Y Situations involving the precise attainment of set limits, tolerances, or standards.

PHYSICAL DEMANDS

Physical demands are those physical activities required of a worker in a job.

The physical demands referred to in this Dictionary serve as a means of expressing both the physical requirements of the job and the physical capacities (specific physical traits) a worker must have to meet the requirements. For example, "seeing" is the name of a physical demand required by many jobs (perceiving by the sense of vision), and also the name of a specific capacity possessed by many people (having the power of sight). The worker must possess physical capacities at least in an amount equal to the physical demands made by the job.

The Factors

1 Lifting, Carrying, Pushing, and/or Pulling (Strength). These are the primary "strength" physical requirements, and generally speaking, a person who engages in one of these activities can engage in all.

Specifically, each of these activities can be described as:

1. Lifting: Raising or lowering an object from one level to another (includes upward pulling)

2. Carrying: Transporting an object, usually holding it in the hands or arms or on the shoulder.

3. Pushing: Exerting force upon an object so that the object moves away from the force (includes slapping, striking, kicking, and treadle actions).

4. Pulling: Exerting force upon an object so that the object moves toward the force (includes jerking).

The five degrees of Physical Demands Factor No. 1 (Lifting, Carrying, Pushing, and/or Pulling), are as follows.

S Sedentary Work Lifting 10 lb maximum and occasionally lifting and/or carrying such articles as dockets, ledgers, and small tools. Although a sedentary job is defined as one which involves sitting, a certain amount of walking and standing is often necessary in carrying out job duties. Jobs are sedentary if walking and standing are required only occasionally and other sedentary criteria are met.

L Light Work Lifting 20 lb maximum with frequent lifting and/or carrying of objects weighing up to 10 lb. Even though the weight lifted may be only a negligible amount, a job is in this category when it requires walking or standing to a significant degree, or when it involves sitting most of the time with a degree of pushing and pulling of arm and/or leg controls.

M Medium Work Lifting 50 lb maximum with frequent lifting and/or carrying of objects weighing up to 25 lb.

H   Heavy Work   Lifting 100 lb maximum with frequent lifting and/or carrying of objects weighing up to 50 lb.

V   Very Heavy Work   Lifting objects in excess of 100 lb with frequent lifting and/or carrying of objects weighing 50 lb or more.

2   Climbing and/or Balancing

1.   Climbing: Ascending or descending ladders, stairs, scaffolding, ramps, poles, ropes, and the like, using the feet and legs and/or hands and arms.

2.   Balancing: Maintaining body equilibrium to prevent falling when walking, standing, crouching, or running on narrow, slippery, or erratically moving surfaces; or maintaining body equilibrium when performing gymnastic feats.

3   Stooping, Kneeling, Crouching, and/or Crawling

1.   Stooping: Bending the body downward and forward by bending the spine at the waist.

2.   Kneeling: Bending the legs at the knees to come to rest on the knee or knees.

3.   Crouching: Bending the body downward and forward by bending the legs and spine.

4.   Crawling: Moving about on the hands and knees or hands and feet.

4   Reaching, Handling, Fingering, and/or Feeling

1.   Reaching: Extending the hands and arms in any direction.

2.   Handling: Seizing, holding, grasping, turning, or otherwise working with the hand or hands (fingering not involved).

3.   Fingering: Picking, pinching, or otherwise working with the fingers primarily (rather than with the whole hand or arm as in handling).

4.   Feeling: Perceiving such attributes of objects and materials as size, shape, temperature, or texture, by means of receptors in the skin, particularly those of the finger tips.

5   Talking and/or Hearing

1.   Talking: Expressing or exchanging ideas by means of the spoken word.

2.   Hearing: Perceiving the nature of sounds by the ear.

6   Seeing   Obtaining impressions through the eyes of the shape, size, distance, motion, color, or other characteristics of objects. The major visual functions are: (1) acuity, far and near, (2) depth perception, (3) field of vision, (4) accommodation, (5) color vision. The functions are defined as follows:

1.   Acuity, far—clarity of vision at 20 feet or more. Acuity, near—clarity of vision at 20 inches or less.

2. Depth perception—three-dimensional vision. The ability to judge distance and space relationships so as to see objects where and as they actually are.

3. Field of vision—the area that can be seen up and down or to the right or left while the eyes are fixed on a given point.

4. Accommodation—adjustment of the lens of the eye to bring an object into sharp focus. This item is especially important when doing near-point work at varying distances from the eye.

5. Color vision—the ability to identify and distinguish colors.

WORKING CONDITIONS

Working conditions are the physical surroundings of a worker in a specific job.

1   Inside, Outside, or Both

I   Inside: Protection from weather conditions but not necessarily from temperature changes.

O   Outside: No effective protection from weather.

B   Both: Inside and outside.

A job is considered "inside" if the worker spends approximately 75% or more of his time inside, and "outside" if he spends approximately 75% or more of his time outside. A job is considered "both" if the activities occur inside or outside in approximately equal amounts.

2   Extremes of Cold Plus Temperature Changes

1. Extremes of Cold: Temperature sufficiently low to cause marked bodily discomfort unless the worker is provided with exceptional protection.

2. Temperature Changes: Variations in temperature which are sufficiently marked and abrupt to cause noticeable bodily reactions.

3   Extremes of Heat Plus Temperature Changes

1. Extremes of Heat: Temperature sufficiently high to cause marked bodily discomfort unless the worker is provided with exceptional protection.

2. Temperature Changes: Same as 2 (2).

4   Wet and Humid

1. Wet: Contact with water or other liquids.

2. Humid: Atmospheric condition with moisture content sufficiently high to cause marked bodily discomfort.

5   Noise and Vibration

Sufficient noise, either constant or intermittent, to cause marked distraction or possible injury to the sense of hearing and/or sufficient vibration (production of an oscillating movement or strain on the body or its extremities from repeated motion or shock) to cause bodily harm if endured day after day.

6   Hazards

Situations in which the individual is exposed to the definite risk of bodily injury.

7   Fumes, Odors, Toxic Conditions, Dust, and Poor Ventilation

1.   Fumes: Smoky or vaporous exhalations, usually odorous, thrown off as the result of combustion or chemical reaction.

2.   Odors: Noxious smells, either toxic or nontoxic.

3.   Toxic Conditions: Exposure to toxic dust, fumes, gases, vapors, mists, or liquids which cause general or localized disabling conditions as a result of inhalation or action on the skin.

4.   Dust: Air filled with small particles of any kind, such as textile dust, flour, wood, leather, feathers, etc., and inorganic dust, including silica and asbestos, which make the workplace unpleasant or are the source of occupational diseases.

5.   Poor Ventilation: Insufficient movement of air causing a feeling of suffocation; or exposure to drafts.

NOTE

1.   Working conditions were recorded as part of each job analysis, and are reflected, when appropriate, in job definitions in Volume I. However, because they did not contribute to the homogeneity of worker trait groups, they do not appear as a component in the Worker Traits Arrangement.

APPENDIX C

OCCUPATIONAL CATEGORIES, AND DIVISIONS

OCCUPATIONAL CATEGORIES

$\left.\begin{array}{c}0\\1\end{array}\right\}$ Professional, technical, and managerial occupations

2   Clerical and sales occupations
3   Service occupations
4   Farming, fishery, forestry, and related occupations
5   Processing occupations
6   Machines trades occupations
7   Bench work occupations
8   Structural work occupations
9   Miscellaneous occupations

TWO-DIGIT OCCUPATIONAL DIVISIONS

Professional, Technical, and Managerial Occupations

$\left.\begin{array}{c}00\\01\end{array}\right\}$ Occupations in architecture and engineering

02   Occupations in mathematics and physical sciences
04   Occupations in life sciences
05   Occupations in social sciences
07   Occupations in medicine and health
09   Occupations in education
10   Occupations in museum, library, and archival sciences
11   Occupations in law and jurisprudence

12 Occupations in religion and theology
13 Occupations in writing
14 Occupations in art
15 Occupations in entertainment and recreation
16 Occupations in administrative specializations
18 Managers and officials, n.e.c.
19 Miscellaneous professional, technical, and managerial occupations

Clerical and Sales Occupations

20 Stenography, typing, filing, and related occupations
21 Computing and account-recording occupations
22 Material and production recording occupations
23 Information and message distribution occupations
24 Miscellaneous clerical occupations
25 Salesmen, services
26
27 } Salesmen and salespersons, commodities
28
29 Merchandising occupations, except salesmen

Service Occupations

30 Domestic service occupations
31 Food and beverage preparation and service occupations
32 Lodging and related service occupations
33 Barbering, cosmetology, and related service occupations
34 Amusement and recreation service occupations
35 Miscellaneous personal service occupations
36 Apparel and furnishings service occupations
37 Protective service occupations
38 Building and related service occupations

Farming, Fishery, Forestry, and Related Occupations

40 Plant farming occupations
41 Animal farming occupations
42 Miscellaneous farming and related occupations
43 Fishery and related occupations
44 Forestry occupations
45 Hunting, trapping, and related occupations
46 Agricultural service occupations

Processing Occupations

50 Occupations in processing of metal
51 Ore refining and foundry occupations

52   Occupations in processing of food, tobacco, and related products
53   Occupations in processing of paper and related materials
54   Occupations in processing of petroleum, coal, natural and manufactured gas, and related products
55   Occupations in processing of chemicals, plastics, synthetics, rubber, paint, and related products
56   Occupations in processing of wood and wood products
57   Occupations in processing of stone, clay, glass, and related products
58   Occupations in processing of leather, textiles, and related products
59   Processing occupations, n.e.c.

Machine Trades Occupations

60   Metal machining occupations
61   Metalworking occupations, n.e.c.
62
63   } Mechanics and machinery repairmen
64   Paperworking occupations
65   Printing occupations
66   Wood machining occupations
67   Occupations in machining stone, clay, glass, and related materials
68   Textile occupations
69   Machine trades occupations, n.e.c.

Bench Work Occupations

70   Occupations in fabrication, assembly, and repair of metal products, n.e.c.
71   Occupations in fabrication and repair of scientific and medical apparatus, photographic and optical goods, watches and clocks, and related products
72   Occupations in assembly and repair of electrical equipment
73   Occupations in fabrication and repair of products made from assorted materials
74   Painting, decorating, and related occupations
75   Occupations in fabrication and repair of plastics, synthetics, rubber, and related products
76   Occupations in fabrication and repair of wood products
77   Occupations in fabrication and repair of sand, stone, clay, and glass products
78   Occupations in fabrication and repair of textile, leather, and related products
79   Bench work occupations, n.e.c.

Structural Work Occupations

80   Occupations in metal fabricating, n.e.c.
81   Welders, flame cutters, and related occupations
82   Electrical assembling, installing, and repairing occupations
84   Painting, plastering, waterproofing, cementing, and related occupations
85   Excavating, grading, paving, and related occupations
86   Construction occupations, n.e.c.
89   Structural work occupations, n.e.c.

Miscellaneous Occupations

90   Motor freight occupations
91   Transportation occupations, n.e.c.
92   Packaging and materials handling occupations
93   Occupations in extraction of minerals
94   Occupations in logging
95   Occupations in production and distribution of utilities
96   Amusement, recreation, and motion picture occupations, n.e.c.
97   Occupations in graphic art work

APPENDIX D

AREAS OF WORK
(ALPHABETIC ARRANGEMENT)

APPENDIX E

WORKER TRAIT GROUPS WITHIN AREAS OF WORK

CLERICAL WORK

ENGINEERING

ENTERTAINMENT

FARMING, FISHING, AND FORESTRY

INVESTIGATING, INSPECTING, AND TESTING

LAW AND LAW ENFORCEMENT

MACHINE WORK

MANAGERIAL AND SUPERVISORY WORK

PHOTOGRAPHY AND COMMUNICATIONS

TRANSPORTATION

WRITING

APPENDIX F

NEW YORK STATE DEPARTMENT OF LABOR
Manpower Services Division

OMB 44-R0722

Estab. & Sched. No. ____________

JOB ANALYSIS SCHEDULE

1. Estab. Job Title BOOKKEEPER, GENERAL LEDGER POSTING AND TRIAL BALANCE

2. Ind. Assign. Retail Trade

3. SIC Code(s) and Title(s) Department Stores - 5311

DOT Title GENERAL LEDGER BOOKKEEPER, UNDER BOOKKEEPER I

Code 210.388

Ind. Desig. Clerical

WTA Group Computing & Related Recording P. 280

4. JOB SUMMARY:

Posts to and maintains general ledger; takes periodic trial balance and closes profit-and-loss statements into general-ledger control account; maintains capital-expenditure and depreciation records and prepares annual fixtures-and-equipment report; prepares profit-and-loss recapitulation; and reconciles general and subsidiary ledgers to provide overall accounting data for use of accountants, auditors, and management of department-store chain and parent company.

5. WORK PERFORMED RATINGS:

	(D)	P	T
Worker Functions	Data	People	Things
	3	6	2

Work Field Accounting-Recording - 232

M.P.S.M.S. Bookkeeping - 893

6. WORKER TRAITS RATINGS:

GED 1 2 3 (4) 5 6

SVP 1 2 3 4 5 (6) 7 8 9

Aptitudes G 3 V 3 N 2 S 4 P 4 Q 2 K 3 F 3 M 3 E 5 C 5

Temperaments D F I J M P (R) S (T) V

Interests (1a) 1b 2a 2b (3a) 3b 4a (4b) 5a 5b

Phys. Demands (S) L M H V 2 3 (4) 5 6

Environ. Cond. (I) O B 2 3 4 5 6 7

FO 92 (4-74)

7. General Education

    a. Elementary ___8___ High School ___4___ Courses _Commercial diploma with at least_
                                                          two years bookkeeping. Compare 8b.

    b. College ___0___ Courses _____

8. Vocational Preparation

    a. College _____ Courses _____

    b. Vocational Education _____ Courses _2 yr. bookkeeping if high school diploma is_

       other than commercial.

    c. Apprenticeship _‾_____

    d. Inplant Training _‾_____

    e. On-the-Job Training _‾_____

    f. Performance on Other Jobs _‾_____

9. Experience _None_____

10. Orientation _Six months to become familiar with company's bookkeeping procedures._

11. Licenses, etc. _‾_____

12. Relation to Other Jobs and Workers

    Promotion: From _‾_____ To _Supervisor (remote)_

    Transfers: From _Statistical Dept. Clerical_ To _Statistical Dept. Clerical_

    Supervision Received _Genl. Ledger Supervisor_

    Supervision Given _None_____

13. Machines, Tools, Equipment, and Work Aids

    See Supplemental Sheet

14. Materials and Products

    None

15. Job Definition:

1. Maintains general ledger: Receives journals and other records, such as petty cash report and computer printout of accounts payable, from personnel of own and other departments, for posting. Totals columns in each book or other record, using ten-key adding machine, and compares debit and credit totals to determine whether addition is correct and record in balance. Returns records for correction by personnel involved if error is discovered. Posts all entries to general-ledger accounts, totals debit and credit columns for each account, computes difference, using subtraction key of adding machine, to obtain account balance, and enters in debit-or credit-balance column. (30%)

2. Takes trial balance: Transfers all general-ledger account balances to trial-balance page monthly and annually, totals debits and credits, and compares totals to determine whether books balance. Compares all general-ledger postings with original journal entries to locate errors if debits and credits do not balance. Makes corrections as necessary. Closes profit-and-loss statement accounts monthly. Posts trial-balance profit-and-loss figures semi-annually to assets-and-liabilities control account to balance books. (30%)

3. Maintains capital-expenditure and depreciation records: Posts fixed-assest purchase figures from accounts-payable ledger to pages of fixed-assets control book according to vendor and type of equipment purchased. Enters purchases from control book to fixed-assets schedule book, distributing to schedule pages according to nature and estimated life of assets purchased. Totals entries in control and schedule books. Enters data from each schedule to one line of monthly capital expenditures report, listing cost figures and identifying data (such as vendor's name, description of asset, life, and schedule number) under appropriate columnar headings for information of auditors and company officers. Adds job costs to miscellaneous costs on each line of report, enters result in "total" column, totals the three columns, adds "job" total to "miscellaneous" total and compares result with sum of "total" column to verify accuracy. (20%)

4. Prepares annual Fixtures-and-Equipment Report: Transfers yearly total cost figure from each page of fixed-asset schedule book to corresponding line of fixtures-and-equipment report by branch store. Divides cost figure of each category by estimated years of life to determine one-year depreciation and enters results in "depreciation" column. Effects computation by depressing keys of electric or electronic calculator to feed in figures and pressing division or multiplication bar to cause machine to automatically divide or multiply. Computes portion of one-year depreciation chargeable to current-year according to asset-acquisition date as recorded in schedule, using calculating machine, and enters result in current-year depreciation-expense column. Totals cost, one-year, and current-year depreciation figures for each life category (3, 5, 8, 10, or 15 years) and enters results on corresponding line of summary sheet to summarize by life estimates. Totals each column to determine sum of cost and depreciation for entire store. Transfers totals of single-store summary sheets to company-wide summary sheet, detailing cost and depreciation by store, and totals cost and depreciation columns to determine grand totals for entire system. (5%)

5. Prepares profit and loss recap: Copies balances of profit-and-loss statement accounts from trial balance to debit and credit columns opposite pre-printed account numbers and names on summary sheet, and takes totals of columns to supply information to statistical department. (5%)

6. Prepares analysis books: Posts voucher and journal expense entries to analysis book by account, distributes and labels entries within each account according to prescribed classification such as donation by name of donee,

real estate taxes by building, and personal property taxes by store, to provide
data for study by auditors. Prepares recapitulation of data by month at year
end.   (5%)

7. Reconciles general and subsidiary ledgers: Receives accounts payable and
receivable reconciliation sheets from each department monthly, with subsidiary
ledger columns completed. Enters general-ledger control account figures in opposite columns, takes totals, takes balance, and compares with subsidiary ledger
comumns. Returns reconciliation sheet to personnel involved for correction if
errors are discovered.   (5%)

16. Definition of Terms

    None

17. General Comments

18. Analyst_____ Date_____ Editor_____ Date_____

    Reviewed By _____ Title, Org. _Accounting Off. Mgr.   3/20/72_____

    National Office Reviewer_____

NEW YORK STATE DEPARTMENT OF LABOR
MANPOWER SERVICES DIVISION

OMB 44-R0722

Physical Demands and Environmental Conditions

ESTAB. JOB TITLE BOOKKEEPER, GENERAL LEDGER POSTING
AND TRIAL BALANCE   ESTAB. & SCHED. NO.

DOT TITLE AND CODE   GENERAL LEDGER BOOKKEEPER   210.388

PHYSICAL DEMANDS		COMMENTS
1. STRENGTH		
a. Standing _____ %		
Walking _5_ %		
Sitting _95_ %		
b. Weight		
Lifting	NP	
Carrying	NP	
Pushing	NP	
Pulling	NP	
2. CLIMBING	NP	
BALANCING	NP	
3. STOOPING	NP	
KNEELING	NP	
CROUCHING	NP	
CRAWLING	NP	
4. REACHING	F	4. Handles, fingers, and reaches for writing
HANDLING	F	materials and calculating-machine keys and
FINGERING	F	controls.
FEELING	NP	
5. TALKING		
Ordinary	O	5. Present but not critical.
Other	NP	
HEARING		
Ordinary Conversation	O	
Other Sounds	NP	
6. SEEING		6. Near acuity and accommodation necessary for
Acuity, Near	C	checking and copying figures.
Acuity, Far	NP	
Depth Perception	NP	
Accommodation	C	
Color Vision	NP	
Field of Vision	NP	

RATINGS: P.D.:   (S) L M H VH 2 3 (4) 5 (6)

Analyst _____ Date _3/20/72_   Estab. Reviewer _____

E.S. Reviewer _____ Date _4/25/72_   Title _____ Date _3/20/72_

FO 94 (4—74)

ENVIRONMENTAL CONDITIONS		COMMENTS
1. ENVIRONMENT		
Inside_____100__%		
Outside_____%		
2. EXTREME COLD WITH OR WITHOUT TEMPERATURE CHANGES	NP	
3. EXTREME HEAT WITH OR WITHOUT TEMPERATURE CHANGES	NP	
4. WET AND/OR HUMID	NP	
5. NOISE Estimated maximum number of decibels	70 db.	
VIBRATION	NP	
6. HAZARDS Mechanical	NP	
Electrical		
Burns		
Explosives		
Radiant Energy		
Other		
7. ATMOSPHERIC CONDITIONS Fumes	NP	
Odors		
Dusts		
Mists		
Gases		
Poor Ventilation		
Other		

RATINGS: E. C.:   (1)   0   B   2   3   4   5   6   7

PROTECTIVE CLOTHING OR PERSONAL DEVICES

None

SUPPLEMENTAL SHEET

Item 13 - Machines, Tools, Equipment, and Work Aids:

    Journals, Ledgers, Trial Balance, and other accounting books.

    Petty cash report.

    Computer printout of accounts payable.

    Ten-key adding machine.

    Automatic electric calculating machine.

    Miscellaneous columnar work sheets and report forms, including
        expense statements and profit-and-loss statements.

    Writing materials.

APPENDIX G

WORKER TRAIT GROUPS OF LOWER LEVELS OF COMPLEXITY

Page [in *DOT 3*, Volume II]	Worker Trait Group	Three-Digit Code
430	Set Up and/or All-Round Machine Operating	.280
		.380
433	Set Up and Adjustment	.780
435	Operating—Controlling	.782
444	Driving—Operating	.883
447	Tending	.885
479	Child and Adult Care	.878
488	Demonstration and Sales Work	.258
		.358
		.458
493	Selling and Related Work	.858
499	Beautician and Barbering Services	.271
		.371
501	Customer Service Work, n.e.c.	.468
		.478
503	Miscellaneous Customer Service Work	.863
		.864
		.865
		.867
		.873
		.874
		.877
505	Accommodating Work	.868
507	Miscellaneous Personal Service Work (Food Serving, Portering, Valeting, and Related Activities)	.868
		.878
509	Ushering, Messenger Service, and Related Work	.868
		.878
511	Animal Care	.874
		.877
514	Motion Picture Projecting, Photographic Machine Work, and Related Activities	.282
		.382
516	Radio and Television Transmitting and Receiving	.282
		.382
519	Transportation Service Work	.363
		.364
		.463

APPENDIX H

COMPARISON OF *DOT* INTERESTS AND TEMPERAMENTS WITH SUPER'S WORK VALUES INVENTORY

The *DOT* authors made a complete review of all relevant literature before considering the interest and temperament factors to be complete. Nevertheless one might well ask whether the *DOT* interest factors are all-inclusive and how they relate to the interest formulations of other authorities. For example, Super's Work Values Inventory lists the following factors (and others). Each line in the first column represents an interest. The opposite entry in the second column lists the specific interest in the *DOT* formulation under which the Super interest can be subsumed. The numbers following each item in columns refer to the interest identification numbers in Appendix B (*DOT 3*, Volume II, p. 654; reproduced here as Appendix B also).

Super[a]	USES Interests
Are looked up to by others	Prestige (5)
Gain prestige in the field	Prestige (5)
Need to have artistic ability	Abstract, Creative (8)
Get the feeling of having done a good day's work	Tangible, productive satisfaction (0) Abstract, creative (8)
Create something new	Abstract, creative (8)
Add beauty to the world	Prestige (5)
Use leadership abilities	
	USES Temperaments
Have freedom in own area	
Have authority over others	
Make own decisions	Direction, control, and planning of an entire activity (4)

265

Super[a]	USES Interests
Use leadership abilities	Direction, control, and planning of an entire activity (4) Evaluation of information against judgmental criteria (9) Preference for activities resulting in prestige or direction, control (4)

[a] Donald E. Super, *Work Values Inventory* (Boston: Houghton Mifflin, 1968).

This is but *one* example of the scope of the *DOT* interest formulation. Incidentally, these interests might well be included in the *DOT* definitions as examples to clarify the scope and depth of each. Research is needed to establish definitively how far the *DOT* approach includes all other current, significant comparable formulations.

APPENDIX I

New York State Department of Labor
Division of Employment

CONFIDENTIAL STAFFING SCHEDULE
(Title Sheet)

Title Sheet No. ___9___

UNIT NAME ___Business Office___

No. Employees in Unit ___14___

Establishment No. _____

JOB NO.	JOB TITLE	IN-EX.	NO. EMPLOYED			DICTIONARY OF OCCUPATIONAL TITLES				TR.	COMMENTS
			M	F	T	TITLE	CODE	SUF. CODE	WTA GROUP		
	Assistant Treasurer		1		1	Treasurer	161.118	010	237		
	Business Manager		1		1	Business Manager, College	186.118	010	237		
	Comptroller		1		1	Controller	186.118	014	237		
	Head Accountant		1		1	Accountant	160.188	010	252		
	Accountant			1	1	Bookkeeper I	210.388	022	280		
	Secretary II			1	1	Secretary	201.368	018	263		
	Bookkeeper, Students Accounts			3	3	Accounting Clerk	219.488	036	280		
	Bookkeeper, Accounts Payable			1	1	Bookkeeping - Machine Operator	215.388	010	280		NCR 3300 (I or II?)
	Payroll Clerk			2	2	Pay-Roll Clerk	215.488	010	280		
	Cashier			2	2	Cashier I	211.368	010	267		

FO 91 (2-72)

New York State Department of Labor
Division of Employment

OMB 44-R0722

CONFIDENTIAL STAFFING SCHEDULE
(Title Sheet)

UNIT NAME Purchasing and Bookstore

Title Sheet No. 24

No. Employees in Unit _____

Establishment No. _____

JOB NO.	JOB TITLE	IN-EX.	NO. EMPLOYED			DICTIONARY OF OCCUPATIONAL TITLES				TR.	COMMENTS
			M	F	T	TITLE	CODE	SUF. CODE	WTA GROUP		
1	Director		1		1	PURCHASING AGENT	162.158	102	484		
		Purchasing									
2	General Services Supervisor		1		1	RECEIVING & SHIPPING FORE-MAN PROPERTY MAN	223.138 964.168	022 014	243 261		
3	Clerk-Typist			1	1	PROCUREMENT CLERK	223.368	014	258		
		Bookstore									
4	Bookstore Manager		1		1	MANAGER, STORE I	185.168	054	245		
5	Bookkeeper			1	1	BOOKKEEPER II	210.388	026	280		
6	Secretary			1	1	PROCUREMENT CLERK	223.368	014	258		
7	Cashier			1	1	CASHIER II	211.468	010	269		

FO 91 (2-72)

New York State Department of Labor
Division of Employment

CONFIDENTIAL STAFFING SCHEDULE
(Title Sheet)

OMB 44-R0722

UNIT NAME ___Computer Center___

No. Employees in Unit ___5___

Title Sheet No. ___30___

Establishment No. _____

JOB NO.	JOB TITLE	IN-EX.	NO. EMPLOYED M	F	T	DICTIONARY OF OCCUPATIONAL TITLES TITLE	CODE	SUF. CODE	WTA GROUP	TR.	COMMENTS
1	Director		1		1	Manager, Electronic Data Processing	169.168	058	245		many titles might apply
2	Programmer			1	1	Programmer, Business	020.188	026	468		Performs secretarial duties as well
5	Keypunch Operator, Verifier			1	1	Keypunch Operator	213.582	010	274		
3	Senior /Console Operator			1	1	Supervisor, Computer Operations	213.138	018	243		
4	Console Operator			1	1	Digital-Computer Operator	213.382	018	274		Assists in Keypunch when necessary

FO 91 (2-72)

APPENDIX J

EMPLOYER'S NAME	SAMPLE OF A POSITION DESCRIPTION		CODE
WAGNER COLLEGE	FINANCIAL-AIDS OFFICER		090.118
ADDRESS	EMPLOYER'S JOB TITLE-DEPARTMENT Director - Financial Aid		CODE
TELEPHONE	PERSON TO SEE-HOW TO REACH	HOURS OF WORK	
		UNION	
INDUSTRY	CODE	RATE OF PAY	SEX AGE

NO.	JOB DUTIES	NO.	SKILLS, KNOWLEDGE, ABILITIES
	Directs and coordinates student Financial-Aid Program at college; determines which student-candidates or students are eligible for financial aid and what type and amount of financial aid is to be awarded:		
1	Interviews student-candidate, student, and/or parents to learn college costs and income to determine financial aid needed to begin or stay in college. Explains eligibility under various Federal and State loan, grant and scholarship programs and college scholarship and grant programs.	1	Must be throughly familiar with requirements under the following federal, state, and college financial aid programs: National Defense student loan program, Educational Opportunities Grant, and College Work Study Program: New York State guaranteed loan program; New York State Scholar Incentive, and New York State Regents Scholarship; various scholarship and grants from the college.
2	Advises student-candidate, student, and/or parents, in person, on phone, or by letter, what forms must be completed or information required and when and where to send or bring completed forms or information in order to apply for, expedite, or receive financial aid.		
3	Counsels student, upon request, on how to overcome certain personal problems, such as relations with parents, drug use, or money problems (i.e. helps student prepare personal budget), in order to stay in college. Refers student to person at college best equipped to help student with certain problems, such as school psychologist.	2	Same as Task #1, and must also know procedures and forms used and routing of forms in applying for financial aid.
4	Evaluates information acquired about student-candidate, student, or parents, such as confidential earnings statement, letters of recommendation, transcript of grades, computer print-out on student grades and expenditures, or athletic or talent appraisals, against requirements of various Federal, State or college Financial Aid Programs, to determine if student is eligible for financial aid, what type of aid and how much will be offered.		

EXPERIENCE	INTERESTS & TEMPERAMENTS
*1 yr. minimum in Financial Aid to students and 2 yrs. in some area of student personnel activities	Interest 2. Talks to students & parents to determine eligibility for financial aid - see task #1. Interest 4. Attempts to find legitimate eligibility to help student secure enough money to attend college - see tasks 3 & 4.
EDUCATION & TRAINING	Interest 5. Has authority to dispense financial aid - see task #4.
*Master's Degree in Student Personnel Administration. (Requires minimum of six months to learn job.)**	Interest 6. Prepares annual report of disposition of funds.

	PROF.	GED	SVP	G	V	N	S	P	Q	K	F	M	E	C	INT	TEMP	PD	EC	REASON FOR VARIANCE (TASK NO. 5)
TAPE		5	8	1	1	2	4	4	2	4	4	4	5	5	4,6	4,5	S,5	I	
FIRM	*5	7	2	2	3	5	5	2	4	4	4	5	4	2,5	2,0	S45	I		

FORM ES 541 (8/1/72) N.Y.S. - DEPT. OF LABOR JOB SPECIFICATION FORM

NO.	JOB DUTIES	NO.	SKILLS, KNOWLEDGE, ABILITIES
5	Supervises and coordinates activities of clerical staff of three or four in recording financial aid transactions maintaining student or student-candidate folders, compiling and computing data for periodic reports, arranging appointments, giving out routine information or advice to students and parents, and typing correspondence.	3	Must know which college personnel are trained or experienced to help students with certain problems.
		4	Same as Tasks # 1 & 2. Also see Comments.
6	Occasionally reviews financial records to determine how much federal funds remain for disposition during remainder of current fiscal year for loans or grants.	5.	See Comments
7	Prepares or assists in preparation of various reports on disposition and request of funds used for financial aid to students or for office budget, such as annual statistical report on disposition of federal funds for student financial aid, annual request and jurisdiction for new federal education aid funds, monthly report on financial aid expenditures and individual student need analysis sheets for Financial Aid Committee meeting, annual report of disposition of college scholarship and grant funds and annual department budget request to college administration.	7	Must know the statutory and/or administrative requirements and format for each required report. Clerical and numerical perception. Must be able to write correctly and effectively.

ENVIRONMENTAL CONDITIONS

1. ENVIRONMENT
   Inside...100.%
   Outside......%
2. EXTREME COLD WITH OR WITH-OUT TEMPERATURE CHANGES........
3. EXTREME HEAT WITH OR WITH-OUT TEMPERATURE CHANGES........
4. WET AND/OR HUMID ....
5. NOISE
   Estimated maximum
   number of decibels ....
   VIBRATION
6. HAZARDS
   Mechanical ....
   Electrical ....
   Burns ....
   Explosives ....
   Radiant Energy ....
   Other ....
7. ATMOSPHERIC CONDITIONS
   Fumes ....
   Odors ....
   Dusts ....
   Mists ....
   Gases ....
   Poor Ventilation ....
   Other ....

PHYSICAL CONDITIONS

1. STRENGTH   WEIGHT
   a. Standing...5..% b. Lifting ....
   Walking .25..% Carrying........
   Sitting .22..% Pushing ....
   Pulling ....
2. CLIMBING ....
   BALANCING ....
3. STOOPING ....
   KNEELING ....
   CROUCHING ....
   CRAWLING ....
4. REACHING ....
   HANDLING ....
   FINGERING ....
   FEELING ....
5. TALKING ....
   Ordinary ....
   Other ....
   HEARING ....
   Ordinary Conversation ....
   Other Sounds ....
6. SEEING ....
   Acuity, Near ....
   Acuity, Far ....
   Depth Perception ....
   Accommodation ....
   Color Vision ....
   Field of Vision ....

DETAILS OF PHYSICAL ACTIVITIES & ENVIRONMENTAL CONDITIONS

Works inside 100%. Handles and fingers forms, correspondence and reports and writes comments and notes frequently. Listens and speaks when interviewing, advising, or counseling students and/or parents.

PROMOTIONAL SOURCES & LINES

To: None
From: Assistant Director

WORKER TRAIT GROUP PAGE NOS.

DIRECT	RELATED
P. 237	P. 245

COMMENTS

Director of Department will make final decision if a difference of opinion with Assistant Director occurs on whether to award financial aid or how much or what work the clerical staff should be doing. Usually the Assistant Director supervises and coordinates activities of clerical staff. The applications for financial aid are divided so that the Director handles upper-class student-candidates and freshman students. In all other respects, job duties are the same for these two positions.

DATE PREPARED   September 22, 1972

BY   Peter A. Thomas

APPROVED BY

EMPLOYER'S NAME		OCCUPATIONAL TITLE		CODE
WAGNER COLLEGE		FINANCIAL-AIDS OFFICER		090.118
ADDRESS		EMPLOYER'S JOB TITLE-DEPARTMENT		CODE
TELEPHONE	PERSON TO SEE-HOW TO REACH	HOURS OF WORK		
		UNION		
INDUSTRY	CODE	RATE OF PAY	SEX	AGE

NO.	JOB DUTIES	NO.	SKILLS, KNOWLEDGE, ABILITIES
3	Attends monthly meeting of Financial Aid Committee to present selected or difficult applications for scholarships, grants, or loans to get advice and consent of committee on whether award should be made and type and amount of financial aid to be offered.	8	Verbal ability to present point of view.

INTERESTS & TEMPERAMENTS

Temperament 4. Supervises and coordinates work of others - See Task #5.
Temperament 5. Interviews students and parents - See Task #1.
Temperament 9. Counsels students on personal problems and makes qualitative judgment about student's willingness to do well in school and pay back loan - See Task #3.
Temperament 0. Determines eligibility based on financial data - See Task #3.

REASON FOR VARIANCE (TASK NO.'S) (cont')
SVP - School believes job requires 3 years experience minimum. Analyst feels 1 year minimum is sufficient.
G,V,N - Analyst believes tape ratings too high for this job.
C - Must discern different color copies of snap out form.
PD-4 - Frequent use of hands and fingers to write and handle forms.

EXPERIENCE

EDUCATION & TRAINING

	PROF.	GED	SVP	G	V	N	S	P	Q	K	F	M	E	C	INT.	TEMP	PD	EC	REASON FOR VARIANCE (TASK NO.'S.)
TAPE																			
FIRM																			

FORM ES 541 (8/1/72)   N.Y.S. - DEPT. OF LABOR   JOB SPECIFICATION FORM

NO.	JOB DUTIES	NO.	SKILLS, KNOWLEDGE, ABILITIES

ENVIRONMENTAL CONDITIONS

1. ENVIRONMENT
    Inside........%
    Outside......%
2. EXTREME COLD WITH OR WITH-
    OUT TEMPERATURE CHANGES........
3. EXTREME HEAT WITH OR WITH-
    OUT TEMPERATURE CHANGES........
4. WET AND/OR HUMID   ....
5. NOISE
    Estimated maximum
    number of decibels   ....
    VIBRATION   ....
6. HAZARDS
    Mechanical   ....
    Electrical   ....
    Burns   ....
    Explosives   ....
    Radiant Energy   ....
    Other   ....
7. ATMOSPHERIC CONDITIONS
    Fumes   ....
    Odors   ....
    Dusts   ....
    Mists   ....
    Gases   ....
    Poor Ventilation   ....
    Other   ....

PHYSICAL CONDITIONS

1. STRENGTH   WEIGHT
    a. Standing.......% b. Lifting ....
    Walking ....%   Carrying........
    Sitting ....%   Pushing ....
                        Pulling ....
2. CLIMBING   ....
    BALANCING   ....
3. STOOPING   ....
    KNEELING   ....
    CROUCHING   ....
    CRAWLING   ....
4. REACHING   ....
    HANDLING   ....
    FINGERING   ....
    FEELING   ....
5. TALKING
    Ordinary   ....
    Other   ....
    HEARING
    Ordinary Conversation ....
    Other Sounds   ....
6. SEEING
    Acuity, Near   ....
    Acuity, Far   ....
    Depth Perception   ....
    Accommodation   ....
    Color Vision   ....
    Field of Vision   ....

DETAILS OF PHYSICAL ACTIVITIES & ENVIRONMENTAL CONDITIONS

PROMOTIONAL SOURCES & LINES

WORKER TRAIT GROUP PAGE NOS.

DIRECT	RELATED

COMMENTS

DATE PREPARED

BY

APPROVED BY

APPENDIX K

DIAGNOSTIC INTERVIEW FORM, NEW YORK STATE EMPLOYMENT SERVICE

A diagnostic interview form from the New York State Employment Service, filled out in handwriting. The form includes sections for:

- 18. ACTIONS TO BE TAKEN BY APPLICANT AND PROGRESSIVE SUMMARY OF CONTACTS OTHER THAN REFERRALS, with handwritten entries describing past work activities (bookstore activities, cash register operation, bookkeeping, switchboard operator, student employee in purchasing department, physician's assistant duties including preparing and administering medication)
- 19. CALLED IN / REFERRAL / EMPLOYER / JOB TITLE / DUR / PAY / RESULT / REMARKS / INTERVIEWER
- A–20 column grid
- 1. PRINT LAST NAME / FIRST NAME / INITIAL / 2. S.S.A. NO.
- OCCUPATIONAL TITLES / CODES
- 3. ADDRESS (STREET, CITY, ZIP CODE): Jersey City, N.J. 07307
- 4. TELEPHONE NUMBER / 5. HEIGHT / WEIGHT / 6. BIRTH DATE: MO. 10 DAY 16 YR. 48
- 7. MARRIED / SINGLE / OTHER
- 12. EDUCATION AND TRAINING (CIRCLE HIGHEST GRADE COMPLETED): GRADE SCHOOL 1 2 3 4 5 6 7 8 / HIGH SCHOOL 1 2 3 4 / COLLEGE 1 2 3 4
- NAME OF SCHOOL: Wagner College / COURSE OR MAJOR: Medical Technology / DEGREE: B.S. / YEAR COMPLETED: 1970
- OTHER TRAINING: Started college as nursing major. Completed 3 yrs. Lost interest because of personal problem. B.S. in Medical Technology.

274

(A) WORK EXPERIENCE LIST (LAST JOB FIRST) THEN LIST OTHER MOST IMPORTANT AND LONGEST JOBS	(B) PRINCIPAL TASKS PERFORMED	(C) APPRAISAL OF APPLICANT'S LIKES AND DISLIKES AND LEVELS OF CAPABILITY	
		(1) LIKES OR DISLIKES	(2) CAPABILITY AND LEVEL OF COMPLEXITY

1
NAME OF FIRM
ADDRESS
KIND OF BUSINESS
EMPLOYED FROM MONTH / YEAR / TO MONTH / YEAR / RATE OF PAY
REASON FOR LEAVING

2
NAME OF FIRM
ADDRESS
KIND OF BUSINESS
EMPLOYED FROM MONTH / YEAR / TO MONTH / YEAR / RATE OF PAY
REASON FOR LEAVING

3
NAME OF FIRM
ADDRESS
KIND OF BUSINESS
EMPLOYED FROM MONTH / YEAR 67 / TO MONTH / YEAR 66 / RATE OF PAY
REASON FOR LEAVING

4
NAME OF FIRM
ADDRESS
KIND OF BUSINESS
EMPLOYED FROM MONTH / YEAR / TO MONTH / YEAR / RATE OF PAY
REASON FOR LEAVING

(D) OTHER DATA: ☐1 SP ☐2 APPEARANCE, MANNER ☐4 OTHER
☐3 TEST RESULTS OTHER THAN GATB

(E) APPLICANT'S JOB PREFERENCES

(F) EMPLOYMENT PROSPECTS

	WORKER FUNCTIONS		
	POTENTIAL	D	P	T
	TEMPERAMENTS	2 4 5		

(G) APTITUDES	G	V	N	S	P	Q	K	F	M	E	C
(H) GED											
(I) PHYSICAL CAPACITIES											
(J) WORKING CONDITIONS											

E.S. 66.4 (1-70)   N.Y.-DEPT. OF LABOR-D.E.   APPLICATION CARD
(over)

APPENDIX L

DIAGNOSTIC INTERVIEW FORM, WAGNER COLLEGE

NAME OF FIRM	(B) PRINCIPAL TASKS PERFORMED	LIKES OR DISLIKES
ADDRESS		
KIND OF BUSINESS		
5 EMPLOYED FROM / TO / RATE OF PAY MONTH YEAR / MONTH YEAR REASON FOR LEAVING		

DATE	ADDITIONAL DATA — SUBSEQUENT INTERVIEWS

A	B	C	D	E	F	G	H	I	J	1	2	3	4	5	6	7	8	9	10		13	14	15	16	17	18	19	20

1. PRINT: LAST NAME FIRST NAME INITIAL	2. S.S.A. NO.	6. DOT OCCUPATIONAL TITLES	CODES

3. EDUCATION AND TRAINING:	GRADE SCHOOL	HIGH SCHOOL	COLLEGE
(CIRCLE HIGHEST GRADE COMPLETED)	1 2 3 4 5 6 7 8	1 2 3 4	1 2 3 4

NAME OF SCHOOL	COURSE OR MAJOR	MINOR	DEGREE	YEAR COMPLETED

4. OTHER TRAINING: (INCLUDE WHERE PERTINENT SUBJECTS LIKED BEST AND LEAST: FOREIGN LANGUAGES, MEMBERSHIP IN PROFESSIONAL SOCIETIES, SPECIAL HONORS.)

7. COMMENTS:

5. DESCRIBE ANY PHYSICAL DISABILITY.

STATE LAW PROHIBITS DISCRIMINATION ON THE BASIS OF AGE, SEX, RACE, CREED OR NATIONAL ORIGIN.

APPLICATION CARD

(A) WORK EXPERIENCE LIST LAST JOB FIRST — THEN LIST OTHER MOST IMPORTANT AND LONGEST JOBS.

(B) PRINCIPAL TASKS PERFORMED

(C) APPRAISAL OF APPLICANT LEVELS OF CAPABILITY

(1) LIKES OR DISLIKES

1
NAME OF FIRM
ADDRESS
KIND OF BUSINESS
EMPLOYED FROM   TO
MONTH   YEAR   MONTH   YEAR   RATE OF PAY
REASON FOR LEAVING

2
NAME OF FIRM
ADDRESS
KIND OF BUSINESS
EMPLOYED FROM   TO
MONTH   YEAR   MONTH   YEAR   RATE OF PAY
REASON FOR LEAVING

3
NAME OF FIRM
ADDRESS
KIND OF BUSINESS
EMPLOYED FROM   TO
MONTH   YEAR   MONTH   YEAR   RATE OF PAY
REASON FOR LEAVING

4
NAME OF FIRM
ADDRESS
KIND OF BUSINESS
EMPLOYED FROM   TO
MONTH   YEAR   MONTH   YEAR   RATE OF PAY
REASON FOR LEAVING

INTERESTS
TEMPERAMENTS

(CONTINUE OVERLEAF)

(D) OTHER DATA [1] SP [2] APPEARANCE MANNER
[3] TEST RESULTS [4] OTHER

(E) CAPABILITY AND LEVEL OF COMPLEXITY

(F) APPLICANT'S JOB PREFERENCES & PLANS

(G) APTITUDES   G V N S P Q K F M E C
(H) GED
(I) PHYSICAL CAPACITIES
(J) WORKING CONDITIONS

(K) WORKER FUNCTIONS   D   P   T
POTENTIAL

N.Y.S. DEPT. OF LABOR

APPENDIX M

SAMPLE OF A WORKER TRAIT GROUP

COMPUTING AND RELATED RECORDING
.388; .488

Work Performed

Work activities in this group primarily involve performing arithmetic computations and preparing numerical records with the aid of typewriters and adding, billing, bookkeeping, and calculating machines. Typical activities are computing wages, interest, and production costs; totaling bank deposit slips; and verifying computations recorded in accounts.

Worker Requirements

An occupationally significant combination of: Intellectual capacity and interest sufficient to acquire an understanding of systematic, numerical, recordkeeping and data-gathering procedures; ability to apply arithmetic principles and correct computational errors; attention to detail to avoid clerical errors; form perception eye-hand coordination; and finger and manual dexterity.

Clues for Relating Applicants and Requirements

Expressed preference for clerical work.
Good grades in arithmetic and pertinent clerical subjects in school.

Training and Methods of Entry

Graduation from high school and business school with average or superior grades in arithmetic frequently is the minimum requirement for entry into this type of work.

For some kinds of work, specialized training on a particular machine is required. For many beginning positions, however, a general knowledge of the work and the equipment involved usually is regarded as sufficient preparation. Often an employer will give a new employee instruction and on-the-job training, ranging anywhere from a few days to several months, depending chiefly on the type of work or the kind of machine involved.

RELATED CLASSIFICATIONS
Accounting, Auditing, and Related Work (.188; .288) p. 252

Paying and Receiving (Banks and Other Establishments) (.368) p. 267

Cashiering (Drug Stores, Theaters, Restaurants, and Related Establishments) (.468) p. 269

Routine Checking and Recording (.588; .688) p. 289

QUALIFICATIONS PROFILE
GED: 3 4
SVP   3 4 5

Apt: **GVN S PQ KFM** EC
        3 3 3   4 4 2   3 3 3   5 5
        2 2   5 3 3   2 2   4

Int: 3
Temp: 3 Y
Phys. Dem: S   L   4   6

278

15	**ENTERTAINMENT AND RECREA-TION**
153.	**Athletics and Sports**
153.488	CLERK-OF-SCALES (amuse. & rec.)
16	**ADMINISTRATIVE SPECIALTIES**
168.	**Inspecting and Investigating, Managerial and Public Service**
168.388	LIABILITY EVALUATOR (gov. ser.)
18	**MANAGERIAL WORK, N.E.C.**
184.	**Transportation, Communication, and Utilities Management**
184.388	WHARFINGER (water trans.) I
20	**STENOGRAPHY, TYPING, FILING, AND RELATED WORK**
209.	**Stenography, Typing, Filing, and Related Work, n.e.c.**
209.488	CIRCULATION CLERK (print. & pub.)
	COUPON CLERK (banking)
	INVOICE-CONTROL CLERK (clerical)
21	**COMPUTING AND ACCOUNT RECORDING**
210.	**Bookkeeping**
210.388	AUDIT CLERK (clerical)
	DISTRIBUTION ACCOUNTING CLERK (light, heat, & power)
	RECONCILEMENT CLERK (banking)
	BILLING CONTROL CLERK (light, heat, & power)
	BOOKKEEPER (clerical) I
	GENERAL-LEDGER BOOKKEEPER (banking)
	NIGHT AUDITOR (hotel & rest.)
	BOOKEEPER (clerical) II
	ACCOUNT-CLASSIFICATION CLERK (clerical)
	CLASSIFICATION-CONTROL CLERK (clerical)
	COMMODITY/LOAN CLERK (banking)
	FIXED-CAPITAL CLERK (light, heat, & power)
	MEDICAL-VOUCHER CLERK (insurance)
	MORTGAGE-LOAN-COMPUTATION CLERK (insurance)
	CHART CALCULATOR (light, heat, & power)
	DIVIDEND-DEPOSIT-VOUCHER QUOTER (insurance)
211.	**Cashiering**
211.488	MONEY COUNTER (amuse. & rec.)
	MONEY COUNTER (ret. tr.: whole. tr.)
214.	**Billing-Machine Work**
214.488	BILLING-MACHINE OPERATOR (clerical)
215.	**Bookkeeping-Machine Work**
215.388	BOOKKEEPING-MACHINE OPERATOR (clerical) I
	BOOKKEEPING-MACHINE OPERATOR (clerical) II
215.488	PAY-ROLL CLERK (clerical)
216.	**Computing-Machine Work**
216.388	BALANCE CLERK (clerical)

	BANK-RECONCILIATION CLERK (clerical)
216.488	ADDING-MACHINE OPERATOR (clerical)
	AUDIT-MACHINE OPERATOR (clerical)
	CALCULATING-MACHINE OPERATOR (clerical)
	POLICY-VALUE CALCULATOR (insurance)
	TESTER, RECORDING AND CHECKING (nonfer. metal alloys)
	FOOD CHECKER (hotel & rest.) I
	FOOD CHECKER (hotel & rest.) II
	FOOD CONTROLLER (hotel & rest.)
	INTERLINE CLERK (r.r. trans.)
217.	**Account-Recording-Machine Work, n.e.c.**
217.388	PROOF MACHINE OPERATOR (banking)
	TRANSIT CLERK (banking)
219.	**Computing and Account Recording, n.e.c.**
219.388	ACCOUNT ANALYST (banking)
	ACTUARIAL CLERK (insurance)
	AIRCRAFT-LOG CLERK (air trans.)
	BILLING CLERK (clerical) II
	BOND CLERK (banking)
	ADVICE CLERK (banking)
	COUPON-COLLECTION CLERK (banking)
	BOX-ESTIMATOR, PAPER BOARD PRODUCTS (paper goods)
	BUDGET CLERK (clerical)
	CITY-COLLECTION CLERK (banking)
	CLEARING-HOUSE CLERK (banking)
	CLERK, CABLE TRANSFER (tel. & tel.)
	CLERK, GENERAL OFFICE (clerical)
	CONTRACT CLERK, AUTOMOBILE (ret. tr.)
	DISTRICT CLERK (clerical)
	MANIFEST CLERK (water trans.)
	SETTLEMENT CLERK (ore dress., smelt., & refin.)
	TAX CLERK (clerical) I
	WARD CLERK (medical ser.)
	C.O.D. CLERK (clerical)
	COLLATERAL-AND-SAFEKEEPING CLERK (banking)
	CONTROL CLERK, AUDITING (insurance)
	COUNTRY-COLLECTION CLERK (banking)
	DEMURRAGE CLERK (r.r. trans.)
	EXCHANGE CLERK (banking)
	FOREIGN-COLLECTION CLERK (banking)
	INSURANCE CLERK (banking) I
	INTEREST CLERK (banking)
	LOAD-CONTROL AGENT (air trans.)
	MAIN-EXTENSION CLERK (light, heat, & power)
	MARGIN CLERK (banking)
	MARGIN CLERK (finan. inst.)
	MEDIA CLERK (bus. ser.)

869.	Miscellaneous Construction Work, n.e.c.
869.388	MEASUREMAN (ret. tr.)
91	**TRANSPORTATION WORK, N.E.C.**
910.	**Railroad Transportation**
910.388	TARIFF INSPECTOR (r.r. trans.)
911.	**Water Transportation**
911.388	RECEIPT-AND-REPORT CLERK (water trans.)
911.488	TONNAGE-COMPILATION CLERK (water trans.)
912.	**Air Transportation**
912.488	TRAFFIC-RATE CLERK (air trans.)
94	**LOGGING**
941.	**Log Inspecting, Grading, Scaling, and Related Work**
941.488	LOG SCALER (logging; paper & pulp; sawmill)

APPENDIX N

WAGNER COLLEGE JOB TITLES BY WORKER TRAIT GROUP AND *DOT* TITLES AND CODES

WTG Page Number	*DOT* code	*DOT* title	Wagner Job Title
237	090.118-010	Academic Dean	Academic Supervisor; Asst. Dean, Academic Affairs; Dean, Academic Affairs; Dean of Faculty
	090.118-014	Alumni Secretary	Director, Alumni Affairs
	090.118-018	Dean of Students	Dean of Students; Dean (Men or Women)
	090.118-026	Financial Aids Officer	Asst. Director, Financial Aid; Director, Financial Aid
	090.168-014	Director of Admissions I	Associate Director of Admissions; Director of Admissions
	090.168-022	Director of Student Affairs	Director, Wagner Union
	099.168-034	Registrar, College or University	Registrar
	100.118-010	Library Director	Head Librarian
	161.118-018	Treasurer	Asst. Treasurer
	166.118-022	Manager, Personnel	Director of Personnel
	186.118-014	Controller	Controller
	189.118-010	Association Executive	Asst. Director of Development; Director of Development
239	165.118 (tent.)		Director of Church Relations; Director of Foundation
243	207.138-010	Chief Clerk, Print Shop	Asst. Supervisor Lettershop; Supervisor, Lettershop
	213.138-010	Supervisor, Computer Operations	Senior Console Operator
	223.138-022	Receiving and Shipping Foreman	General Services Supervisor

WTG Page Number	DOT Code	DOT Title	Wagner Job Title
	231.138-010	Mailing Supervisor	Asst. Supervisor, Postal Center
	235.138-014	Telephone Operator, Chief	Chief Operator
245	090.168-010	Department Head, College or University	Director of Graduate Studies and Professional Programs
	100.168-030	Librarian, Reference Library	Reference Librarian
	169.168-014	Administrative Assistant	Asst. to Director, Graduate Studies; Asst. to President; Secretary II, Library
	169.168-058	Manager, Electronic Data Processing	Director, Computer Center
	169.168-062	Manager, Office	Recorder, Registrar's Office
	185.168-054	Manager, Store I	Bookstore Manager
	187.168-094	Manager, Front Office	Asst. Director, Wagner Union
250	166.268-014	Employment Interviewer I	Affirmative Action Assistant
	166.268-030	Personnel Recruiter	Asst. Director of Admissions
	166.268-034	Placement Officer	Placement Officer
252	160.188-010	Accountant	Head Accountant
258	205.368-014	Employment Clerk	Clerk-Typist (Personnel)
	205.368-026	Personnel Clerk	Clerk-Typist (Personnel)
	223.368-014	Procurement Clerk	Clerk-Typist (Purchasing); Secretary (Bookstore)
	249.368-050	Library Assistant	Library Asst., Periodicals
261	964.168-014	Property Man	General Services Supervisor
263	201.368-018	Secretary	Administrative Assistant (Alumni Affairs); Faculty Secretary; Faculty Secretary (Education); Registrar's Assistant; *Secretary:* Admissions; Athletic Department;

WTG Page Number	DOT Code	DOT Title	Wagner Job Title
			Chaplain's Office; Nursing Department Director; Nursing Department Faculty; Dean of Academic Affairs
			Secretary I: Development Office; President's Office
			Secretary II: Bregenz Program; Business Office; Assistant Dean of Academic Affairs; Dean of Faculty; Assistant Dean of Students; Dean of Students; Development Office; Asst. Director of Development; Director of Development; Financial Aid Office; Graduate Studies; Personnel; Vice Pres President's Office; Registrar; Security Department; Special Programs
			Secretary III: Asst. to President; President's Confidential Secretary
			Supervising Secretary, Admissions
265	222.368-014	Expediter I	Library Asst., Ordering Department
267	211.368-010	Cashier I	Cashier (Business Office)
269	211.468-010	Cashier II	Cashier (Bookstore)
271	222.387-018	Receiving Clerk	General Services Manager (Chemistry Department)

WTG Page Number	DOT Code	DOT Title	Wagner Job Title
274	213.382-018	Digital-Computer Operator	Console Operator
	213.582-010	Key-Punch Operator	Key-Punch Operator
	234.582-010	Addressing-Machine Operator	Graphotype Operator
276	100.388-010	Cataloger	Assistant Cataloger
	206.388-022	File Clerk II	Alumni Records Clerk; Library Asst., Catalog
	209.388-022	Clerk-Typist	Clerk-Typist: Development Office; Financial Aid Reception
280	210.388-022	Bookkeeper I	Accountant (Business Office)
	210.388-026	Bookkeeper II	Bookkeeper (Bookstore)
	215.388-010	Bookkeeping Machine Operator I	Bookkeeper, A/P, Business Office
	215.488-010	Payroll Clerk	Payroll Clerk-Business Office
	219.388-066	Clerk, General Office	Clerk-Typist (Financial Aid); Registrar's Assistant; Registrar's Assistant, Records; Secretary (Chemistry Department); Transcript Clerk
	219.488-010	Accounting Clerk	Bookkeeper, Students' Accounts (Business Office)
289	209.588-018	Clerk, General	File Clerk (Lettershop)
	231.588-014	Mail Clerk	Mail Clerk
291	235.862-026	Telephone Operator	Operator
206	045.108-010	Counselor II	HEOP Counselor
	045.108-018	Director of Guidance	Assistant to Director, Special Programs; Director Special Programs
	045.108-038	Residence Counselor	Resident Coordinator; Resident Director
	099.108-014	Foreign Student Advisor	Coordinator, Bregenz Program
360	381.887-026	Porter I	Porter (Biology Department)

WTG Page Number	DOT Code	DOT Title	Wagner Job Title
416	372.168-010	Guard, Chief	Chief of Security
435	207.782-014	Offset-Duplicating Machine Operator	Offset Printer
	208.782-014	Embossing Machine Operator II	Graphotype Operator
468	020.188-026	Programmer, Business	Programmer-Secretary
482	164.068-010	Advertising Assistant	Director of Publications
	165.068-018	Public-Relations Man I	Director of News Bureau
484	162.158-102	Purchasing Agent	Director of Purchasing

APPENDIX O

SUPERVISORY REVIEW			Date	
Employee Current Job Title:		Period	From	To
		Department		

I have the following comments regarding this employee:

1. Performs the following duties best:

2. Could probably perform the following higher or other duties:
   a. New Duties

   b. Training Needed or Desirable.

3. Other Comments:

Supervisor   Title:

APPENDIX P

```
┌─────────────────────────────────────────────────────────────────┐
│              REQUEST FOR CONSIDERATION                          │
│              FOR POSSIBLE JOB OPENING                           │
│                                    Date                         │
├─────────────────────────────────────────────────────────────────┤
│ Job Title:                  Department:                         │
│ D.O.T. Code                 W.T.G. p.                           │
├─────────────────────────────────────────────────────────────────┤
│ I would like to be considered for this job if and when an       │
│ opening occurs.  I believe my qualifications (listed below)     │
│ support this request.                                           │
│                                                                 │
│ Experience                           Education                  │
│                                                                 │
│                                                                 │
│                                                                 │
│ Training                             Personal Traits            │
│                                                                 │
│                                                                 │
│ Other Comments:                                                 │
│                            Signature:_____          │
│                            Present Department                   │
├─────────────────────────────────────────────────────────────────┤
│ Reason for submitting this request                              │
│   In response to Notification of Job Opening No. ____           │
│      On my own initiative                                       │
│ Form "B"                                                        │
└─────────────────────────────────────────────────────────────────┘
```

APPENDIX Q

NOTICE OF JOB OPPORTUNITY AT WAGNER COLLEGE

Job Title: _____

A vacancy exists or is expected for this job.

A description of the job duties is attached.

If you think you can perform these duties and want to be considered, ask the Personnel Office for Form B. When you obtain Form B, enter in the space provided, information about your experience, education, and training.

The Personnel Office will consider all candidates in filling this vacancy.

APPENDIX R

WAGNER COLLEGE JOB TITLES CLASSIFIED BY *DOT* TITLES AND MAJOR CENSUS CATEGORIES (SAMPLE PAGES)

Census Category	*DOT* Title	*DOT* Code	WTG page	Wagner Title	Number of Positions	Total	F	N	SS
							Job Seekers at Staten Island NYSES Office[a]		
OFFICIALS AND MANAGERS	Manager, Front Office	187.168	245	Asst. Dir., Wagner Union	3	117	35	1	3
(cont'd)	Manager, Office	169.168	245	Recorder, Registrar's Office	1	117	35	1	3
	Manager, Store I	185.168	245	Bookstore Manager	1	117	35	1	3
	Purchasing Agent	162.158	484	Director of Purchasing	1	13	5	0	0
	Registrar, College	090.168	237	Registrar	1	33	6	1	1
	Treasurer	161.118	237	Asst. Treasurer	1	33	6	1	1
PROFESSIONALS	Academic Dean	090.118	237	Academic Supervisor	1	33	6	1	1

290

Accountant	160.188	252 Head Accountant	1	25	3	2	1
Advertising Assistant	164.068	482 Dir. of Publications	1	8	1	1	0
Cataloger	100.388	276 Asst. Cataloger, Library	2	175	147	24	5
Controller	186.118	237 Controller	1	33	6	1	1
Counselor II	045.108	296 HEOP Counselor	1	25	6	3	1
Employment Interviewer I	166.268	250 Affirmative Action Asst.	2	8	5	1	1
Foreign Student Advisor	099.108	296 Coordinator, Bregenz Program	1	25	6	3	1
Librarian, Reference Library	100.168	245 Reference Librarian	2	117	35	1	3
Library Director	100.118	237 Head Librarian	1	33	6	1	1
Manager, Electronic Data Proc.	169.168	245 Dir., Computer Center	1	117	35	1	3
Manager, Personnel	166.118	237 Dir. of Personnel	1	33	6	1	1
Personnel Recruiter	166.268	250 Asst. Dir. of Admissions	4	8	5	1	1

Census Category	DOT Title	DOT Code	WTG page	Wagner Title	Number of Positions	Job Seekers at Staten Island NYSES Office[a]			
						Total	F	N	SS
OFFICIALS AND MANAGERS	Manager, Front Office	187.168	245	Asst. Dir., Wagner Union	3	117	35	1	3
	Placement Officer	166.268	250	Placement Officer	1	8	5	1	1
	Programer, Business	020.188	468	Programer-Secretary	1	6	0	0	0
	Public-Relations Man I	165.068	482	Dir. of News Bureau	1	8	1	1	0
	Residence Counselor	045.108	296	Residence Coordinator	1	25	6	3	1
	"	045.108	296	Resident Director	4	25	6	3	1
OFFICE AND CLERICAL	Accounting Clerk	219.488	280	Bookkeeper, Students' Acct's	3	249	140	18	6
	Addressing-Machine Operator	234.582	274	Graphotype Operator	1(CJ1)	31	17	4	1
	Bookkeeper I	210.388	280	Accountant, Business Office	1	249	140	18	6
	Bookkeeper II	210.388	280	Bookkeeper, Bookstore	1	249	140	18	6

	Code	Dept Code					
Bookkeeping-Machine Operator	215.388	280 Bookkeeper, Accounts Payable	1	249	140	18	6
Cashier I	211.368	267 Cashier, Business Office	2	18	10	6	0
Cashier II	211.468	269 Cashier, Bookstore	1	29	11	2	1
Chief Clerk, Print Shop	207.138	243 Asst. Supervisor, Letter Shop	1	28	8	0	1
"	207.138	243 Supervisor, Letter Shop	1	28	8	0	1
Clerk, General	209.588	289 File Clerk, Letter Shop	1	251	157	34	12
Clerk General Office	219.388	280 Clerk-Typist, Finan. Aid Off.	1	249	140	18	6
"	219.388	280 Registrar's Assistant	1	249	140	18	6
"	219.388	280 Registrar's Assistant, Rec.	3	249	140	18	6
"	219.388	280 Secretary II, Chem. Dept.	1	249	140	18	6
"	219.388	280 Transcript Clerk, Reg. Off.	1	249	140	18	6
Clerk-Typist	209.388	276 Clerk-Typist Development Off.	1	175	147	24	5

293

Census Category	DOT Title	DOT Code	WTG page	Wagner Title	Number of Positions	Total	F	N	SS
						Job Seekers at Staten Island — NYSES Office[a]			
OFFICIALS AND MANAGERS	Manager, Front Office	187.168	245	Asst. Dir., Wagner Union	3	117	35	1	3
	"	209.388	276	Clerk-Typist, Finan. Aid Rec.	1	175	147	24	5
	Digital-Computer Operator	213.382	274	Console Operator	1	31	17	4	1
	Embossing Machine Operator II	208.782	435	Graphotype Operator	(CJI)[b]	77	44	6	10
	Employment Clerk	205.368	258	Clerk-Typist, Personnel Dept.	1	65	50	1	3
	Expediter I	222.368	265	Library Assistant, Ordering	1	16	9	0	0
	File Clerk II	206.388	276	Alumni Records Clerk	1	175	147	24	5
	"	206.388	276	Library Assistant Catalog	1	175	147	24	5
	Key-Punch Operator	213.582	274	Key-Punch Operator	1	31	17	4	1

Job Title								
Library Assistant	249.368	258	Library Assistant, Periodicals	11	65	50	1	3
Mail Clerk	231.588	289	Mail Clerk, Postal Center	1	251	157	34	12
Mailing Supervisor	231.138	243	Asst. Supervisor, Postal Center	1	28	8	0	1
Offset Duplicating Mach. Oper.	207.782	435	Offset Printer	1	77	44	6	10
Payroll Clerk	215.488	280	Payroll Clerk, Business Office	2	249	140	18	6
Personnel Clerk	205.368	258	Clerk-Typist, Personnel Dept.	1	65	50	1	3
Procurement Clerk	223.368	258	Clerk-Typist, Purchasing	1	65	50	1	3
"	223.368	258	Secretary, Bookstore	1	65	50	1	3
Receiving-and-Shipping For.	223.138	243	Gen'l Services Sup., Pur.	1(CJ2)[b]	28	8	0	1
Receiving Clerk	222.387	271	Gen'l Services Mgr. Chem Dept.	1	50	2	7	1
Secretary	201.368	263	Admin. Asst. Alumni Affairs	1	154	154	4	2

Census Category	DOT Title	DOT Code	WTG page	Wagner Title	Number of Positions	Job Seekers at Staten Island NYSES Office[a]			
						Total	F	N	SS
	"	201.368	263	Faculty Secretary	1	154	154	4	2
	"	201.368	263	Faculty Secretary, Educ. Dept.	2	154	154	4	2
	"	201.368	263	Registrar's Assistant	1	154	154	4	2
	"	201.368	263	Secretary, Admissions Office	3	154	154	4	2

[a] F = female; N = negro; SS = Spanish speaking.   [b] = combined job

APPENDIX S

VARIANCES IN WORKER TRAIT FACTORS BETWEEN WAGNER COLLEGE AND *DOT* 3 RATINGS TITLES ARRANGED BY WAGNER DEPARTMENT

WTG page	DOT Code	DOT Title	Wagner Title	GED			SVP			Interest			Temperament			Physical Demands			Working Conditions			Aptitudes
				0	±1	2+	0	±1	2+	0	1	2+	0	1	2+	0	1	2+	0	1	2+	
237	090.168	Dir. of Admissions I	Dir. of Admissions	x			x					x			x			x			x	$S - 1$
237	090.168	Dir. of Admissions I	Assoc. Dir. of Admissions	x				−2			x	x			x			x			x	$G - 1\ v - 1$ $N - 2\ S - 1$
250	166.268	Personnel Recruiter	Asst. Dir., Admissions	x			x					x			x			x			x	$N - 1\ S - 1$
263	201.368	Secretary	Supervisory Secretary, Admissions	x				+1				x			x			x			x	$G - 1\ C - 1$
263	201.368	Secretary	Secretary, Admissions Office	x			x					x			x			x			x	$G - 1$
263	201.368	Secretary	Secretary, Athletic Department	x			x					x			x			x			x	—
360	181.887	Porter I	Porter, Biology Department	x				+1				x			x			x			x	$N + 1\ Q + 1$
263	201.368	Secretary	Secretary II, Bregenz	x			x					x			x			x			x	—

WTG page	DOT Code	DOT Title	Wagner Title	GED 0	GED ±1	GED 2+	SVP 0	SVP ±1	SVP 2+	Interest 0	Interest 1	Interest 2+	Temperament 0	Temperament 1	Temperament 2+	Physical Demands 0	Physical Demands 1	Physical Demands 2+	Working Conditions 0	Working Conditions 1	Working Conditions 2+	Aptitudes
296	099.108	Foreign Student Advisor	Coordinator, Bragenz	x			x					x	x			x			x	x		N − 1
237	161.118	Assistant Treasurer	Assistant Treasurer		−1		x					x	x			x			x			G − 1 N − 1
237	186.118	Controller	Controller	x				+1				x	x			x			x			G − 1
252	160.188	Accountant	Head Accountant	x			x					x	x			x			x			G − 1 N − 1 / S − 1 Q − 1
280	210.398	Bookkeeper I	Accountant Business Office	x					+2			x	x			x			x			S − 1
263	201.368	Secretary	Secretary II, Business Office	x			x					x	x			x			x			F − 1 C − 1
280	219.488	Accounting Clerk	Bookkeeper, Student Accounts	x			x					x	x			x			x			—
280	315.388	Bookkeeping Mach. Oper.	Bookkeeper, Accounts Payable	x			x					x	x			x			x			S − 1
280	215.488	Pay-Roll Clerk	Payroll Clerk, Business Office	x			x					x	x			x			x			S − 1 M + 1
267	211.368	Cashier I	Cashier, Business Office	x			x					x	x			x			x			N − 1 S − 1
263	201.368	Secretary	Secretary, Chaplain's Office	x			x					x	x			x			x			—
271	222.387	Receiving Clerk	Gen. Svces Mgr., Chem. Department	x					+2			x	x			x	x		x			P − 1 M + 1

280	219.388	Clerk, Gen. Office	Secretary II, Chemical Department	x	x	x	x	x	x	x	x	$P + 1$ $Q + 1$
245	169.168	Manager, EDP	Director, Computer Center	x	x	x	x	x	x	x	x	$Q + 2$
468	020.188	Programmer, Business	Programmer-Sect'y Computer Center	x	x	x	x	x	x	x	x	$K + 1$ $E + 1$ $M + 1$ $E - 1$ $C - 1$
274	213.582	Key-Punch Operator	Key-Punch Operator Computer Center	x	x	x	x	x	x	x	x	$C + 1$
243	213.138	Supervisor, Computer Operations	Senior Console Operator, Computer Center	x	x	x	x	x	x	x	x	$P + 2$
274	213.382	Digital-Computer Operator	Console Operator	x	x	x	x	x	x	x	x	$E - 1$
237	090.118	Academic Dean	Dean of Academic Affairs	x	x	x	x	x	x	x	x	—
237	090.118	Academic Dean	Asst. Dean, Academic Affairs	x	x	x	x	x	x	x	x	$Q + 2$
263	201.368	Secretary	Secretary, Dean of Acad. Affairs	x	x	x	x	x	x	x	x	$M + 1$
263	201.368	Secretary	Secretary Asst. Dean, Acad. Affairs	x	x	x	x	x	x	x	x	$G - 1$ $N - 1$
237	090.118	Academic Dean	Dean of Faculty	x	x	x	x	x	x	x	x	—
263	201.368	Secretary	Secretary, Dean of Faculty	x	x	x	x	x	x	x	x	—
237	090.118	Dean of Students	Dean of Students	x	x	x	x	x	x	x	x	—
237	090.118	Dean of Students	Dean	-1	x	x	x	x	x	x	x	—
263	201.368	Secretary	Secretary II, Dean of Students	x	x	x	x	x	x	x	x	$G - 1$ $N - 1$

WTG page	DOT Code	DOT Title	Wagner Title	GED			SVP	Interest			Temperament			Physical Demands			Working Conditions			Aptitudes
				0	±1	2+	±1	0	1	2+	0	1	2+	0	1	2+	0	1	2+	
263	201.368	Secretary	Secretary II, Asst. Dean of Students	x			x			x			x			x		x	x	—
237	189.118	Association Executive	Dir. of Development	x			x			x			x			x			x	$V - 1$ $Q + 1$
237	189.118	Association Executive	Asst. Dir. of Development	x			x			x			x			x			x	$V - 1$
239	T 165.118 No DOT Coverage		Director of Foundation and Corporate Support																	
237	090.118	Alumni Secretary	Director of Alumni Affairs Development Office	x			−1			x			x			x			x	$N + 1$ $Q + 1$
263	201.368	Secretary	Secretary II, Registrar's Office	x			+1			x			x			x			x	$P - 1 F + 1$
237	090.168	Registrar	Registrar	x			x			x			x			x			x	—
245	169.168	Manager, Office	Recorder, Registrar's Office	x			−1			x			x		x	x			x	—
280	219.388	Clerk, General Office	Transcript Clerk, Registrar's Office	x			x		x			x				x			x	—
296	045.108	Residence Counselor	Resident Coordinator Towers	x			x			x			x			x			x	$N + 1$
296	045.108	Residence Counselor	Resident Director, Guild Hall	x			x			x			x			x			x	$N + 2$

300

Score	DOT	Title	Position								Adjustments
416	322.168	Guard, Chief	Chief of Security	x	+2	x	x	x	x	x	$V+1$ $S+1$ $Q+2$
263	201.368	Secretary	Secretary II, Security Dept.	x	−1	x	x	x	x	x	$G-1$ $N-1$ $F-1$ $V-1$ $P-1$
237	090.118	Academic Dean	Academic Supervisor, Special Programs	x	x	x	x	x	x	x	—
296	045.108	Director of Guidance	Director, Special Programs	x	x	x	x	x	x	x	—
296	045.108	Director of Guidance	Assistant to Director, Special Programs	x	x	x	x	x	x	x	—
296	045.108	Counselor II	HEOP Counselor, Spec. Programs	x	x	x	x	x	x	x	—
263	201.368	Secretary	Secretary II, Special Programs	x	x	x	x	x	x	x	$F-1$ $C-1$
291	235.862	Telephone Operator	Operator	x	x	x	x	x	x	x	$P-2$ $Q+1$ $S-1$
243	235.138	Telephone Operator, Chief	Chief Operator	−1	−3	x	x	x	x	x	—
245	187.168	Manager, Front Office	Assistant Director, Wagner Union	x	x	x	x	x	x	x	$G-1$ $V-1$
237	090.163	Director of Student Affairs	Director, Wagner Union	x	−1	x	x	x	x	x	$S+1$ $Q+2$
250	166.268	Placement Officer	Placement Officer	x	x	x	x	x	x	x	$C-1$

APPENDIX T

REQUEST FOR SUPERVISOR'S APPRAISAL OF POSITION DESCRIPTIONS

1. Do you consider the job specifications to be useful for the following purposes:

    (a) To inform workers of their job duties and the standards of performance expected?

    (b) As a basis for your supervisory review, including initiating remedial actions?

    (c) As a basis for selecting new employees?

    (d) As a basis for promoting employees?

2. Other comments.

APPENDIX U

FOLLOW—UP QUESTIONNAIRE
OF THE INTERVIEW

We have interviewed 50 members of the Wagner staff thus far in accordance with our Affirmative Action Program. To help us to improve the remaining interviews, it would be helpful if you would give us your reaction to *your* recent interview. Please answer *all* questions which apply to you. You need not sign your name to this sheet.

Did you find this interview rewarding?   ☐ Yes   ☐ No
If you did, was it because

☐ It convinced you that you were in the right field of work?
☐ It helped you to clear up your own thinking about your career goals?
☐ It made you aware of other suitable careers you had never considered before?
☐ It indicated that Wagner was interested in your growth and development?

If you did not find the interview rewarding, please tell us why. (If you need more space, use the other side of this sheet.)

Other comments and suggestions:

APPENDIX V

COMPARISON OF VARIOUS TYPES OF POSITION DESCRIPTIONS

This appendix presents examples of four position descriptions/job specifications indicating differing degrees of detail for *Librarian*.

Position Description

EXAMPLE 1

EMPLOYER'S NAME		OCCUPATIONAL TITLE		CODE
		LIBRARIAN, REFERENCE LIBRARY		100.168
ADDRESS		EMPLOYER'S JOB TITLE-DEPARTMENT		CODE
		Reference Librarian – Library		
TELEPHONE	PERSON TO SEE-HOW TO REACH	HOURS OF WORK		
		UNION		
INDUSTRY		CODE	RATE OF PAY	SEX	AGE

NO.	JOB DUTIES	NO.	SKILLS, KNOWLEDGE, ABILITIES
	Takes charge of Reference Collection. Selects materials for and maintains the collection, and assists, advises, guides and instructs students and other library patrons in using the collection and the library's other resources sources. Publicizes the library's resources by means of bulletins and lectures:	1, 4, 5, 6, 7	Administrative ability and professional knowledge to take charge of reference collection of a college library.
1	Selects materials for and maintains the Reference Collection. Keeps abreast of reference publications by reading library journals, recommends purchase of reference books and participates, with faculty and other library staff, in the selection of other library materials. Locates and makes available less commonly used materials not in College library, contacting outside libraries for this purpose.	1, 2, 5	Verbal ability to review library journals, give individual research assistance to faculty and students and to lecture to student groups.
2	Acts as Reader's Adviser and provides answers to inquiries requiring specific information. Provides bibliographical and other research assistance. Answers correspondence and in-person inquiries on special reference services.		
3	Assists Catalog Department in maintenance of card catalog. Provides information to Catalog Librarian about needed additional cross-references and changes in subject headings. (See Comments)		
4	Assists Acquisitions Department in acceptance of gift books and arranges for disposal of surplus or obsolete books. Verifies against catalog to determine whether prospective donated books are already in stock and in sufficient quantity. Organizes periodic displays of surplus books for distribution to interested students or		

EXPERIENCE	INTERESTS & TEMPERAMENTS
Minimum of 2 years experience as Reader's Advisor plus periodicals experience in a public library.	INTEREST 2 – Business contact with faculty, students, other library patrons, and with staff of other libraries and institutions. INTEREST 5 – Prestige as result of administrative functions.
EDUCATION & TRAINING	INTEREST 6 – Communicates via lectures and informational bulletins with prospective library patrons regarding library resources and answers individual requests in person, by (cont'd)

	GED	SVP	G	V	N	S	P	Q	K	F	M	E	C	INT	TEMP	PD	EC	REASON FOR VARIANCE (TASK NO.'S.)
PROF.																		GED: No tasks requiring higher than ass assigned level. (cont'd)
TAPE	6	7	2	2	3	4	3	2	4	4	4	5	3	256	159	L145	I	
FIRM	5	7	2	1	4	4	3	2	4	4	4	5	5	256				

FORM ES 541 (8/1/72)   N.Y.S. - DEPT. OF LABOR   JOB SPECIFICATION FORM

NO.	JOB DUTIES	NO.	SKILLS, KNOWLEDGE, ABILITIES

faculty. Compiles lists of unwanted books for circulation and distribution to other institutions.

5 Publicizes the Reference Collection and other library resources by means of information bulletins and bibliographies, assisting in the publication of the Library Handbook, and by lecturing student groups on library facilities and resources. Proofreads bulletin material prior to final printing.

6 Maintains Government Depository Library collection of books and pamphlets of Federal, State and City publications and makes this material available to the general public. Informs Catalog Librarian of noteworthy material in this area for incorporation into college catalog. (See Comments)

7 Trains and gives specific assignments and direction to part-time student clerical workers.

Works under general supervision of Head Librarian.

ENVIRONMENTAL CONDITIONS

1. ENVIRONMENT
   Inside...100..%
   Outside......%
2. EXTREME COLD WITH OR WITH-OUT TEMPERATURE CHANGES.........
3. EXTREME HEAT WITH OR WITH-OUT TEMPERATURE CHANGES.........
4. WET AND/OR HUMID ....
5. NOISE
   Estimated maximum
   number of decibels ..60..
   VIBRATION ....
6. HAZARDS
   Mechanical ....
   Electrical ....
   Burns ....
   Explosives ....
   Radiant Energy ....
   Other ....
7. ATMOSPHERIC CONDITIONS
   Fumes ....
   Odors ....
   Dusts ....
   Mists ....
   Gases ....
   Poor Ventilation ....
   Other ....

DATE PREPARED   8/29/72

BY   David Knapp

APPROVED BY

PHYSICAL CONDITIONS

1. STRENGTH   WEIGHT
   a. Standing...50..% b. Lifting..20..
   Walking ...20..% Carrying..20..
   Sitting ...30..% Pushing ....
                    Pulling ....
2. CLIMBING ....
   BALANCING ....
3. STOOPING ...0....
   KNEELING ....
   CROUCHING ...0....
   CRAWLING ....
4. REACHING ...F....
   HANDLING ...F....
   FINGERING ...F....
   FEELING ....
5. TALKING   F
   Ordinary
   Other
   HEARING   F
   Ordinary Conversation ....
   Other Sounds ....
6. SEEING   F
   Acuity, Near
   Acuity, Far
   Depth Perception
   Accommodation ...F....
   Color Vision ....
   Field of Vision ....

DETAILS OF PHYSICAL ACTIVITIES & ENVIRONMENTAL CONDITIONS

Stands (50%) at reference desk and at shelves walks (20%) to shelves, files and stacks to locate books and materials. Sits (30%) to compile bibliographies, write informational bulletins, review materials and answer (cont'd)

PROMOTIONAL SOURCES & LINES

No promotion within the library. May transfer to Periodicals Librarian.

WORKER TRAIT GROUP PAGE NOS.

DIRECT	RELATED
P. 245	P. 237

COMMENTS

(1) Catalog Librarian position was vacant at time of this specification. Deals with assistant cataloger for tasks 3 and 6.
Reference Librarian position requires a friendly, outgoing personality.

EMPLOYER'S NAME			OCCUPATIONAL TITLE	CODE
			LIBRARIAN, REFERENCE LIBRARY	100.168
ADDRESS			EMPLOYER'S JOB TITLE-DEPARTMENT	CODE
			Reference Librarian - Library	
TELEPHONE	PERSON TO SEE-HOW TO REACH		HOURS OF WORK	
			UNION	
INDUSTRY		CODE	RATE OF PAY	SEX AGE

DETAILS OF PHYSICAL ACTIVITIES & ENVIRONMENTAL CONDITIONS (cont'd) | NO. | SKILLS, KNOWLEDGE, ABILITIES

correspondence. Lifts up to 20 lbs. of books occasionally, with frequent carrying of materials up to 10 lbs. Stoops and crouches occasionally to retrieve and replace books and files from lower shelves and drawers. Reaches for, grasps, handles and fingers books, library materials files, bibliographies, pens, pencils, and to use telephone. Talks to groups and individuals and listens to their questions and comments. Near acuity and accommodation needed to proofread informational bulletins and to retrieve information from files.

INTERESTS & TEMPERAMENTS
INTEREST 6 - correspondence.
INTEREST 7 - Interest in technical aspects of Library Science.
TEMPERAMENT 1 - Variety of duties with frequent interruptions to answer individual requests for assistance.
TEMPERAMENT 4 - Plans, directs, and controls Reference Collection activities of acquisition, maintenance of books and materials; publicizes available resources to prospective patrons.
TEMPERAMENT 5 - Deals with faculty, students, and staff of other institutions, rendering individual research assistance and securing the loan of materials not in the college library.

REASON FOR VARIANCE (TASK NO.'S)
Aptitudes: V -- tasks 1,2,5
            N - no tasks present involving higher level.
Temperaments: 4 -- tasks 1,4,7
P.D. -- see Physical Conditions and Details of Physical Activities.

EXPERIENCE

EDUCATION & TRAINING

PROF.	GED	SVP	G	V	N	S	P	Q	K	F	M	E	C	INT.	TEMP	PD	EC	REASON FOR VARIANCE (TASK NO.'S.)
TAPE																		
FIRM																		

FORM ES 541 (8/1/72)   N.Y.S. - DEPT. OF LABOR   JOB SPECIFICATION FORM

NO.	JOB DUTIES	NO.	SKILLS, KNOWLEDGE, ABILITIES

ENVIRONMENTAL CONDITIONS

1. ENVIRONMENT
   Inside........%
   Outside......%
2. EXTREME COLD WITH OR WITH-
   OUT TEMPERATURE CHANGES........
3. EXTREME HEAT WITH OR WITH-
   OUT TEMPERATURE CHANGES........
4. WET AND/OR HUMID   ....
5. NOISE
   Estimated maximum
   number of decibels   ....
   VIBRATION   ....
6. HAZARDS
   Mechanical   ....
   Electrical   ....
   Burns   ....
   Explosives   ....
   Radiant Energy   ....
   Other   ....
7. ATMOSPHERIC CONDITIONS
   Fumes   ....
   Odors   ....
   Dusts   ....
   Mists   ....
   Gases   ....
   Poor Ventilation   ....
   Other   ....

PHYSICAL CONDITIONS

1. STRENGTH   WEIGHT
   a. Standing.......% b. Lifting ....
      Walking ....%   Carrying........
      Sitting ....%   Pushing ....
                           Pulling ....
2. CLIMBING   ....
   BALANCING   ....
3. STOOPING   ....
   KNEELING   ....
   CROUCHING   ....
   CRAWLING   ....
4. REACHING   ....
   HANDLING   ....
   FINGERING   ....
   FEELING   ....
5. TALKING
   Ordinary   ....
   Other   ....
   HEARING
   Ordinary Conversation   ....
   Other Sounds   ....
6. SEEING
   Acuity, Near   ....
   Acuity, Far   ....
   Depth Perception   ....
   Accommodation   ....
   Color Vision   ....
   Field of Vision   ....

DETAILS OF PHYSICAL ACTIVITIES & ENVIRONMENTAL CONDITIONS

PROMOTIONAL SOURCES & LINES

WORKER TRAIT GROUP PAGE NOS.

DIRECT	RELATED

COMMENTS:

DATE PREPARED

BY

APPROVED BY

Example 2

NEW YORK STATE ANNOUNCES
OPPORTUNITIES IN GOVERNMENT
SENIOR LIBRARIANS

Salaries vary with location

NEW YORK STATE RESIDENCE NOT REQUIRED

Citizenship may be waived by a municipal Civil Service Commission.

NO. 23-670 SENIOR LIBRARIAN II, ASSISTANT LIBRARY DI-
RECTOR I, LIBRARY DIRECTOR II
NO. 23-671 SENIOR LIBRARIAN III, ASSISTANT LIBRARY DI-
RECTOR II, LIBRARY DIRECTOR III
NO. 23-672 SENIOR LIBRARIAN III (Adult Services)
NO. 23-673 SENIOR LIBRARIAN III (Audio-Visual Services)
NO. 23-674 SENIOR LIBRARIAN III (Children's Services)
NO. 23-675 *SENIOR LIBRARIAN III (Reference Services)*
NO. 23-676 SENIOR LIBRARIAN III (Technical Processing)
NO. 23-677 SENIOR LIBRARIAN III (Young Adult Services)
NO. 23-678 SENIOR LIBRARIAN III (Other Specialties)

Location of Positions

These positions are with Municipal, School District, and Cooperative Library Systems in New York State. Salaries vary depending on location and level of responsibility.

Minimum Qualifications

On or before the date of the written tests, candidates for ALL examinations must have completed five years of college training at a regionally accredited college or university, or one recognized by New York State, one year of which shall have been professional library training in a recognized library school.

In addition, candidates must have had satisfactory professional experience in a library of recognized standing, acquired after the completion of professional library training, for the required number of years as specified below:

For Examination No. 23-670: four years
For Examination No. 23-671: six years
For Examination Nos. 23-672 through 23-678: six years including three years in each specialized service for which you apply.

Note: Possession of a New York State professional public librarian's certificate is required for appointment to a position. Application forms for these certificates may be obtained by writing to the Library Development Division, New York State Education Department, 99 Washington Avenue, Albany, New York 12225.

Subject of Examinations

Written test will be given for all nine examinations, which will cover knowledge, skills, and/or abilities in such areas as: library organization, administration, and budgeting; library services and operating procedures; supervision; and public and interpersonal relations. Eligibility for the specialized services will be determined on the basis of the candidates's experience.

Duties

A Senior Librarian II serves as head of a major library department in a library serving a population of 50,000 to 250,000 or assistant department head in a library serving a population of 250,000 to 1,000,000.

An Assistant Library Director I serves as assistant director of a library serving a population of 25,000 to 50,000.

A Library Director II serves as director of a library serving a population of 15,000 to 25,000.

A Senior Librarian III plans and directs the work of a major library department in a library serving a population of 250,000 to 1,000,000; or has charge of specialized services.

An Assistant Library Director II acts as assistant director of a library serving a population of 50,000 to 250,000.

A Library Director III serves as a director of a library serving a population of 25,000 to 50,000.

Examinations to be held November 11, 1972.

Example 3

LIAISON OFFICER (nonprofit organ.) *see* NATIONAL SERVICE OFFICER.

LIBRARIAN (library) 100.168. Maintains library collection of books, periodicals, documents, films, recordings, and other materials, and assists groups and individuals to locate and obtain materials: Furnishes information on library activities, facilities, rules, and services. Explains use of reference sources, such as bibliographic indexes and reading guides, to locate information. Describes or demonstrates procedures for searching catalog files and shelf collections to obtain materials. Searches catalog files and shelves to locate information. Issues and receives materials for circulation or for use in library. Assembles and arranges displays of books and other library materials. Performs variety of duties to maintain reference and circulation matter, such as copying author's name and title on catalog cards and selecting and assembling pictures and newspaper clippings. Answers correspondence on special reference subjects. May compile book titles, according to subject matter of designated interests, to prepare reading lists. May select, order, catalog, and classify materials. May be designated according to specialized function as CIRCULATION LIBRARIAN: READERS'-ADVISORY-SERVICE LIBRARIAN. When engaged in locating information on specific subjects, is known as REFERENCE LIBRARIAN.

BOOKMOBILE LIBRARIAN (library). Provides library services from mobile library within given geographical area. Surveys community needs and selects books and materials for library. Publicizes visits to area to stimulate reading interest. May prepare special collections for schools and other groups. May arrange bookmobile schedule. May drive bookmobile.

CHILDREN'S LIBRARIAN (library). Assists children in selecting and locating library materials, and organizes and conducts activities for children to encourage reading and use of library facilities: Confers with teachers, parents, and community groups to stimulate children's discriminate reading by organizing such activities as reading courses, bookfairs, and story hours. Shows films, tells stories, and gives book talks to encourage reading. Conducts library tours to acquaint children with library facilities and services.

PATIENTS' LIBRARIAN (library) hospital librarian. Analyzes reading needs of patients and provides library services for patients and employees in hospital or similar institution: Furnishes readers' advisory services on basis of knowledge of current reviews and bibliographies. Reviews requests, and selects books and other library materials for ward trips according to mental state, educational background, and special needs of patients. Assembles book reviews for hospital bulletins or newspapers, and circulates reviews among patients. Provides handicapped or bedridden patients with reading aids, such as prism glasses, page turners, bookstands, or talking books, and with phonograph records.

YOUNG-ADULT LIBRARIAN (library). Conducts young adult program in library to provide special activities for high school and college-age readers: Organizes young adult activities, such as chess clubs, creative writing club, and photography contests. Contacts speakers, writes and distributes advertising, and meets young adult club representatives to prepare group programs. Delivers talks on books to stimulate reading. Addresses groups, such as parent-teacher associations and civic organizations, to inform community of activities. Conducts library tours of high school classes to aquaint students with library facilities and services. Compiles lists of young adult reading materials for individuals, high school classes, and branch libraries. Issues and receives library materials, such as books and phonograph records.

LIBRARIAN (motion pic.) 223.387. Keeps library of stock and process films in motion-picture studio for future use or reference: Receives, catalogs, and stores films by title or scene reference. Selects and issues requested items to studio personnel. May cut and assemble portions of positive films, using hand-powered sprocket machine.

—(print. & pub.) *see under* FILE CLERK (clerical) II.

—(radio & tv broad.) *see* MUSIC LIBRARIAN.

LIBRARIAN, CLERICAL (print. & pub.) *see* LIBRARIAN *under* FILE CLERK (clerical) II.

LIBRARIAN, HEAD (library) *see* LIBRARY DIRECTOR.

LIBRARIAN, REFERENCE LIBRARY (library) 100.168. Manages library or section containing specialized materials for industrial, commercial, or governmental organizations, or for such institutions as schools and hospitals: Arranges special collections of technical books, periodicals, manufacturers' catalogs and specifications, film strips, motion pictures, microcards, and journal reprints. Searches literature, compiles accession lists,

and annotates or abstracts materials. Assists patrons in research problems. May translate or order translation of materials from foreign languages into English. May be designated according to subject matter specialty of library or department as ART LIBRARIAN; BUSINESS LIBRARIAN; ENGINEERING LIBRARIAN; LAW LIBRARIAN: MAP LIBRARIAN; MEDICAL LIBRARIAN.

LIBRARIAN, SPECIAL COLLECTIONS (library) 160.168. Collects books, pamphlets, manuscripts, and rare newspapers to provide source material for research: Organizes collections according to field of interest. Examines reference works and consults specialists preparatory to selecting materials for collections. Compiles bibliographies. Appraises books, using references, such as bibliographies, book selection records, and special catalogs on incunabula (printing prior to 1600). Publishes papers and bibliographies on special collections to notify scholars of available materials. Lectures on booklore, such as history of printing, bindings, and illuminations. May plan and arrange displays for library exhibits. May index and reproduce materials for sale to other libraries.

LIBRARY ADMINISTRATOR (library) *see* LIBRARY DIRECTOR.

LIBRARY ASSISTANT (library) 219.368. book-loan clerk; circulation clerk; desk attendant; library attendant; library clerk; library helper. Compiles records, sorts and shelves books, and issues and receives library materials, such as books, films, and phonograph records: Records identifying data and due date on cards by hand or using photographic equipment to issue books to patrons. Inspects returned books for damage, verifies due-date, and computes and receives overdue fines. Reviews records to compile list of overdue books and issues overdue notices to borrowers. Sorts books, publications, and other items according to classification code and returns them to shelves, files, or other designated storage area. Locates books and publications for patrons. Issues borrower's identification card according to established procedures. Files cards in catalog drawers according to system. Repairs books, using mending tape and paste and brush. Answers inquiries of nonprofessional nature on telephone and in person and refers persons requiring professional assistance to LIBRARIAN. May type material cards or issue cards and duty schedules. May be designated according to type of library as BOOKMOBILE CLERK; BRANCH-LIBRARY CLERK; or according to assigned department as LIBRARY CLERK, ART DEPARTMENT; or may be known according to tasks performed as LIBRARY CLERK, BOOK RETURN.

LIBRARY ATTENDANT (library) *see* LIBRARY ASSISTANT.

LIBRARY CLERK (library) *see* LIBRARY ASSISTANT.

LIBRARY CLERK, ART DEPARTMENT (library) *see* LIBRARY ASSISTANT.

LIBRARY CLERK, BOOK RETURN (library) *see* LIBRARY ASSSISTANT.

LIBRARY CLERK, TALKING BOOKS (library) 209.588. Selects Talking Books for mailing to blind library patrons: Compares borrower's written request with list of available titles. Selects books, following borrower's request, or selects substitute titles, following such criteria as age, education, interest, and sex of borrower. Obtains books from shelves. Types address label to prepare books for mailing. May type records, such as material or issue cards. May receive and inspect Talking Books returned to library [CLERK, BRAILLE-AND-TALKING BOOKS].

LIBRARY DIRECTOR (library) 100.118. Librarian, head; library administrator; library superintendent; manager, library. Plans and administers program of library services: Submits recommendations on library policies and services to governing body, such as board of directors or board of trustees, and implements policy decisions. Analyzes, selects, and executes recommendations of subordinates, such as department chiefs or branch supervisors. Analyzes and coordinates departmental budget estimates and controls expenditures to administer approved budget. Reviews and evaluates orders for books, films, and phonograph records, examines trade publications and samples, interviews publishers' representatives, and consults with subordinates to select materials. Administers personnel regulations, interviews and appoints job applicants, rates staff performance, and promotes and discharges employees. Plans and conducts staff meetings and participates in community and professional committee meetings to discuss library problems. Delivers book reviews and lectures to publicize library activities and services. May examine and select materials to be discarded, repaired, or replaced. May be designated according to governmental subdivision served as CITY - LIBRARY DIRECTOR; COUNTY-LIBRARY DIRECTOR.

LIBRARY HELPER (library) *see* LIBRARY ASSISTANT.

LIBRARY SUPERINTENDENT (library) *see* LIBRARY DIRECTOR.

EXAMPLE 4   EMPLOYER MASTER ORDER DESCRIPTION

Library Assistant II—249.368

Definition   Performs a variety of clerical duties under general supervision involving responsibilities requiring a knowledge of library procedures and policies.

Typical Duties

Tracing through files, catalogs, shelf lists and stacks for incomplete or incorrect reference, missing books, or other material.

Keeps various records and compiles data for reports.

Interprets circulation policies to readers.

Procures and issues library materials at loan desk or reserve desk.

Does preliminary checking of bibliographies.

Prepares preliminary catalog entries for professional cataloguers.

Makes corrections and additions to catalog upon direction of professional cataloguer.

Assists in conducting inventories of holdings.

May direct and train Library Assistants I and student assistants in library routines.

May supervise other workers in unpacking, checking, and listing books.

Maintains record of payments for serial publications.

Prepares invoices for final processing.

Perform related duties as assigned.

Qualifications

High school graduation and 1–2 years of library experience.

May require minimum typing ability of 30 wpm.

Approved 7/1/64
Revised   2/1/69

APPENDIX W

WAGNER COLLEGE

STATEN ISLAND, NEW YORK 10301

OFFICE OF THE PRESIDENT

January 5, 1973

Mr. Clement J. Berwitz
Chief of Occupational Analysis and Industrial Services
Manpower Services Division
New York State Department of Labor
370 Seventh Avenue
New York, New York 10001

Dear Mr. Berwitz:

I believe that the Wagner College Affirmative Action Plan which you developed working with M. Charlyne Cox our Director of Personnel represents a milestone in the evolution of Equal Employment Opportunity technique. It is my conviction that this equitable and feasible plan should help us to achieve the goals of the legislation, regulations and policy which created it.

May I express my appreciation to you, your staff and the concerned Department of Labor officials for the assistance which you gave us in making Affirmative Action a reality at Wagner College. It is my expectation that the Wagner plan may well serve as a prototype for other establishments sincerely interested in Equal Employment Opportunity.

Sincerely,

Arthur O. Davidson

AOD:lm

BIBLIOGRAPHY

Baer, Max F., and Roeber, Edward C. *Occupational Information: The Dynamics of Its Nature and Use.* Chicago: Science Research Associates, 1964.

Bakke, E. Wight. *The Mission of Manpower Policy.* Kalamazoo, Mich.: W. E. Upjohn Institute for Employment Research, April 1969.

Bakke, E. Wight. *A Positive Labor Market Policy.* Columbus, Ohio: Charles E. Merrill, 1963.

Berelson, Bernard, and Steiner, Gary A. *Human Behavior.* New York: Harcourt Brace, 1964.

Becker, Gary. Jovanovich, *Human Capital.* New York: Columbia University Press, 1964.

Becker, Joseph M., Haber, William, and Levitan, Sar A. *Programs to Aid the Unemployed in the 1960's.* Kalamazoo, Mich.: W. E. Upjohn Institute for Employment Research, January 1965.

Berkey, Arthur L., and Drake, William E. "An Analysis of Tasks Performed in the Ornamental Horticulture Industry." Ithaca, N.Y.: New York State College of Agriculture and Life Sciences, Cornell University, June 1972 (Xerox copy).

Berkey, Arthur L., Drake, William E., and Legacy, James W. "A Model for Task Analysis in Agri-Business." Ithaca, N.Y.: New York State College of Agriculture and Life Sciences, Cornell University, June 1972 (Xerox copy).

Berwitz, Clement J. "Beyond Motivation". *Harvard Business Review,* May–June, 1960. Vol. 38 No. 3.

Berwitz, Clement J. "The Work Committee." *Harvard Business Review.* Vol. 30, no. 1 (January–February 1952), pp. 110–124.

Berwitz, Clement J. "*DOT,* An Information, Instrumentation and Retrieval System." *Newsletter of the New York Personnel and Guidance Association.* Vol. 6, no. 6 (April 1971), p. 11.

Borrow, Henry. "An Integral View of Occupational Theory and Research." In Henry Borrow (ed.), *Man in a World at Work.* Boston: Houghton Mifflin, 1964.

Budke, Eugene Wesley. *Review and Synthesis of Information on Occupational Exploration.* Columbus, Ohio: ERIC Clearinghouse on Vocational and Technical Education, the Center for Vocational and Technical Education, Ohio State University, 1971.

Burack, Elmer H. *Strategies for Manpower Planning and Programming.* Morristown, N.J.: General Learning Press, 1972.

Burt, Samuel M., and Streiner, Herbert E. *Toward Greater Industry and Government Involvement in Manpower Development.* Kalamazoo, Mich.: W. E. Upjohn Institute for Employment Research, September 1968.

Byham, William C., and Spitzer, Morton Edward. *The Law and Personnel Testing.* New York City, N.Y. American Management Association, 1971.

Calia, Vincent F. "Vocational Guidance After the Fall." *Personnel and Guidance Journal.* Vol. 45, no. 4 (December 1966), pp. 320–327.

Carrol, Bonnie. *Job Satisfaction.* Ithaca, N.Y.: New York State School of Industrial and Labor Relations, Cornell University, February 1969.

Champagne, Joseph E., and King, Donald C. "Job Satisfaction Factors Among Underprivileged Workers." *Personnel and Guidance Journal.* Vol. 45 (1967), pp. 429–434.

Chayes, Antonia Handler. "Make Your Equal Opportunity Program Court-proof." *Harvard Business Review.* September–October 1974, pp. 81–89.

Costello, Timothy W., and Zalkind, Sheldon S. *Psychology in Administration.* Englewood Cliffs, N.J.: Prentice-Hall, 1963.

Cost Benefit Analysis of Manpower Policies: Proceedings of a North American Conference. Industrial Relations Centre, Queen's University, Kingston, Ontario.

Crites, John O. *Vocational Psychology.* New York: McGraw-Hill Book Company, 1969.

Diamond, Daniel E., and Bedrosian, Hrach. *Industry Hiring Requirements and the Employment of Disadvantaged Groups.* New York: New York University School of Commerce, 1970.

Eckerson, A. B. "The New *Dictionary of Occupational Titles.*" *Vocational Guidance Quarterly.* Vol. 12 (1963), pp. 40–42.

Ellis, Allan B., and Tiedeman, David V. "Can a Machine Counsel?" Cambridge, Mass.: Harvard University Graduate School of Education, December 1968 (Xerox copy).

Ferguson, Lawrence L. "Better Management of Managers' Careers." *Harvard Business Review.* Vol. 44, no. 2 (March–April 1966), pp. 139–152.

Fine, Sidney, A. *The 1965 Third Edition of the Dictionary of Occupational Titles.* Kalamazoo, Mich.: W. E. Upjohn Institute for Employment Research, December 1968.

Fine, Sidney, A. *Guidelines for the Design of New Careers.* Kalamazoo, Mich.: W. E. Upjohn Institute for Employment Research, September 1967.

Fine, Sidney, and Wiley, Wretha W., *An Introduction to Functional Job Analysis.* Kalamazoo, Mich.: W. E. Upjohn Institute for Employment Research, 1971.

Fryklund, Verne C. *Occupational Analysis Techniques and Procedures.* New York: Bruce Publishing Company, 1970.

Giblin, Edward J., and Ornati, Oscar A. "A Total Approach to EEO Compliance." *Personnel.* September–October 1974, pp. 32–43.

Gilpatrick, Eleanor G. "A Proposed System of Occupational Coding. *Monthly Labor Review.* Vol. 91, no. 10 (October 1968), pp. 47–53.

Gilpatrick, E. G., and Corliss, Paul K. *The Occupational Structure of New York City Municipal Hospitals.* New York: Frederick A. Praeger, 1970.

Gilpatrick, Eleanor. *Structural Unemployment and Aggregate Demand.* Baltimore: Johns Hopkins Press, 1966.

Ginzberg, Eli. *Manpower Agenda for America.* New York: McGraw-Hill Book Company, 1968.

Gordon, Robert. *The Goal of Full Employment.* New York: John Wiley & Sons, 1967.

Gordon, Robert. *Toward a Manpower Policy.* New York: John Wiley & Sons, 1967.

Greene, Stanley, Priebe, John, and Morrison, Richard. "The 1970 Census of Population Occupational Classification System." *Statistical Reporter.* no. 70-6 (December 1969), pp. 77–84.

Haber, William, and Kruger, Daniel H. *The Role of the United States Employment Service in a Changing Economy.* Kalamazoo, Mich.: W. E. Upjohn Institute for Employment Research, February 1964.

Health Services Mobility Study. "First Progress Report for Phase IV." New York: Research Foundation, City University of New York, 1973 (Xerox copy).

Herzberg, Frederick. "One More Time—How Do You Motivate Employees?" *Harvard Business Review.* Vol. 46, no. 1 (January–February 1968), pp. 53–62.

Herzberg, Frederick, Mausner, Bernard, and Snyderman, Barbara Bloch. *The Motivation to Work,* 2nd ed. New York and London: John Wiley & Sons, 1962.

Holland, John L. *The Psychology of Vocational Choice.* Waltham, Mass.: Blaisdell Publishing Company, 1966.

Hopkins, Jesse T. *The Emergence of a New Public Employment Service.* Albany, N.Y.: J. B. Lyon Company, 1935.

Hoskins, John E. *PROOF Occupational Selection Handbook.* Detroit, Mich.: Goodwill Industries of Greater Detroit, 1968.

Impellitteri, John T. *The Development and Evaluation of a Pilot Computer-Assisted Occupational Guidance Program.* University Park, Pa.: Vocational Education Department of the Pennsylvania State University, July 31, 1968.

Jakubauskas, Edward B., and Palomba, Neil A. *Manpower Economics.* Reading, Mass.: Addison-Wesley Publishing Company, 1973.

Katzell, Raymond A. "Personal Values, Job Satisfaction, and Job Behavior." In Henry Borrow (ed.), *Man in a World at Work.* Boston: Houghton Mifflin, 1964.

Leavitt, Harold J. *Managerial Psychology,* 2nd ed. Chicago: University of Chicago Press, 1964.

Lecht, Leonard. *Manpower Needs for National Goals in the 70's.* New York: Frederick A. Praeger, 1969.

Leontief, Wassily. *Input-Output Economics.* New York: Oxford University Press, 1966.

Lester, Richard. *Manpower Planning in a Free Society.* Princeton N.J.: Princeton University Press, 1966.

Levitan, Sar A., Mangum, Garth L., and Marshall, Ray. *Human Resources and Labor Markets.* New York: Harper & Row, 1972.

Levitan, Sar A. "Our Evolving National Manpower Policy." *Conference Board Record* Vol. 9 (May 1972), pp. 20–23.

Levitan, Sar A., and Taggart, Robert, III. *Social Experimentation and Manpower Policy.* Baltimore: Johns Hopkins Press, 1971.

Loughary, John W., Freisen, Deloss, and Hurst, Robert A. "A Computer Based Automated Counseling Simulation System." *Personnel and Guidance Journal.* Vol. 45, no. 1 (September 1966), pp. 6–15.

McKinsey and Company. "A Study of the Programs of the New York State Employment Service." New York: McKinsey and Company, April 1963 (Xerox copy).

Mangum, Garth. *MDTA: Foundation of Federal Manpower Policy.* Baltimore: Johns Hopkins Press, 1968.

Mangum, Garth. *The Emergence of Manpower Policy.* New York: Holt, Rinehart & Winston, 1969.

Miller, Delbert C., and Form, William H. *Industrial Sociology,* 2nd ed. New York: Harper & Row, 1965.

Neeb, R. W., Cunningham, J. W., and Pass, J. J. *Human Attributes Requirements of Work Elements.* Raleigh: Center for Occupational Education, North Carolina State University, 1971.

Neff, Walter S. *Work and Human Behavior.* New York: Atherton Press, 1968.

Olmsted, Michael S. *The Small Group,* New York: Random House, 1959 12th printing, January 1967.

Osipow, Samuel. *Theories of Career Development.* 2nd ed. Englewood Cliffs, N.J.: Prentice-Hall, 1973.

Patton, John A., Littlefield, C. L., and Self, Stanley Allen. *Job Evaluation.* Homewood, Illinois: Richard D. Irwin, Inc., 1964.

Pati, Gopal C., "Affirmative Action Program, Its Realities and Challenges," *Labor Law Journal.* Vol. 24 (June 1973), pp. 351–361.

Piersen, Glen N., Whitfield, Edwin, and Glaeser, George. *Career Information, the VIEW System.* San Diego, Calif.: San Diego County Department of Education, n.d.

Prien, E. P., and Ronan, W. W. "Job Analysis, A Review of Research Findings." *Personnel Psychology.* Vol. 24, no. 3 (November 3, 1971), pp. 371–396.

Riccabono, J. A., and Cunningham, J. W. *Work Dimensions Derived Through Systematic Job Analysis.* Raleigh: Center for Occupational Education, North Carolina State University at Raleigh, 1971.

Scoville, James G. *The Job Content of the U.S. Economy 1940–1970.* New York: McGraw-Hill Book Company, 1969.

Scoville, James G. *Manpower and Occupational Analysis.* Lexington, Mass.: Lexington Books, D. C. Heath and Company, 1972.

Seligman, Daniel. "How Equal Opportunity Turned into Employment Quotas." *Fortune,* Vol. 37, no. 3 (March 1973), pp. 160–168.

Shartle, Carroll L. "Occupational Analysis, Worker Characteristics, and Occupational Classification Systems." In Henry Borrow (ed.), *Man in a World at Work.* Boston: Houghton Mifflin, 1964.

E. F. Shelley and Company. *Upgrading the Work Force—Problems and Possibilities.* Manpower Administration, U.S. Department of Labor, Contract 82-34-70-26, January 1971.

Sheppard, Harold L. *The Nature of the Job Problem and the Role of the New Public Employment Service.* Kalamazoo, Mich.: W. E. Upjohn Institute for Employment Research, January 1969.

Sinha, Nageshwar. *Manpower Planning.* Minneapolis: Minneapolis Industrial Research Center, University of Minnesota, 1970.

Super, Donald E. *The Psychology of Careers.* New York: Harper & Row, 1957.

State of New York. *The Buffalo Project on Health Manpower Programs,* three volumes. Albany: The Governor's Advisory Committee on Youth and Work, 1971.

State of New York, Department of Labor. "Manpower Requirements of Lower Level Jobs in New York State." Albany: New York State Department of Labor, Division of Research and Statistics, July 1971 (typewritten copy).

State of New York, Department of Labor. *Minority Manpower Statistics.* Albany: New York State Department of Labor, Division of Research and Statistics, August 1973.

Stead, William H., and Masincup, W. Earl. *The Occupational Research Program of the United States Employment Service.* Chicago: Public Administration Service, 1943.

State of New York, Department of Labor. *Women in the Labor Force.* Albany: New York State Department of Labor, Division of Research and Statistics, April 1972.

Super, Donald E. *Computer-Assisted Counseling.* Compiled by Donald E. Super with the collaboration of Martin J. Bohn, Jr. New York: Teachers College Press, 1970.

Super, Donald E., Overstreet, Phoebe L., Morris, Charles N., Dubin, William, and Heyde, Martha B. *The Vocational Maturity of Ninth Grade Boys.* New York: Teachers College, Columbia University Bureau of Publications, 1960.

Swerdloff, Sol. "Sweden's Manpower Programs." *Monthly Labor Review.* Vol. 89 (January 1966), pp. 1–6.

"Technology in Guidance." *Personnel and Guidance Journal,* Vol. 49, no. 3 (November 1970), pp. 172–263.

Tenopyr, Mary L. "Research Roundup." *Personnel Administration.* Vol. 35, no. 1 (January-February 1972), pp. 52–53.

Ulman, Lloyd. "Labor Markets and Manpower Policies in Perspective." *Monthly Labor Review.* Vol. 95 (September 1972), pp. 22–28.

Ulman, Lloyd, ed. *Manpower Programs in the Policy Mix.* Baltimore: Johns Hopkins Press, 1973.

Ulman, LLoyd. "The Uses and Limits of Manpower Policies." *Public Interests.* No. 34, (Winter 1974) pp. 83–105.

U.S. Civil Service Commission. "Manpower Planning and Utilization." Washington, D.C., 1971.

U.S. Congress. *Whither the U.S. Employment Service?* Digest of Hearings on H.R. 11976, 8547, J.J. Res. 607, before the Select Committee on Labor House Committee on Education and Labor, July-August 1964, Chamber of Commerce of the United States.

U.S. Congress, House of Representatives. *The Role and Mission of the Federal State Employment Service in the American Economy.* Committee on Education and Labor, Eighty-Eighth Congress, Second Session, December 1964. Washington, D.C.: Government Printing Office, 1965.

U.S. Congress, Senate. *Toward Full Employment: Proposals for a Comprehensive Employment and Manpower Policy in the United States.* Committee on Labor and Public Welfare, Washington D.C.: Government Printing Office, 1964.

U.S. Congress, Senate. *Employment and Training Opportunities Act of 1970.* Report of the Committee on Labor and Public Welfare on S. 3867. Washington, D.C.: Government Printing Office, August 20, 1970.

U.S. Department of Commerce, Bureau of the Census. *Classified Index of Industries and Occupations, 1970 Census of Population.* Washington, D.C.: Government Printing Office, September 1971.

U.S. Department of Health, Education, and Welfare. *Computer-Based Vocational Guidance Systems.* Washington, D.C.: Government Printing Office, 1969.

U.S. Department of Health, Education, and Welfare, Office of the Secretary, Office for Civil Rights. *Higher Education Guidelines.* Executive Order 11246. Washington, D.C.: Government Printing Office, October 1972.

U.S. Department of Labor, *Dictionary of Occupational Titles,* Vol. I, *Definitions of Titles,* 3rd ed. Washington, D.C.: Government Printing Office, 1965.

U.S. Department of Labor. *Dictionary of Occupational Titles,* Vol. II, *Occupational Classifications,* 3rd ed. Washington, D.C.: Government Printing Office, 1965.

U.S. Department of Labor. *Manpower Report of the President.* Washington, D.C.: Government Printing Office, March 1972.

U.S. Department of Labor. *Revisions in Occupational Classification System.* Washington, D.C.: Government Printing Office. Reprinted from *Employment and Earnings,* February 1971.

U.S. Department of Labor. *Selected Characteristics of Occupations by Worker Traits and Physical Strength, Supplement 2 to the Dictionary of Occupational Titles, Third Edition.* Washington, D.C.: Government Printing Office, 1968.

U.S. Department of Labor. *Selected Characteristics of Occupations (Physical Demands, Working Conditions, Training Time), Supplement to the Dictionary of Occupational Titles, Third Edition.* Washington, D.C.: Government Printing Office, 1966.

U.S. Department of Labor, Bureau of Employment Security. *Counselor's Handbook.* Washington, D.C.: Government Printing Office, 1967.

U.S. Department of Labor, Bureau of Labor Statistics. *Job Redesign for Older Workers, Ten Case Studies.* Bulletin No. 1523. Washington, D.C.: Government Printing Office, 1967.

U.S. Department of Labor, Manpower Administration. "The Employment Service as a Comprehensive Manpower Agency." Washington, D.C.: June 25, 1969 (mimeograph copy).

U.S. Department of Labor, Manpower Administration. *Federal Policy on Equal Employment Opportunity in State and Local Personnel Systems.* General Administration Letter No. 1488 (mimeograph copy).

U.S. Department of Labor, Manpower Administration. *Handbook for Analyzing Jobs.* Washington, D.C.: Government Printing Office, 1972.

U.S. Department of Labor, Manpower Administration. *A Handbook for Job Restructuring.* Washington, D.C.: Government Printing Office, 1970.

U.S. Department of Labor, Manpower Administration. *Hiring Standards and Job Performance.* Manpower Research Monograph 18. Washington, D.C.: Government Printing Office, 1970.

U.S. Department of Labor, Manpower Administration. *Relating General Educational Development to Career Planning.* Washington, D.C.: Government Printing Office, 1971.

U.S. Department of Labor, Manpower Administration. *Job Analysis for Human Resources Management.* Manpower Research Monograph no. 36. Washington, D.C.: Government Printing Office, 1974.

U.S. Department of Labor, Manpower Administration. *Task Analysis Inventories.* Washington D.C.: Government Printing Office, 1973.

U.S. Department of Labor, Manpower Administration. *Training and Reference Manual for Job Analysis.* Washington, D.C.: Government Printing Office, May 1965.

U.S. Equal Employment Opportunity Commission. *Affirmative Action and Equal Employment,* 2 volumes. Washington, D.C.: January 1974.

Vickery, Lawrence L. *Report of the National Employers' Committee for Improvement of the State Employment Service.* Washington, D.C.: Department of Labor, Manpower Administration, July 1972.

Walker, James W. "Evaluating the Practical Effectiveness of Human Resources Planning Applications." *Human Resources Management.* Vol. 13 (Spring 1974), pp. 19–27.

Walther, R. H. "The Functional Occupational Classification Project: A Critical Appraisal." *Personnel and Guidance Journal.* Vol. 38 (1960), pp. 698–706.

Weber, Arnold, R. *The Role and Limits of National Manpower Policies.* Madison Wis.: Industrial Relations Research Association, *Proceedings,* 1965.

Wikstrom, Walter S. *Manpower Planning Evolving Systems.* New York: Conference Board, 1971. Work in America; report of a special task force to the Secretary of Health, Education, and Welfare. Prepared under auspices of the W. E. Upjohn Institute for Employer Research, Kalamazoo, Mich.

Wiley, Wretha W., and Fine, Sidney A. *A Systems Approach to New Careers.* Kalamazoo, Mich.: W. E. Upjohn Institute for Employment Research, November 1969.

Wilson, Michael. *Job Analysis For Human Resource Management: A Review of Selected Research and Development*. Washington, D.C.: Manpower Management Institute, January 1974, Grant No. 21-11-73-40, Manpower Administration, Department of Labor.

Wool, Harold. "What's Wrong with Work in America?" *Monthly Labor Review*. Vol. 96, no. 3 (March 1973), pp. 38–44.

Zalenznik, A. C., Christensen, C. R., and Roethlisberger, F. J. *The Motivation, Productivity and Satisfaction of Workers*. Cambridge, Mass.: Harvard University Graduate School of Business Administration, 1958.

INDEX